PHOTOSHOP LIGHTROOM CLASSIC 2025

A Step-by-Step Guide to Stunning Photo Editing

ZANE MAVERICK

TABLE OF CONTENTS

INTRODUCTION

Part 1: Getting Started with Lightroom Classic

Hello and welcome to "Photoshop Lightroom Classic 2025: A Comprehensive Guide from Beginner to Advanced." This guide is designed to help photographers of all levels use Adobe Lightroom Classic to its fullest. Lightroom Classic is one of the most powerful digital photography tools. It has a lot of features that can help you become a better photographer, from organizing and editing your photos to making beautiful visual stories.

The structure of this guide is designed to give you clear, step-by-step instructions, useful tips, and unique ideas, whether you are new to editing photos or want to improve your skills.

You will learn how to quickly and easily add photos, organize them, and take care of your library. This will keep your process smooth and productive. We will look at the different editing tools and methods that Lightroom Classic has to offer so that you can improve your photos in a precise and creative way. We will also talk about more advanced topics, like how to make custom presets, how to master color correction, and how to use the masking tools.

There are illustrated examples, useful tasks, and real-life situations in this guide that will help you put what you've learned to use right away and make your work better. You will know how to use Lightroom Classic 2025 to its fullest by the end of this journey. This will allow you to make your picture dreams come true.

We're glad you picked this guide. Let's start learning how to use Photoshop Lightroom Classic 2025 to edit photos properly.

CHAPTER ONE

INTRODUCTION TO LIGHTROOM CLASSIC

Overview of Lightroom Classic

Adobe Lightroom Classic is a strong program that photographers use to edit and organize their pictures. This app makes your photos look better and keeps your files neat. It makes it easy to add pictures and sort them. You can sort your photos into albums and folders, tag them, and rate your favorites. So, no matter how many pictures you have, it's easy to find them and keep track of them.

Lightroom Classic has many tools for editing pictures that can help you make them better. The colors, brightness, and contrast can be changed. Images can also be cropped and straightened, and spots or items that you don't want can be removed. The software also has presets, which are settings that have already been made and can be used on photos with just one click.

Lightroom Classic has more advanced tools, such as masking and color grading, for people who want to go deeper. You can give your photos a unique look or make precise adjustments to certain parts of them using these features.

To save and share your pictures after editing them in Lightroom Classic, just click on "Save." You can export your pictures in some different sizes and types, then print them out or share them on social media right away.

One of the best things about Lightroom Classic is that it uses non-destructive editing. This means that your original picture doesn't change, and you can always undo an edit.

It's easy to use Lightroom Classic with other Adobe programs, like Photoshop. You can switch pictures between the two apps to use the best features of each one.

Key Features
Remove distractions in photos with Generative Remove

With the new **Generative Remove feature**, which is driven by Adobe Firefly's cutting-edge generative AI technology, you can easily get rid of things that aren't important in your pictures. Using the brush mask, this tool lets you highlight any object. Adobe Firefly will then remove the object and automatically fill in the area so it fits in with the rest of the content.

Choose the Remove tool and you will find both the Generative AI and Object Aware choices. This is where you can get to this useful tool. This makes it easier than ever to get your pictures looking like they were taken by a professional. You can get Early Access to the Generative Remove feature on all Lightroom platforms right now. This lets you try out the future of photo editing.

The Generative Remove tool also uses machine learning to understand the context of your photos. This makes sure that the generated fill looks natural and fits in with the rest of your picture. This tool works seamlessly with your workflow, whether you're editing on a desktop, computer, or phone. It's a flexible option for all your editing needs.

With Adobe Firefly's Generative Remove, you can quickly and easily get beautiful photos with no distractions, which will improve the quality and effect of your photography as a whole.

Note: Lightroom's "**Heal**" tool is now called the "**Remove**" tool. When you choose the Remove tool, you get access to the Remove, Heal, and Clone tools.

Add aesthetic blur to your photos with Lens Blur

The AI-powered Lens Blur tool was previously offered in Early Access. It is now fully available with better features. With just a few clicks, this tool makes it easy to give your photos a professional look by adding blur and bokeh to them. The May 2025 release of Lightroom Classic includes adaptive presets that make it even simpler to achieve stunning visual effects.

Advanced AI is used by the Lens Blur tool to figure out the depth and context of your photos. This makes the blur effect look natural and in the right place. This makes the main subject of your shot stand out while softening the background slightly, like what you'd get with a high-end camera lens.

One great thing about the Lens Blur tool is that it lets you blur several shots at once with the same settings. This is great for photographers who want all of their pictures to have the same style, like in a wedding album, a portrait session, or a catalog of products. It saves time and makes sure that all of your pictures look the same.

More ways to custom the blur effect are available with the new Lens Blur tool. You can change the shape and size of the bokeh (the light spots that aren't in focus) as well as how strong the blur is and where it shows up in the picture. You can get the exact look you want this way.

The AI-powered Lens Blur tool now has new and better features that make editing photos easier and help you make high-quality pictures. It is now an important part of your Lightroom Classic toolkit.

Tethered Capture with Sony

Lightroom Classic now supports tethered capture for Sony cameras. In other words, you can take pictures and change the camera settings right from Lightroom Classic. With the floating tether bar, you can:

- Capture photos in real-time
- Apply presets instantly
- Control the settings on your camera, such as White Balance, Shutter Speed, Aperture, and ISO.

This integration makes live picture sessions run more smoothly and quickly, so photographers don't have to keep switching between their camera and computer.

Filter by Exported Images

You can now filter your pictures in Lightroom Classic based on their export status. How to do it:

- **Smart Collections:** Make a Smart Collection and use the Exported status and other metadata to filter your pictures.
- **Library Filter Panel**: To filter out the exported pictures, use the Library Filter Panel, which can be found under Attribute.

In the picture's metadata, Lightroom Classic also keeps track of the last time an image was exported, which you can view. On top of that, you can change an image's export state if you need to. Whether your photos have been exported or not, this function makes it easy to handle and arrange them.

Other feature enhancements and changes

- Increased the reliability and speed of the sync process by making major changes to the infrastructure.
- Enabled Apple Neural Engine for AI Denoise on Macs running macOS 14.0 or later.
- New preview level organization.
- Made the Develop module more responsive and easier to navigate.

System Requirements

Desktop System Requirements

Windows:

Minimum:

- **Processor:** Intel, AMD, or ARM processors with 64-bit support; 2 GHz or faster.
- **Operating System:** Windows 10 (64-bit) version 1909 or later.
- **RAM:** 8 GB.
- **Hard Disk Space:** 2 GB available; additional space required during installation and sync.

- **Monitor Resolution:** 1280 x 768.
- **Graphics Card:** GPU with DirectX 12 support; 2 GB VRAM.
- **Internet:** Required for software activation, validation, and access to online services.

Recommended:

- **Processor:** Intel, AMD, or ARM processors with 64-bit support; 2 GHz or faster.
- **Operating System:** Windows 10 (64-bit) version 1909 or later.
- **RAM:** 16 GB or more.
- **Hard Disk Space:** 2 GB available; additional space required during installation and sync.
- **Monitor Resolution:** 1920 x 1080 or greater.
- **Graphics Card:** GPU with DirectX 12 support; 4 GB VRAM for 4K or greater displays.

macOS:

Minimum:

- **Processor:** Multicore Intel processor with 64-bit support or M1 Apple Silicon processor.
- **Operating System:** macOS Catalina.
- **RAM:** 8 GB recommended.
- **Hard Disk Space:** 2 GB available; additional space required during installation and sync.
- **Monitor Resolution:** 1280 x 768.
- **Graphics Card:** GPU with Metal support; 2 GB VRAM.
- **Internet:** Required for software activation, validation of subscriptions, and access to online services.

Recommended:

- **Processor:** Multicore Intel processor with 64-bit support or M1 Apple Silicon processor.
- **Operating System:** macOS Big Sur (version 11) or later.
- **RAM:** 16 GB.
- **Hard Disk Space:** 2 GB available; additional space required during installation and sync (Lightroom does not install on case-sensitive file systems or removable flash storage devices).
- **Monitor Resolution:** 1920 x 1080 or greater.
- **Graphics Card:** GPU with Metal support; 4 GB VRAM for 4K or greater displays.

Mobile System Requirements

iOS:

iOS Devices:

Lightroom Classic is designed to work with any iPhone or iPad that runs iOS. If your device is an iPhone or iPad that supports iOS, you're good to go. Essentially, if your Apple device can run iOS, you can use Lightroom Classic on it.

Android Devices:

For Android users, the requirements vary depending on the performance you want from the app.

Minimum Requirements:

- **Processor:** Your device should have at least a quad-core processor running at 1.5 GHz. This means your device should be able to handle multiple tasks efficiently, as the processor is the brain of your phone.
- **RAM:** The device should have at least 2 GB of RAM. RAM is like your phone's short-term memory, which helps it run apps smoothly.
- **Internal Storage:** You need at least 8 GB of storage space. This is where your apps and files are stored, so having enough space is crucial.

- **Android OS:** Your device should be running Android 8.x (Oreo) or later. This is the version of the operating system, and having a newer version ensures compatibility with the latest features.

Recommended Requirements:

- **Processor:** For better performance, a quad-core processor with 2.2 GHz and ARM v8 architecture is recommended. This means your phone can handle more demanding tasks with ease.
- **RAM:** 6 GB or more is recommended. This ensures that you can run multiple apps simultaneously without your phone slowing down.
- **Internal Storage:** 64 GB or more is recommended. This provides ample space for storing your photos, apps, and other data.

Lightroom Classic System Requirements (Version 11.0 or later, October 2021 Release)

Windows:

For users on Windows, the requirements ensure that Lightroom Classic runs smoothly and efficiently.

Minimum Requirements:

Processor: You need an Intel or AMD processor that supports 64-bit and runs at 2 GHz or faster. This ensures that the software can handle complex tasks.

- **Operating System:** Windows 10 (64-bit) version 1909 or later. This is important because older versions of Windows might not support all the features of the latest Lightroom Classic.
- **RAM:** At least 8 GB of RAM is necessary. This allows your computer to handle the software without lag.
- **Hard Disk Space:** You need 4 GB of available space, with additional space required during installation. This is where the software and your photos will be stored.

- **Monitor Resolution:** A resolution of 1024 x 768 is the minimum. This refers to how clear and detailed the display on your monitor will be.
- **Graphics Card:** A GPU (Graphics Processing Unit) with DirectX 12 support and 2 GB GPU memory is necessary. The GPU helps in rendering images and videos faster.

Recommended Requirements:

- **Processor:** Same as the minimum, but a faster processor is always better for smoother performance.
- **Operating System:** Again, Windows 10 (64-bit) version 1909 or later.
- **RAM:** 16 GB or more is recommended for handling more complex edits and multitasking.
- **Hard Disk Space:** The same 4 GB available, with additional space for installation.
- **Monitor Resolution:** 1920 x 1080 or greater. This provides a clearer and more detailed display.
- **Graphics Card:** For 4K displays or higher, a GPU with 4 GB memory is recommended. For full GPU acceleration, 8 GB dedicated GPU memory or 16 GB shared memory is ideal.

macOS:

For macOS users, the requirements ensure that Lightroom Classic functions optimally.

Minimum Requirements:

- **Processor:** A multicore Intel processor with 64-bit support or Apple Silicon processor. This ensures your Mac can handle the software's demands.
- **Operating System:** macOS Catalina (version 10.15) or later. Newer versions of the OS are necessary for compatibility.
- **RAM:** 8 GB of RAM is required to run the software efficiently.

- **Hard Disk Space:** 4 GB of available space, with more needed during installation.
- **Monitor Resolution:** 1024 x 768 is the minimum resolution, which affects the clarity of your screen.
- **Graphics Card:** A GPU with Metal support and 2 GB GPU memory is required for rendering images.

Recommended Requirements:

- **Processor:** Same as the minimum but having a faster processor improves performance.
- **Operating System:** macOS Catalina (version 10.15) or later is recommended.
- **RAM:** 16 GB or more is recommended for more intensive tasks.
- **Hard Disk Space:** Same 4 GB available, with additional space for installation.
- **Monitor Resolution:** 1920 x 1080 or greater is recommended for better visual clarity.
- **Graphics Card:** For 4K or higher displays, a GPU with 4 GB memory is recommended. For full GPU acceleration, having 8 GB dedicated GPU memory or 16 GB shared memory is ideal.

Installation

1. **Visit Adobe's Website:** Go to Adobe's Lightroom Classic page.
2. **Sign In or Create an Adobe ID:** You'll need to create an Adobe ID if you don't already have one. Sign in if you already have one.
3. **Download Lightroom Classic:** Press the "Download" button. If it's not already on your computer, this will also put the Creative Cloud desktop app on it.
4. **Install the Application:** Open the file you downloaded and install Lightroom Classic by following the steps shown on the screen.
5. **Launch Lightroom Classic:** After setting up Lightroom Classic, you can open it from your desktop or the Creative Cloud app.

Differences Between Lightroom Classic and Lightroom CC

Adobe's photo editing software comes in two different versions, Lightroom Classic and Lightroom CC. Each is designed to meet the wants and workflows of a different set of users. If you know how they are different, you can pick the right tool for managing and editing photos.

Interface and Usability

The desktop layout of Lightroom Classic is very traditional, and it comes with a lot of tools for editing and organizing photos. This version is made for people who like a strong PC setting and are used to working with a more complicated interface. It's great for people who have a lot of photos and need advanced editing tools.

Lightroom CC, on the other hand, has a modern, simpler design that focuses on being easy to use and accessible. Users who want a more natural experience on computers, tablets, and smartphones will find it most useful. Users can easily edit and handle their pictures with the help of the streamlined design.

Storage and Accessibility

Some of the biggest changes are in how the different versions handle storage. Your photos are kept on your computer's hard drive with Lightroom Classic because it focuses on local storage. With this setup, you can handle your files in great depth, and you can even put pictures into folders and collections the way you like. It's especially helpful for people who want to have full control over where their files are stored and how their directories are organized.

But Lightroom CC is in the cloud. All of your pictures are immediately sent to Adobe's cloud storage, where they can be viewed on any internet-connected device. Accessing and editing pictures on the go is made easier with this tool. To keep your work current, the cloud storage also makes it simple to sync pictures and changes between different devices.

File Management and Organization

You have to do more to manage files with Lightroom Classic. You can put pictures on your hard drive into specific folders and make collections to group photos together based on different factors. This method gives you a lot of power over your photo library, which is helpful when you have a lot of pictures and a lot of different ways to organize them.

Cloud storage makes it easier to handle files with Lightroom CC. Photo storage in the cloud is automatically sorted, so you don't have to handle your folders by hand. This setup makes it easier to view and sync photos across devices, but compared to Lightroom Classic, it gives you less control over how files are organized.

Editing Capabilities

Lightroom Classic and Lightroom CC both have strong editing tools, but they can be used in different ways and have different features. Professional photographers will find that Lightroom Classic has a lot of advanced editing choices and tools. It lets you make fine changes and gives you a lot of power over picture processing.

With Lightroom CC, editing photos is easier because the tools are made to be simple and easy to use. It has a lot of the same basic editing tools as Lightroom Classic, but it might not have as many choices for fine-tuning photos. But it works well for people who like to edit photos more simply.

Integration and Workflow

Adobe Photoshop and Lightroom Classic work together perfectly, so it's easy to move photos between the two for more detailed editing. This is a great feature for people who use both Lightroom and Photoshop as part of their work.

Lightroom CC works with other Adobe Creative Cloud apps too, but its cloud-based environment is what makes it so great. This setup makes it easier for people to work together and share since they can work on their photos from different places and devices.

CHAPTER TWO

NAVIGATING THE INTERFACE

The Lightroom Workspace

There are seven main panels in Lightroom Classic, which makes it an easy-to-use program for editing photos.

Platform Differences:

- **macOS:** The menu bar stays at the top of the screen.
- **Windows:** On Windows, the menu bar is below the title bar.

Even though these are small differences, the general layout and functions are the same on both macOS and Windows. This means that users of either operating system will have a smooth experience.

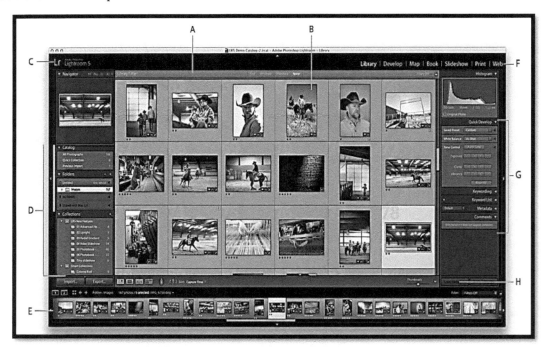

A. Library Filter bar **B.** Image display area **C.** Identity plate **D.** Panels for working with source photos **E.** Filmstrip **F.** Module Picker **G.** Panels for working with metadata, keywords, and adjusting images **H.** Toolbar

Top panel

On the left side of the top panel is the identity plate, and on the right side is the Module Picker. Customize this identity plate with your company name or logo. During background processes in Lightroom, a progress bar takes its place for a short time. If you click on the progress bar, a choice will appear that shows you what Lightroom is doing at the moment.

You can click on the names of the modules in the Module Picker on the right to move between them. In the Module Picker, the name of the module that is currently being used is always highlighted. You will see module tips when you start any Lightroom module. These tips will help you get around the area and work flow. Click the Close button to close the tips. From the Help menu, choose [Module name] Tips to reactivate the tips for any module.

The Work Area

The central preview and work area in Lightroom is where you will spend most of your time. From this page, you can choose, evaluate, arrange, compare, edit, and preview your pictures while you work. This main window changes to show book layouts, slide shows, web galleries, and print designs as needed as you switch between parts.

The Toolbar

The Toolbar is located below the work area. It has a different set of tools and settings for each module. You can change how the Toolbar looks for each module separately to suit your needs. There are many tools and features you can use to change viewing modes, add text, set ratings, flags, or labels, and move between preview pages. You can show or hide certain settings, or you can hide the Toolbar until you need it. To change how the Toolbar looks, press the T key.

Observing the Toolbar for the Library module, which has the view mode buttons on the left and some task-specific tools and controls that can be customized by selecting from the menu on the far right. When you change the view, the menu options change.

In the Select Toolbar Context menu, tools and features that can be seen in the Toolbar are marked with a check mark next to their names. The tools and settings in the Toolbar are set up in the same way they are in the menu, from top to bottom. There are many of the same choices in the buttons and on the computer that you can find in the Toolbar.

The Filmstrip

You can get to all the pictures in your library or collection from the Filmstrip at any point in your work. Without having to go back to the Library module, you can use the Filmstrip to quickly move through a collection of pictures or switch between sets. Press F6 or choose **"Show Filmstrip"** from the **Window** > **Panels menu** to show the Filmstrip at the bottom of the workspace. Working with pictures in the Filmstrip is a lot like working with them in the Grid view of the Library module. You can rate, flag, and name colors, apply metadata develop presets, and rotate, move, or remove pictures.

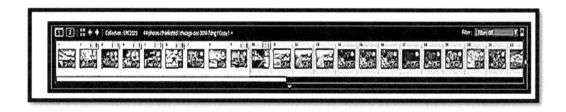

The pictures in the Filmstrip are the same as those in the Library module's Grid view. If you look for pictures, it can show you all of them in the library, just the ones in a certain folder or collection, or a filtered set of them.

The Side Panels

The side panels will change automatically to show you the right tools and resources as you move through each module. The layout can be explained by saying that the panels on the left side of each module help you move around, view previews, find, and select images, while the panels on the right side let you edit or adjust the settings for the image you've selected. This is how the side panels are usually set up. Users of Lightroom Classic 2025 can now switch between panel groups in any module, not just the Develop module.

On a mac, go to the menu bar in Lightroom Classic. On Windows, go to the "Edit" menu. To change the interface, go to **Preferences** > **Interface** and pick either **Swap Only Develop Left and Right Panel Groups** or **Swap Left and Right Panel Groups**. In the Library module, the left panels (Catalog, Folders, Collections, and Publish Services) help you find pictures and put them in order. You can make changes to the picture you've chosen in the right panels, which are Quick Develop, Keywording, Keyword List, Metadata, and Comments.

When you're in the Develop module, you can choose Develop presets on the left and change their settings on the right. In the Slideshow, Print, and Web modules, you can pick a layout template from the list on the left and change how it looks on the right.

Customizing the Interface
Modules

In Lightroom Classic, each module is equipped with its own unique set of tools that are designed to function exclusively within that particular module. For example, if you're looking to create and print contact sheets from a recent photo shoot, you would need to navigate to the Print module, where you'll find all the necessary tools to complete the task.

It's worth noting that not every module will be used frequently by everyone. In fact, you might discover that there are some modules you rarely, if ever, need to access. The majority of Lightroom users tend to spend most of their time in the Library and Develop modules, as these are the areas where essential tasks such as organizing and editing photos take place.

Interestingly, Lightroom also offers the option to simplify your workspace by hiding any modules you don't use regularly. This allows you to streamline the interface and focus only on the tools that matter most to your workflow. This customization can make navigating the software more efficient and less cluttered.

Right-clicking on the module panel will bring up a menu that you can use to choose which modules to keep visible:

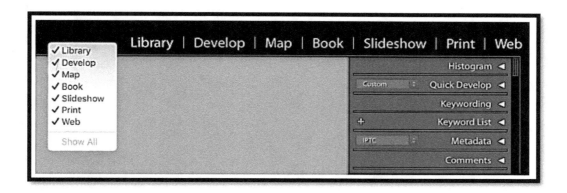

In Lightroom Classic, the visibility of different panels is controlled by a small tick mark next to each panel's name. If you want to hide a particular module from your workspace, you simply need to click on the module's name in the menu to uncheck it. This will make that module invisible in your workspace.

For instance, the **Book and Slideshow modules** are ones that I rarely use, so I have unchecked them in my own Lightroom setup to keep my workspace more streamlined. However, if you ever need to access a module that you've hidden, you don't need to worry—these modules aren't gone forever. You can always find the hidden ones in the Window menu.

To open a hidden module, you can also use specific keyboard shortcuts, which provide a quick way to bring them back into view. It's important to note that when you do this, Lightroom will automatically add the previously hidden module back to the Module

Picker. This means the module will reappear alongside the others in your workspace, allowing you to access it easily whenever you need it.

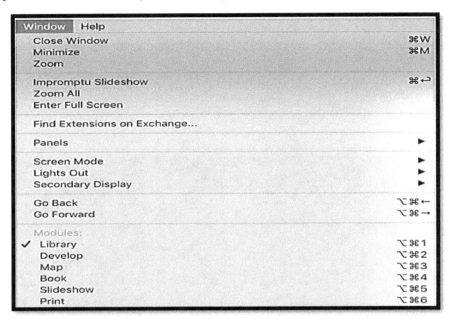

Panels

The following can be seen in the picture above:

A.   Library Filter bar

B.   Image Display area

C.   Identity Plate area

D.   Panels displaying photos

E.   Filmstrip

F.   Module Picker

G.   Panels for working with metadata, keywords, adjustments

H.   Toolbar

To show only the panels you want, you can adjust your workspace to do that.

To manage the visibility of panels in Lightroom Classic, you can use a few handy keyboard shortcuts that make navigating the interface more efficient.

If you want to open or close all the panels within a group at once, you can do so by holding down the **Command key on a Mac or the Ctrl key** on Windows while clicking. This action will toggle the entire group of panels, saving you time compared to adjusting them individually.

For situations where you only want to open or close a single panel, there's a quick way to do that as well. Simply hold the Option key on a Mac or the Alt key on Windows and click on the panel header. This will toggle just that one panel, leaving the others in the group unaffected.

If you want to hide or show both groups of side panels simultaneously, you can either press the **Tab key** or go to the **Window** menu, then choose **Panel**, followed by **Toggle Side Panels**. This is useful when you need a larger workspace to focus on your photos without the distraction of side panels.

Additionally, if you want to hide all of the panels in Lightroom, including the side panels, the Module Picker, and the Filmstrip, you can press Shift-Tab. Alternatively, you can access the same command by going to the Window menu, selecting Panels, and then choosing Toggle All Panels. This action gives you a completely uncluttered workspace, perfect for when you need to focus entirely on your images.

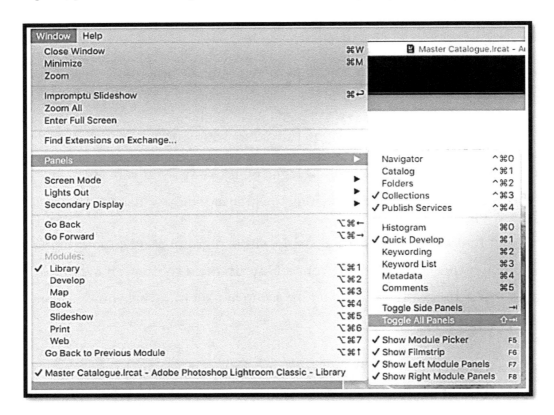

You can hide a panel from view if you don't use it very often. To do this, **Control-Click** (Mac) or **Right-Click** (Windows) on any panel header in the group and pick the panel name.

Change the Screen Mode

You can also change how the screen looks to hide the menus, panels, and title bar.

Pick -> **Window -> Screen Mode**, and pick an option from the drop-down menu.

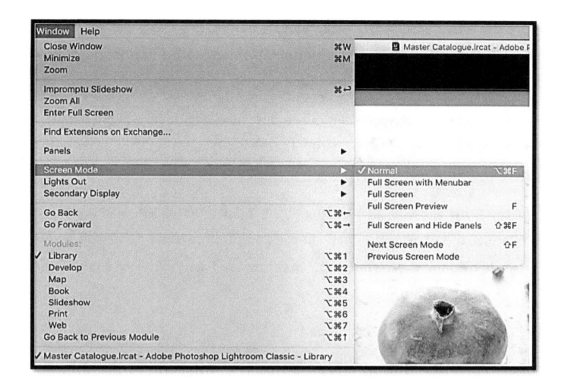

Switching between different viewing modes in Lightroom Classic is straightforward and can be done with a simple keystroke. By pressing the F key, you can toggle through the three main viewing modes: Normal mode, Full Screen with **Menubar, and Full Screen** mode. This makes it easy to adjust your workspace to suit your needs.

Be cautious with the Full Screen mode and Full Screen with Hide Panels mode on macOS. Both of these modes will hide the Dock, which might also cause the **Minimize, Maximize, and Close** buttons for the application to become hidden. If you encounter this, pressing the F key once or twice will cycle through the viewing modes until you see these controls again.

If you want to bring back the panels and menu bar while in a fullscreen mode, you can press **Shift+Tab** followed by the **F** key. This will make the panels and menu bar visible again, giving you quick access to the tools and options you need.

To switch from Full Screen with Menubar or Full Screen Mode back to the normal screen mode, use the shortcut **Command+Option+F on a Mac or Ctrl+Alt+F** on Windows. This will return you to the standard windowed view.

For a more streamlined view that hides the title bar, menus, and panels, press **Shift+Command+F** on a Mac or **Shift+Ctrl+F** on Windows. This provides a clean workspace with minimal distractions.

Lastly, if you want to adjust the lighting in the Lightroom Classic workspace, you can select Window, then Lights Out, and choose an option to dim or hide the workspace. You can cycle through these choices by pressing the F key, allowing you to adjust the lighting according to your preference

Identity Plate

Through the **Identity Plate Setup**, you can give your Lightroom your photography business's logo.

With this cool customization, you can look more professional when dealing with clients and using tethered capture. It won't change the way you do your work in any way.

To customize your Identity Plate in Lightroom Classic, follow these steps depending on your operating system:

On a Mac, start by clicking on "Lightroom" in the menu bar at the top of your screen. From the drop-down menu, select **"Identity Plate Setup**." If you're using Windows, you'll need to go to **"Edit**" in the top menu and choose "Identity Plate Setup."

Once you're in the Identity Plate Setup window, look for the option labeled "Personalized and Custom" under the **"Identity Plate**" section. Click on this option to begin customizing your Identity Plate.

If you want to use an image as your Identity Plate, click on **"Use a Graphical Identity Plate**" and then select **"Locate File**." This will allow you to navigate to the location on your computer where your image is saved and select it for use as your Identity Plate.

Even if you don't have a logo or image to use, you can still personalize the text on your Identity Plate. Adjust the text's font size, color, and background to give it a custom appearance that fits your style or branding. This customization can help make your Identity Plate stand out, even without a graphical element.

CHAPTER THREE

IMPORTING AND ORGANIZING PHOTOS

Import Photos Into Lightroom Classic

Step 1: Open the Import Dialog

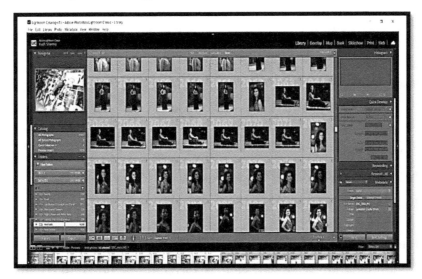

Open Lightroom Classic and click on the "**Import**" button in the bottom left corner of the library module to start adding pictures. You can also use the menu bar to go to "**File**" > "**Import Photos and Videos**."

Step 2: Select the Source

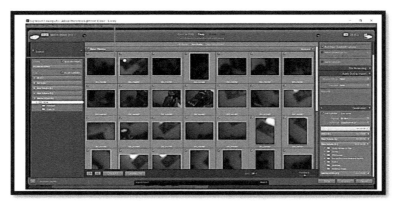

In the import dialog box, you choose where the pictures came from in the left-hand panel. You can bring in pictures from a hard drive, an external drive, a camera, or a memory card. Lightroom Classic can import many types of files, such as RAW, JPEG, TIFF, and PSD.

When you put in your SD card, this window will usually open itself if Lightroom is already running.

Step 3: Choose Import Settings

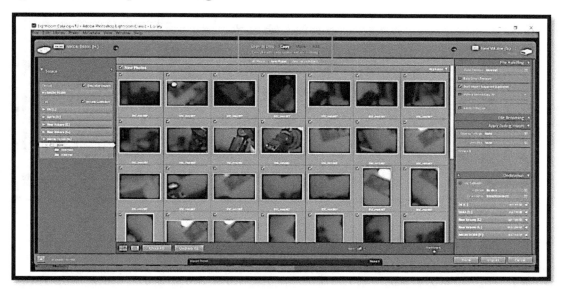

They are "**Copy as DNG**," "**Copy**," "**Move**," and "**Add**." They are at the top of the import text box. Pick the one that works best for you:

- **Copy as DNG:** This option changes RAW files to Adobe's DNG format and copies them to a certain place.
- **Copy**: Files are copied to a new place without their format being changed.
- **Move:** Moves the files to a new location.
- **Add:** This option keeps the photos where they are and adds them to the Lightroom catalog.

Most of the time, you'll pick Copy because it's the best and safest choice.

Step 4: Apply Import Settings

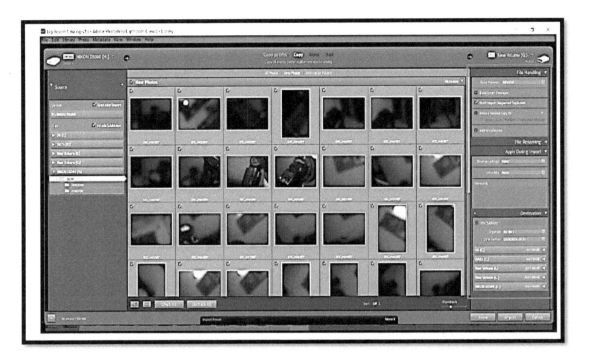

As you import the pictures, you can apply some settings in the panel on the right:

- **File Handling**: Choose how Lightroom manages previews and duplicates.
- **File Renaming**: Rename files when you import them for better organization.
- **Apply During Import**: Add keywords, metadata, and develop settings.

I don't use any of these settings very often, to be honest. A lot of the time, I don't change the names of my shots until much later in the editing process.

Step 5: Choose Destination

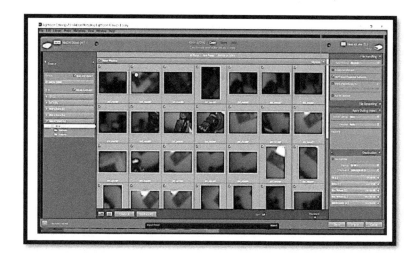

You can tell Lightroom Classic where to store the photos you import below the import settings. You can choose a folder that already exists or make a new one. Putting your pictures into folders by date, event, or subject can make it easier to find them later.

You will likely be moving your photos to an external hard drive, which is where most photographers like to keep all of their photos. That's because pictures can take up a lot of space on your computer very quickly.

Step 6: Import the Photos

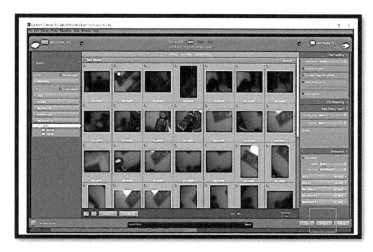

Select everything you want, then click the "**Import**" button in the bottom right corner of the text box. Based on your settings, Lightroom Classic will start to import your pictures. In the upper left part of the screen, you can see how things are going.

Additional FAQ Related to Importing in Lightroom

Where does Lightroom store imported photos?

Lightroom does not store any photos. It only syncs with the photos that have already been imported. The actual photos are not moved. Making a Lightroom Catalog is how this is done.

Can Lightroom import folders?

Yes, you can also just drag and drop the whole folder into the Lightroom import window to import it. When you do that, make sure you check the box that says "**Include subfolders**." This will make sure that everything is imported since the pictures are often in the category subfolders.

What happens if I move around photos in my storage location after importing?

Lightroom can only sync with the original files, so if you move a picture from where it is stored, Lightroom will lose track of it. After that, an empty mark will appear next to the thumbnail of that picture. After that, you'll need to right-click on that thumbnail and choose where the new picture is stored so that Lightroom can sync it again.

Additional Tips

- **Previewing and Selecting**: Before importing, you can look at the photos you want to import and remove the ones you don't want to import.
- **Presets**: You can save settings for later use by using import presets, which makes your work go faster.
- **Backup**: Think about setting up a second place for backups while the import is going on. You can do this by selecting the "**Make a Second Copy to**" option located below the "**Destination**" choice.

What is a Lightroom Catalog?

In a sense, a catalog is just a collection of all your pictures. The pictures you bring into Lightroom are put into a collection when you do this. One album is usually enough for all of your pictures, but you can make more than one if you want to.

But a lot of people don't know that Lightroom doesn't store pictures in the catalog itself. It only syncs your hard drive's pictures with Lightroom. In other words, it only keeps track of the pictures you've imported and connects Lightroom to where your photos are on your computer or external hard drive.

There will be no photos if you delete them from the hard drive. There is no "back-up" in the catalog because the pictures were never stored there. The catalog will lose track of the deleted photos, and in Lightroom, you'll only see a missing icon on the thumbnails of the deleted photos.

Lightroom catalog is like a smart robot that helps you keep track of all your photos in Adobe Lightroom. You can't see this robot, but it works like one in the background to keep everything in order and simple to find.

What Does This Robot Do?

The Lightroom Catalog Robot doesn't hold your pictures. It keeps a full record of where each picture is saved on your external hard drive, what it looks like, and what Lightroom changes you've made to it. What if you had a robot that remembered where you put everything in your room and what changes you made? That's what this robot does for your pictures.

Keeping Photos and Changes in Sync

When you edit a photo in Lightroom Classic, the original image file on your hard drive remains completely unchanged. Instead of altering the original picture, Lightroom works by saving a set of instructions on how you want the image to be adjusted. Think of it like telling a robot exactly how you want the photo to look, but without actually changing the original file.

The original picture on your hard drive acts as a master copy, preserving its initial state. All of your edits are applied in a non-destructive way, meaning they only affect how the image is displayed within Lightroom. This way, the original file remains intact, and you can always revert back to it if needed. Lightroom simply keeps track of your adjustments and applies them when you view or export the photo, without modifying the original image itself.

Seeing Your Photos Through the Robot
The Lightroom Catalogue Robot allows you to view your images in Lightroom. You can see and organise them using it as a kind of window, despite the fact that they are on your external hard drive. The robot ensures that this window always displays the most recent data and updates to your images.

Finding Photos Fast
It's easy for this robot to find pictures for you. Tell it what you want, like a picture with a certain rating or keyword, and it will find it quickly in your collection. When someone knows every picture you have and can quickly bring it to you, it's like having a helper.

Backing Up: Keeping Your Edits Safe
Making a backup of your Lightroom catalogue is crucial. It's similar to copying the robot's memory. You can restore all of your modifications and organization using this backup in the event that something goes wrong.

Creating and Managing Catalogs
1. Startup Lightroom
2. From the box that comes up, click the **"Create a New Catalog"** button.

3. It will open a new box. In the first field that says "Save As," type the name of the catalog.

4. You can choose which folder on your computer or external hard drive the catalog will go to, or Lightroom will store it where it is supposed to be (Pictures).

5. Press "**Create**"

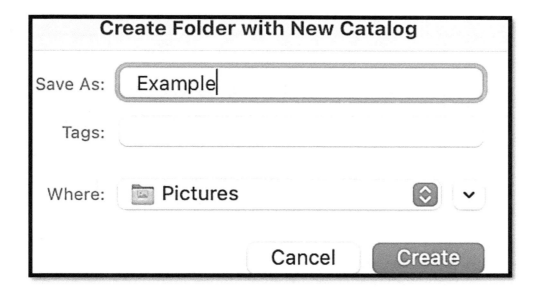

6. With the name you gave the catalog, a new folder will be made, and the catalog will be inside it.

Or make a new Lightroom catalog while you're in an old one.

- Click "**File**" in the Lightroom menu bar.

- Click on "**New Catalog**" next.

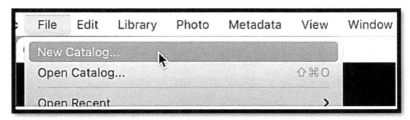

- Do the steps 3 through 6 above.

Lightroom catalog settings

Take some time to change some of the catalog settings after you've made your Lightroom catalog.

In the top menu bar, click on **"Lightroom Classic."** Then, scroll down and click on **"Catalog Settings"** to bring up the Catalog Settings box.

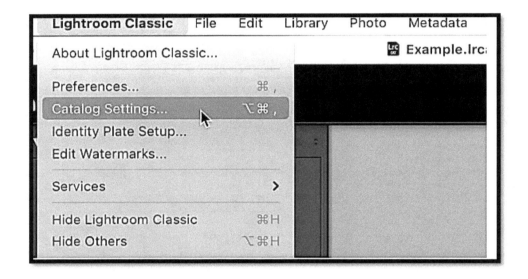

Lightroom catalog settings – backup

The most important setting for catalogs is to back up your Lightroom catalogs so that you don't lose all of your hard work if the catalog gets damaged. Go to the General tab of Catalog Settings.

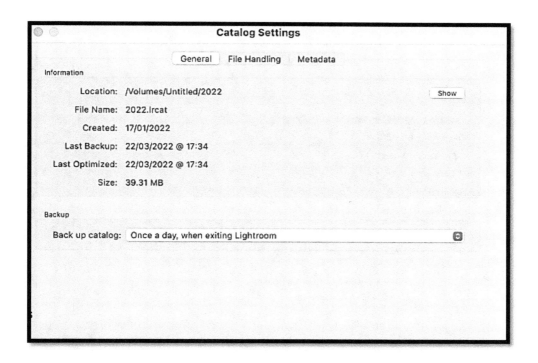

How often you back up will depend on how often you use your catalog, or how often you edit pictures.

It's possible to set it to back up every time you close it, but you'll quickly have a huge number of backup catalogs. Otherwise, you'll quickly run out of room on your hard drive if you don't regularly delete old catalog files.

Here are my ideas for backup frequencies:

- Editing daily —backing up once a day when you close Lightroom
- Editing or adding images weekly —back up once a week when you close Lightroom

You can change how often your catalog is backed up at any time in the catalog settings:

There is an area with a blue button in the General tab of the dialog box. Click it to see your choices and pick the one that works best for you.

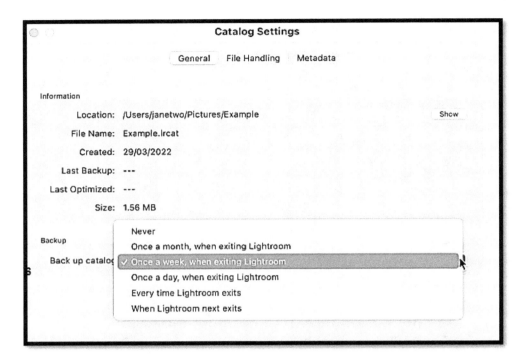

Or change backup frequency when you close Lightroom and get the "Back Up Catalog" prompt

Keep in mind that Lightroom only does a backup of your catalog.

You need to back up your pictures on at least two different drives or in the cloud. (I said it because it's that important.)

Lightroom catalog settings – file handling

In Lightroom Classic, the File Handling tab in the Catalog Settings dialog box provides several options to optimize how the software manages your photo files and previews, enhancing your overall workflow.

One key feature to consider is enabling the "Smart Previews" option during import. When you check this box, Lightroom creates smaller versions of your photos, allowing you to work on your images even if the original files are not connected or accessible.

This can be especially useful if you're working with large batches of photos or if you're using an external drive that's not always connected.

Another useful option is to choose "Build 1:1 Previews" during import. This setting generates previews of your photos at their actual size, which allows you to view and edit them with greater detail right from the start. Although building these large previews can make the import process take a bit longer, it can significantly speed up your workflow later. Without this setting, Lightroom would need to generate these previews on-the-fly when you zoom in on an image, which can be time-consuming.

Importantly, Lightroom is set by default to automatically delete these 1:1 previews after 30 days. This means once your photos have been edited and you no longer need the high-resolution previews, Lightroom will remove them to save disk space. You'll still have standard previews for browsing, but these are smaller and take up less space.

To ensure that 1:1 previews are deleted after 30 days, check that this option is enabled in the File Handling tab. If you prefer a different setup or have specific needs, you can adjust these settings to fit your workflow. Just make sure to select "Build 1:1 Previews" during import if you want to benefit from detailed previews without waiting for them to generate later on.

Lightroom catalog settings – metadata

Metadata can significantly impact the file size of your images and the size of your Lightroom catalog. To manage this efficiently and reduce unnecessary data, you can adjust the settings in the Metadata tab.

Including metadata in your exported JPEG files can be very useful, especially when sharing photos on social media or discussing your camera settings. For this reason, I keep the option to include metadata checked. However, even though metadata is included during export, I use an image optimizer afterward to strip this information before posting my photos to The Lens Lounge. This helps to maintain privacy and keep file sizes manageable for online sharing.

GPS coordinates are another metadata element that may or may not be useful depending on your photography style. As a portrait photographer, I find that GPS information is not necessary for my work, so I make sure this option is unchecked. However, if you're a nature or landscape photographer, you might find GPS data valuable for tracking the locations where your photos were taken.

Another feature is "**Detect faces**," which can identify and tag people in your photos. Even though I specialize in portrait photography, I don't find this feature essential for my workflow, so I leave it unchecked. However, if you frequently photograph family or events and want to organize your photos by the people in them, this feature could be beneficial.

By customizing these settings, you can control the amount of metadata associated with your photos, which can help reduce file and catalog sizes and make your workflow more efficient.

Catalog Settings

General | File Handling | Metadata

Editing

☑ Offer suggestions from recently entered values ⬚ Clear All Suggestion Lists

☑ Include Develop settings in metadata inside JPEG, TIFF, PNG, and PSD files

☐ Automatically write changes into XMP

Warning: Changes made in Lightroom will not automatically be visible in other applications unless written to XMP.

Address Lookup

☐ Look up city, state and country of GPS coordinates to provide address suggestions

☐ Export address suggestions whenever address fields are empty

Face Detection

☐ Automatically detect faces in all photos

EXIF

☐ Write date or time changes into proprietary raw files.

About the Library Module

Panel 1 is inside the Library Module, Panel 2 is inside, and Panel 3 is inside. These are the first two things on the menu. The library panel stands out in the upper left part of the screen. There are two parts to the Library panel: The Collections Section and the Library Section. The left menu makes it simple to get to the Library section. Check out all of the pictures in the Library Module. The way Collections works is the same as the way Library works, so feel free to look through all of the Library Items there.

The Library Module has a cool function that lets you quickly switch between sections and collections from the Library Section. People who have a lot of images in their library will love this feature because it lets them quickly switch between **"Select to Import"** and **"Select to Load"** without leaving the library section.

40

People who like to look at all of their pictures can easily do so in the Library module, even if the photos are in different collections. Double-click on "**Sort By**" and "**Sort By Age**" to do this. In the library module, go to the Collection section and click on a picture to see all the photos there.

Using Picture Lock: Command Bar in the Library Module

The picture lock is in the top left part of the home screen of the Library module. This drop-down menu lets you save a picture. The picture lock tool in the Lightroom Library Module is a great way to keep new and unpublished photos in a certain library. With Picture Lock, all of your pictures that haven't been published are put in a new folder in the library module. You can still look at the photos in your library, but you won't be able to import or export them.

To lock a picture to the same library, double-click on it. This will stop it from being unlocked. When working with a multi-layer folder system that has many folders, you can protect a picture that is inside one of the nested folders. You can also get to the picture lock command bar from the Library section. **Make sure to use the picture lock choices that were given.**

- Show the Picture Lock icon.
- Lock from one folder only.
- Lock to any location in the library
- Lock from any library

The folder name in the library module is now fixed in the Library section.

Mastering the Command Bar in the Library Module

The second part is easy to find on the Navigation Bar (also called the Command Bar) in the top right area of the Library Module. As the name suggests, this is a full list of every change you can make to your library. Since there are 3 settings for the Command

Bar, there isn't just one guide for it. You can try out all three settings for each part of the list if you'd like. We like the left Option 1 button the best.

- **Disable**

  To turn this section off, just click the button at the bottom. In the top left part of the screen, the library module will have a navigation bar. It can handle organizing your files well. In any case, it won't be able to hide and show the library navigation. The "**Clear Library**" menu is the only way to change libraries. It's in the top left corner of the Library Module.

- **Options**

  Depending on the section you are working on, use these settings to quickly move between the different sections of the library module.

- **Gallery**

  This lets you look through all of the pictures in the library, which are in the bottom part. It shows previews of the pictures, icons for the layers, and links that let you open the pictures in different places, like an HDR Slideshow or Photoshop Presets. Keep in mind that the Gallery option doesn't have an icon, so it might not be easy to find at first. You have to press the List button to see it. Press and hold down the navigation bar in the Library Module to get to the Gallery section.

Library Module's Gallery Section

Press the menu button in the upper right corner to switch to the Gallery option. Just click on the button in the bottom right corner to go to the Gallery section. The Gallery section works in the same way that the Library module does.

Locate a suitable gallery image.

To begin editing a library or photo, you must first pick a picture from your library or photo collection. Some people think it's simple, but it's one of the hardest things to do when you're editing pictures. Drag and drop the picture where you want it on the surface with the mouse.

After choosing the picture, go to the Gallery section of your Library module and click on Project Settings. On the left side of the picture is an icon that looks like a small circle. This is the picture you want to get. If you tap on it, the image's features will show up. Here are some things that will help you narrow down your choices. Using different tool settings, you can zoom in, change the image's size, change its color, crop it, resize it, and rotate it.

Using Compare View

Once you know where the blurry parts are in your photos, it's time to fix them so they are clear. You will decide which way to use based on the differences you see in your pictures.

One way to fix blurry photos is to change the exposure or sharpness settings for all of them. Another way is to fine-tune the settings for specific parts of your photos to make them clearer and more contrasty. If you have a good eye, the first choice might work best if you have many clear pictures. You could get a lot of blurry pictures if you don't.

When you use this method, you can change the sharpness and exposure settings for different parts of your photos to make blurry ones look better. With the second choice, you can look at different parts of your photos side by side and change the settings for brightness and sharpness to fix blurry photos. Change the sharpness and exposure levels for every part of the picture at the same time. This will save you time.

How to Find Your Best Photos Using Compare View In Lightroom

Follow these steps to use the second option: In Lightroom Classic, find the list of adjustments and choose "Compare View." When you're done, the edited picture will replace the original photo. To save the picture, just click on it or drag the top picture to your clipboard. The second picture should be added to the list. It's easier to see how different parts of your picture compare with this feature. You can change the settings to make parts of the picture that aren't in focus stand out more. You can save the first picture by clicking on it, or you can drag the next picture to your clipboard if you'd rather. The Exposure and Contrast sliders let you improve the look of your photos' highlights and shadows.

Organizing Photos with Folders and Collections

If you're like me, I get confused when I see a restaurant's big menu. It's much easier to decide what to eat when the menu is small.

The same goes for pictures.

When you can see a small collection of images at a glance it's easier to cherry-pick the ones you want.

In this case, Lightroom Collections are more important than Folders. In a collection, you can view a group of pictures at once instead of going through all the photos in a folder.

Not only that, though. Collections are more than that.

To begin, Lightroom has four different types of collections, and each one is used for a different task.

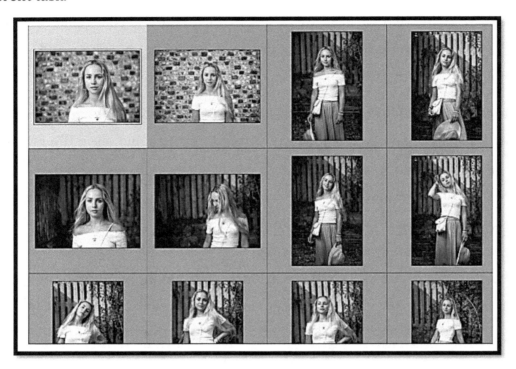

What's the difference between Folders and Collections in Lightroom?

Lightroom Folders

- A folder is where your pictures live, and you can only get to it from the Library module.
- Folders show how your filing system is organized. Photos on your computer are kept there. When you move or delete a folder, the computer will also move or delete it.
- Photos can only show up in one folder at a time.

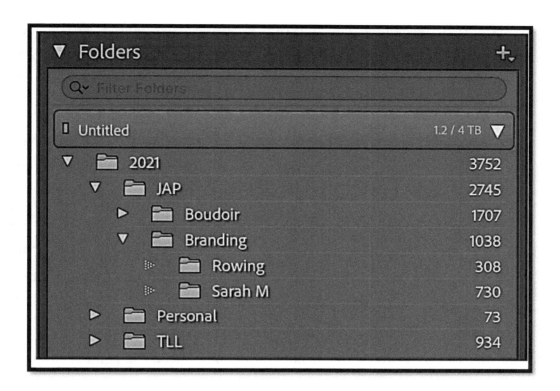

Lightroom Collections

- When you create a virtual copy of a photo in a Collection within Lightroom, this virtual copy will also appear in the Folder where the original photo is stored.

This means that while the Collection serves as a temporary workspace for organizing and viewing your photos, the virtual copies are still linked to their original locations in the Folder.

- You can access and manage your Collections from any Lightroom module, which makes it a flexible way to organize your photos without having to worry about deleting them. Collections act as a temporary holding place for your images, allowing you to group and view them as needed.

- If you delete a photo from a Collection, the original file remains in the Folder. To completely remove the photo from Lightroom, you must also delete it from the Folder. This can be a bit cumbersome, especially if you frequently create virtual copies to compare different edits of the same image. It's easy to end up with multiple versions of the same photo if you're not careful.

- To avoid clutter and keep your catalog organized, remember to delete unwanted photos from both the Collection and the Folder. Failing to do so can result in a buildup of duplicate images, which can overwhelm your library.

- Additionally, removing a Collection will not affect the photos within it or the Folder they are stored in. Collections are simply organizational tools and do not alter the actual files or their locations

You can include photos from lots of different folders into one collection. And a photo can appear in several collections, but in only one folder.

Putting pictures for a photo book into collections is a great way to narrow down your choices before you go to the book module to design your book.

Kinds of Lightroom collections
There are four types of Lightroom collections:

1. Collections
2. Quick Collections
3. Target Collections

4.   Smart Collections

1.   Collections

These are collections that you create and populate manually.

How Collections work

Most of the time, you'll use these Lightroom collections to view a group of pictures from a shoot. Collections are very useful because, unlike Folders, they can be reached from the Develop module.

To create a Collection:

- Click the plus sign next to Collections.
- From the drop-down menu, choose "**Create Collection.**"
- Give your collection a name and check or uncheck the Include selected photos box
- If you want it to be included in a Collection Set, check that box and specify the Collection Set

2. **Quick Collections**

Photographs will be added to this Lightroom collection when you press the B key or right-click and choose "Add to Quick Collection."

Simply put, Quick Collections are great for quickly making short-term collections.

How Quick Collections work

When I write an article Lounge, I make a "Quick Collection" of photos from different shoots that I might use before I choose the best ones.

- The Library grid view makes it quick and easy to look through my folders.
- Click on the pictures I'm thinking about
- I like to use computer shortcuts so I can add pictures to the Quick Collection quickly. To do this, click B or right-click and choose Save Quick Collection.
- Next, save the Quick Collection as a Collection.
- After that, I view the Collection and make my final selection for the article by removing photos.

To save a Quick Collection as a Collection:

- Click on Quick Collection with the right mouse button.
- iFrom the drop-down menu, choose **Save Quick Collection.**
- Gve your collection a name.
- Make sure the box that says "**Clear Quick Collection After Saving**" is checked.
- You can click **Save** and it will show up in your Collections panel.

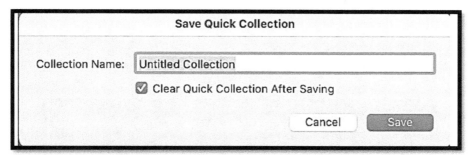

Target Collections

You don't have to use Quick Collections to turn any regular collection into a Target Collection. To set a collection as a target, right-click on its name and choose "**Set as Target Collection**" from the menu that appears.

Once you've set up a Target Collection in Lightroom Classic, you can easily add photos to it with a simple keystroke or a quick menu option. When you select a photo and press the B key (or right-click and choose "Add to Target Collection"), the photo will be added directly to the Target Collection you've designated, rather than the Quick

Collection. This feature is handy for quickly organizing images into a specific collection without having to navigate through multiple menus.

If you want to remove a photo from the Target Collection, simply press the B key again or right-click the photo and select "Remove from Target Collection" from the menu. This action will remove the image from the Target Collection, but it will remain in its original location or other collections.

Target Collections are particularly useful for efficiently managing and organizing photos for various purposes. For example, you can use a Target Collection to:

- Compile a list of your client's favorite images from a recent shoot.

- Gather images you plan to include in a photo book, making it easier to keep track of your selections.

- Create virtual copies of images sized specifically for Instagram stories or other social media platforms, helping you streamline your content preparation process.

Once you've finished using a Target Collection in Lightroom Classic and no longer need to add photos to it, you can easily remove the target function. This will stop new photos from being added to the collection when you press the B key, but the collection itself will remain intact and accessible.

To remove the Target Collection functionality, right-click on the name of the collection in the Collections panel. From the context menu that appears, deselect the option labeled "Set as Target Collection." This action will deactivate the target function for that collection.

After doing this, any new photos you select and press B for will default back to the Quick Collection, as it was before you set up the Target Collection. This allows you to manage your workflow efficiently without accidentally adding new images to a collection that is no longer relevant.

3. **Smart collections**

According to their settings, these Lightroom collections populate automatically.

Lightroom comes with six smart collections already set up:

- Colored Red (or whatever colors you've used)
- Five Stars
- Past Month
- Recently Modified
- Video Files
- Without Keywords

How to use smart collections in Lightroom

You can use the metadata of your pictures to filter the Smart Collection, in addition to the default ones, to build your own. For instance, you can make a Smart Collection of all the pictures you've taken:

- With a particular lens
- On a particular day
- Or of a particular person

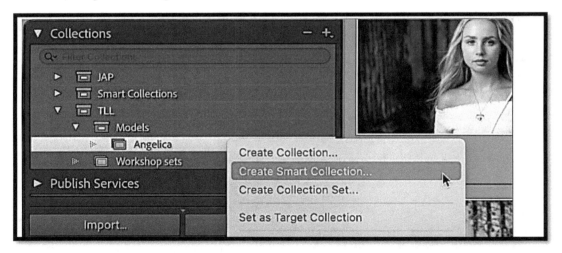

There are a lot of things on this list that can be used to put pictures in a smart collection, whether they are in the metadata or something you type in (like keywords or people tags).

Here's how to create a Smart Collection:

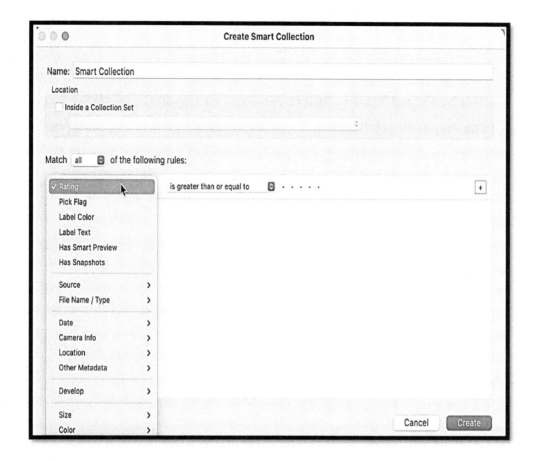

- When you click the plus sign next to Collections,
- From the drop-down menu, choose **"Create Smart Collection."**
- Set the settings for the Smart Collection, give it a name, and click **Create**.

What's the difference between a Collection and a Smart Collection in Lightroom?

Collections

- You gather photos into Collections by hand.
- In a regular Lightroom Collection, you can rearrange pictures as much as you want.

Smart Collections

- Smart Collections are configured to compile images on their own. For example, you can put all of your five-star pictures into a Smart Collection. A picture will appear there if you award it five stars. It will be removed from the Smart Collection if you alter the rating from five stars to anything else.

- It is not possible to manually organize photos in a Smart Collection. You can still arrange them using the default settings for things like label color, star rating, and capture time.

Where are Lightroom collections stored?

You can get to collections in the Library and Develop modules via the Collections panel on the left side of the screen.

Lightroom Collections do not hold image data. Similar to a technique to access a collection of images from one or more folders, collections.

How do I organize my Lightroom collections?

Lightroom Collections can be individual Collections or can be organized into Collection Sets.

For instance, I have Collection Sets for The Lens Lounge and my portrait photography company, which are further subdivided into Collection Sets for various genres (boudoir, model portfolios, personal branding, etc.).

How to create a Collection Set:

- Click the plus sign next to Collections.

- From the drop-down box, choose Create Collection Set.

- Give the Collection Set a name.

- Check the box and choose which Collection Set it will go into if it's going into a Collection Set. If not, uncheck the box.

- Press "**Create**"

Applying Keywords

Keywords are image metadata that customers add that tell you what's in a photo. They help you figure out what pictures are in the catalog and how to find them. Keywords can be read by Adobe programs like Adobe Bridge, Photo Shop, and Photo Shop Elements, as well as other programs that accept XMP metadata after they have been applied to pictures.

There are several ways to add keywords to pictures in Lightroom Classic. It's possible to type or choose keywords in the Keywording panel, or you can drag pictures to certain keywords in the Keyword List panel.

Photos that have keywords show up with a thumbnail badge in the Grid view. In the Keyword List panel, you can view all of the catalog's keywords. At any time, you can add, edit, rename, or delete keywords. It's possible to choose synonyms and export choices when you're making or editing keywords. Keywords and their synonyms are similar concepts. When you choose Photos that have keywords that have similar words, the similar words show up in the Keywording panel when you choose **Keyword** > **Will Export.**

Keywords can have other keywords inside them. For instance, the keyword animals might have the keywords cats and dogs in it. On the other hand, the keyword dogs could include things like Australian Shepherd, Border Collie, and more.

Create keywords

1. In the Grid view, pick one or more pictures, or In the Loupe, Compare, or Survey view, select a single photo in the Filmstrip and do any of the following:
   - Type your keywords into the box that says "**Click Here To Add Keywords**" in the **Keywording** panel. After that, press Return (Mac OS) or Enter (Windows). Don't do the rest of the steps in this process.
   - In the **Keyword List** panel, click the plus sign (+).
2. Type a name for the keyword in the **Create Keyword Tag** box.
3. Type synonyms for the keyword. For each word, put a comma between it.
4. Pick any of the options that are shown.

Edit keywords

1. In the Library module, right-click (Windows) or control-click (Mac OS) on a keyword in the **Keyword List** panel. This will bring up a menu where you can choose **Edit Keyword Tag.**
2. Inside the **Edit Keyword Tag** box, you can change the keyword name, add synonyms, or set any of the keyword choices that are shown.

Export Synonyms

Includes synonyms associated with the keyword when exporting photos.

Rename keywords

1. In the Library module, right-click (Windows) or control-click (Mac OS) on a keyword in the **Keyword List** panel. This will bring up a menu where you can choose **Edit Keyword Tag.**

2. Change the keyword's name in the **Edit Keyword Tag** box, then click **Save**.

Add keywords to photos

You can add keywords to pictures in the Library module's **Keywording** panel. You can type in a new keyword or use keywords from a set. You can drag pictures to keywords in the **Keyword List** panel to add keywords to them as well.

The changes you make to photos with keywords are saved in Lightroom Classic, but they aren't saved to the files until the **Automatically Write Changes Into XMP** option is chosen in the **Catalog Settings** dialog box. If you want to save the keywords by hand, go to **Metadata > Save Metadata To File.**

1. If you want to add keywords to more than one picture at once, pick them all in the Grid view. You can also pick out a single picture from the Filmstrip in Loupe, Compare, or Survey view.

    Note: It is possible to pick more than one picture in the Filmstrip in Loupe, Compare, or Survey view. The keywords will only be added to the active photo.

2. Do any of these things:

    o   Type keywords into the box that says "**Click Here To Add Keywords**" in the Keywords area of the **Keywording** panel. Use commas to separate keywords. If you want to show a hierarchy of keywords, use |, <, or >. For example, animal | dog, animal > dog, or dog < animal.

    o   In the **Keywording** panel, click on a keyword in the **Keyword Suggestions** area. Several things go into making keyword suggestions, such as the keywords that have already been used on the chosen picture and on other photos that were taken within a reasonable amount of time.

- o In the **Keyword Set** area of the **Keywording** panel, click on a keyword from a keyword set.
- o In the **Keyword List** panel, click the target box to the left of a keyword. A tick means that the chosen picture has that keyword in it.
- o (Grid view only) Drag photos to keywords in the **Keyword List** panel. You can also drag a keyword from the **Keyword List** panel to the pictures you've chosen.

Note: When you import pictures into Lightroom Classic, you can also add keywords to them.

The **Keyword List** panel shows how many photos use the tag when new keywords are added to photos.

Copy and paste keywords

1. Pick out the picture with the keywords you want to copy in the Grid view.
2. Choose the keywords in the applied tags area of the **Keywording** panel, Right-click (Windows), or Control-click (Mac OS) and select **Copy**.
3. In the Grid view, pick out the pictures that you want to add keywords to.
4. Click in the applied tags area of the **Keywording** panel and right-click (Windows) or Control-click (Mac OS) and choose **Paste**.

Remove or delete keywords from photos or the catalog

1. In the Grid view, pick one or more pictures. In the Loupe, Compare, or Survey view, select one photo in the Filmstrip and do one of the following:
   - o Select **Keyword Tags** > **Enter Keywords** in the **Keywording** panel to remove keywords from pictures. Then, in the panel's text box, pick out one or more keywords and delete them. It's possible to pick more than one

picture in the Filmstrip while in Loupe, Compare, or Survey view. The keywords will only be removed from the active photo.

o   Right-click (Windows) or Control-click (Mac OS) on the keyword in the **Keyword List** panel and select **Delete** from the menu. This will remove the keyword from pictures and the catalog for good. You can also pick keywords and click the minus sign (-) at the top of the **Keyword List** panel.

Note: If you remove keywords by mistake, press Ctrl+Z (Windows) or Command+Z (Mac OS) right away to undo it.

o   Select **Metadata > Purge Unused Keywords** to get rid of any keywords that aren't being used from the catalog.

Note: Once you use the Purge Unused Keywords command to delete keywords, you can't get them back.

The **Keyword List** panel changes to show how many photos still use the tag after you remove keywords from them.

Add or remove keywords using the Painter tool

Once you've set up your keyword shortcuts in Lightroom Classic, you can efficiently apply these keywords to your photos using the Painter tool. Here's how to use it effectively:

1.   **Enable the Painter Tool:**

o   In the Library module, if the Painter tool isn't visible in the toolbar, you can access it by going to Metadata and selecting "Enable Painting."

o   Alternatively, in Grid view, select the Painter tool directly from the toolbar. If you don't see it immediately, you may need to add it to your toolbar.

When the Painter tool is activated, your cursor will change to a painter icon. If you still can't see the Painter tool icon in the toolbar, make sure it is enabled from the menu.

2. **Select Keywords:**
   - In the Painter tool's menu, choose "Keywords" if that's what you want to apply. This allows you to add specific keywords to your selected photos.

3. **Enter Keywords:**
   - Type the keyword or keywords you wish to apply in the toolbar box. These keywords will be added to the photos you select using the Painter tool.

4. **Apply Keywords:**
   - **Single Photo:** Click on a single photo with the Painter tool to apply the keyword to that image.

   - **Multiple Photos:** Click and drag across multiple photos in the Grid view to apply the keyword to all selected images.

   - **Remove Keywords:** If you need to remove a keyword, hold down the Alt key on Windows or the Option key on Mac OS. The Painter tool will switch to an eraser function. Click on the photo or drag across several photos to remove the keyword.

Tip: To quickly filter photos by keyword in Grid view, click the white arrow next to the keyword in the Keyword List panel. This will display only the photos with that keyword, making it easier to review or remove them.

5. **Turn Off Painter Tool:**

- Once you're done, click the circular well in the Painter tool menu to disable it. The Painter icon will reappear in the toolbar, indicating that the tool is turned off.

Using the Painter tool is a quick and efficient way to manage keywords across your photos, helping you keep your catalog organized and easily searchable.

Working with keyword sets and nesting keywords

You work with keyword sets in the Keyword Set section of the Keywording panel. A keyword set is a collection of keywords assembled for a particular purpose. Sort the terms you'll need for the project into three categories: special occasion, project, and family and friends. There are three fundamental sets of keyword presets in Lightroom Classic.

You can use these sets in any way you want. Based on them, you can make your own sets. When you're in charge of several library collections, keyword sets can help you keep important keywords close at hand. A keyword tag can be part of more than one keyword set. Go to **Lightroom Preferences** and click on the **Presets** tab. This will show you the Lightroom presets in the **Keyword Set** menu. Press "**Restore Keyword Set Presets**" in the **Lightroom Defaults** menu. Please keep in mind that we will use some examples in this part.

The steps:

1. If you need to, you can make the Keyword Set area in the Keywording panel bigger. Then, pick Wedding Photography from the Keyword Set menu. It will be easy to organize the pictures from a big event with this list of keywords. Check out the other Lightroom keyword sets to see what other groups they have. You can make your own sets of keywords from these templates and save them as a new preset. Setting up sets of keywords is a great way to keep things

in order. Putting tags in a tree-like structure based on how they connect is a good way to keep them in order.

2. Find the **Syracuse keyword** in the Keyword List panel. Click and drag it to the New York keyword. The New York keyword instantly widens to show the tag "Syracuse" nested inside it.

3. Move your files from the keywords list to the Collections keyword. When the Collections tag is expanded, the nested tags will be shown.

4. We'd like to add the keyword "Chicago" to the Tour keyword to show some pictures. Click on the Tour keyword and then on the plus sign (+) in the upper left area of the Keyword List panel to add a new keyword tag.

5. In the dialog box for making a Keyword Tag, type "**Chicago**" in the text box that says "Keyword Name." Make sure that the first three choices under Keyword Tag Options are chosen, as shown in the image below, and then click on **Create**.

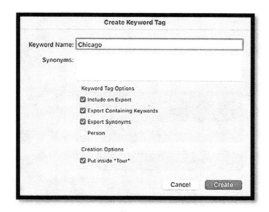

○   When you export your pictures, don't forget to include the keyword tag.

○   When exporting photos, the parent tag is included in the export containing keywords.

○   The export synonyms feature includes any words that are similar to the keyword tag when you export your pictures.

6. In the Folders panel, pick a folder. Then, pick all the pictures in that folder except for the last two. From the Keyword List, add the Chicago keyword tag to any of the pictures you've chosen in the Grid view.

Here's a helpful suggestion: In the Metadata menu, you can find the Export Keywords and Import Keywords options. These can be used to move keyword lists between computers or share them with friends who also use Lightroom. Make sure that the new Chicago and Tour keyword tags have checkmarks next to them as you look through the Keyword List. On the right, you can also see how many pictures are next to each entry. In other words, these two keyword tags were used on all of the pictures that were picked.

Searching by keyword

Metadata like ratings, flags, and labels help you organize your pictures properly. Then it's simple to set up advanced filters to find the exact photo you need. It's possible to find pictures in your library by searching or filtering them with keywords. To have two panels open at the same time in either of the side panel groups, just right-click on the header of any panel in the group and uncheck Solo mode from the menu that appears.

The steps:

1. If you haven't already, go to **Library > Show Photos In Subfolders**. If you need to, you can collapse any other panels in the group on the left panel so that you can see the Catalog and Folder panels. Click on the folder in the Folders panel, then select **Edit > Select None** or use **Command+D/Ctrl+D**.

2. Slide the Thumbnails slider in the Toolbar to make the thumbnails smaller. This will let you see more images in the Grid view. Choose **View > Show Filter Bar** or press the Backslash key (\) to show the Filter bar above the Grid view.

3. To view the expanded Keyword List panel's contents, collapse any other panels in the right panel group as necessary.

4. Move your mouse over the other keyword in the Keyword List panel and click on the white arrow that shows up next to the image count.

The fact that All Photographs are chosen in the left panel group shows that your entire catalog was searched for photos with the keyword tag you opened. The Metadata filter has been activated in the Filter bar at the top of the work area. The Grid view now only shows pictures in your library that are tagged with the opened keyword tag.

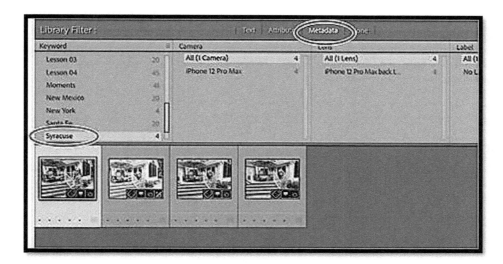

In the Grid view, you can only see four pictures that have the tag. You will search differently now.

5. Click on All in the Keywords column, and then click on Text in the Filter bar at the top In the Text filter menus, choose Any Searchable Field from the first menu and Contains All from the second menu. Pay close attention to the options in each menu. After that, type Tour into the box on the right and press **Enter** or **Return**.

Tip: Press the lock button on the right side of the Filter bar while choosing a different image source in the Catalog, Folders, or Collections panel. This will keep your current filter settings. You can only see nine photos in the Grid view at the moment. The Library filters are at their most powerful when you set up more complicated filters based on a mix of criteria. The thing you did should have shown you what's possible.

6. To turn off the filters, click "**None**" at the top of the Filter bar. Pick out the folder in the Folders panel. Then, press **Command+D** or **Ctrl+D** or go to **Edit > Select None.**

Using flags and ratings

With the Attribute filters in the Filter bar, you can quickly find your pictures and put them in the right place. These filters are based on things like ratings and flags. When you click on Attribute, the Library Filter bar will get bigger. This will reveal controls to sort images by flag status, edit status, star rating, color label, copy status, or any combination of these.

Flagging images

Putting together a group of pictures can begin with assigning flags to separate the good ones from the bad ones (and the ones that haven't been flagged). You have the option to mark an image as a pick, reject, or leave it unflagged.

Here are the steps:

1. At the very top of the Filter bar, click on **Attribute**. When the Filter bar gets bigger, the Attribute filter controls show up. The Toolbar lets you add ratings, flags, and color labels in both the Grid and Loupe views. The controls below the pictures let you change any of these things when you're in the Compare or Survey views. In the Photo menu, you can flag, rate, or color label a selected image.

2. Simply press the **T key** to show the Toolbar below the Grid view. Press the triangle on the right side of the Toolbar and choose Flagging from the menu. This will show the Flag as Pick and Set as Rejected buttons in the Toolbar.

3. Find a folder in the Folders panel and pick it.

4. When you're in Grid view, pick a picture from this group of pictures. If you choose the Flags option under Cell Icons in the **Library View Options** dialog box, a gray flag icon will appear in the top left corner of the image cell. In this case, the picture has not been flagged. If you can't see the flag icon, move the

mouse over the image cell or turn off the option in the Library View Options box that makes clickable things only show up when the mouse is over them. You can press Command+J or Ctrl+J to get to the **View Options** box or go to **View > View Options**.

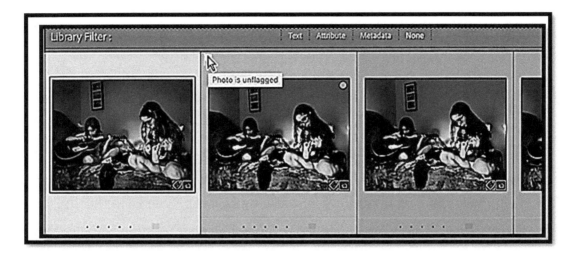

5. You can either click on the flag badge in the image cell or the Flag as Pick button in the Toolbar to mark the flag as "Flagged." To remind you, the picture now has a white flag icon in the top left corner of the image cell.

6. In the Attribute Filter bar, press the white flag icon. In the Grid view, only the picture that has been flagged is shown. Now, the screen only shows the flagged images from the folder you opened.

    TIP: You can quickly sort your pictures by whether they have been marked or not by going to **Library > Refine Photos**. In the **Refine Photos** box, go to **Library > Refine Photos** and click **Refine**. This action will mark any photos that aren't flagged as rejects and return the picks to being unflagged.

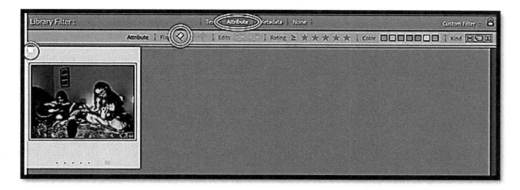

In Lightroom Classic 2025, you can make notes on a picture in a number of different ways. Press the P key on your keyboard or go to **Photo > Set Flag > Flagged** to make a picture a pick. To switch from **"Unflagged" to "Pick**," just click on the flag icon in the picture cell's top left area. Find Photo > Set Flag > refused and press the X key. You can also option-click or alt-press the flag icon in the upper left corner of the image cell to mark it as refused.

Press the U key or go to Photo > Set Flag > Unflagged to get rid of a flag in a picture. Right-click on the flag icon in the top left corner of an image cell and select Flagged, Unflagged, or Rejected from the menu that comes up. Now the image's flag state has changed.

7.   In the Attribute Filter bar, make sure the white flag is still chosen. Then, click on the gray flag button in the middle. Now that all photos marked as picks and photos not marked as picks can be seen in the Grid view, we can see all the pictures in the Sabine-guitar folder.

8.   To turn off the Attribute filters, click on None in the Filter bar.

Assigning ratings

Putting each picture on a scale from one to five stars is a good way to keep them organized while you're reviewing them.

These are the steps:

1. Click on a folder in the Folders panel. In the Grid view, make sure that the Sort menu on the Toolbar is set to Capture Time. After that, click on the second picture to choose it.

2. When you press the 3 key on your keyboard, the words "Set Rating To 3" will briefly show up on the screen. The photo now has three stars in the lower left corner of the image cell. To make sure you can see the stars, go to View > View Options and make sure that **Rating And Label** are chosen in the Bottom Label or Top Label menu in the Compact Cell Extras display settings.

3. If you need to change the rating, click on the triangle on the right side of the Toolbar and select Rating from the menu that appears. The stars in the Toolbar show the rating that was just given to the currently selected image. If more than one image with a different rating is chosen, the Toolbar will show the rating of the first image chosen. To rate photos in the Metadata panel, either right-click on a photo's thumbnail and choose **Set Rating** from the menu that appears or choose Photo > Set Rating from the menu that appears.

4. It's easy to change the rating for a chosen picture—just press a key between 1 and 5 to give it a new rating, or press the 0 key to remove the rating. For this image, press the 0 key.

Applying Metadata

The information that is linked to image files is called metadata. It helps you organize and manage your photo library better. Your camera automatically creates important metadata, like the date and time of the capture, the exposure time, the focal length, and the camera settings. You can also add your own metadata, which will help you organize and search your catalog better.

Giving your photos keywords, ratings, and color labels showed how knowledgeable you were. Lightroom also follows the **International Press Telecommunications Council (IPTC)** rules for information, which cover things like credits, origins, descriptions, and categories. The Metadata panel in the right panel group lets you see or change the information about an image.

These are the steps:

1. Click on your picture folder in the Folders panel. In the Grid view, pick any picture you want.

    There is a Customize button next to the Default setting on the Metadata Set menu at the bottom of the Metadata panel. If you click it, you can pick which fields to show in that setting.

2. To get the best view of the Metadata panel, collapse the other panels in the right panel group or hide the Filmstrip. In the title of the Metadata panel, find the Metadata Set menu and choose "**Default**."

    The default metadata set shows a lot of information about the image. If you click the "Customize" button, you can add information from many other fields as well. The camera made a lot of the metadata, which can help you organize your photos. For example, you can sort photos by the date they were taken, look for photos taken with a certain lens, or tell the difference between photos taken on different cameras. The default set only shows a small part of an image's metadata.

3. Choose EXIF and IPTC from the Metadata Set menu. Go to the next page of the Metadata panel to learn about the different kinds of data that can be added to a picture.

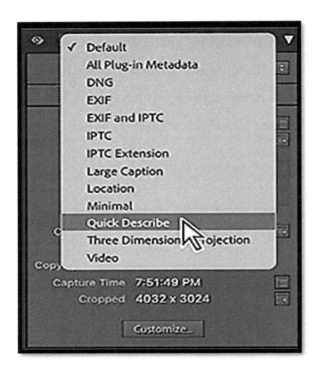

4. To finish this task, go to the Metadata Set menu and choose Quick Describe.

The Metadata panel shows details like the filename, copy name (for a virtual copy), folder, rating, and various EXIF and IPTC metadata as part of the Quick Describe metadata set. This panel lets you give a photo a title and caption, add a copyright notice, share information about the photographer and the location of the photo, and change the star rating.

5. Give the picture three stars by clicking on the third dot next to Rating in the Metadata panel. Next, type "Sabine and Ethan at the Game" in the Title text box and press Return or Enter.

6. Click on either of the two photos that look a lot alike to add it to the list. Then, click on **Selected Photos** at the top of the Metadata panel. You'll see that both files have the same folder name, size, and camera model. However, things that aren't shared by both images will now show up as <mixed>. If you change any of the items in the Metadata panel, it will affect both of the chosen images, even if their values are different.

If you need a more detailed caption for your files, choose the Large Caption Metadata Set. This is important for photojournalists and people who take pictures for sports. It will give you more room for the title, which will make it easier to write.

Storing metadata

Data is stored using the Extensible Metadata Platform (XMP) standard, which is built on top of XML. When working with camera raw files, which have their own file format, XMP is not integrated into the original files.

A feature that makes it easy for metadata to move between Adobe programs and publishing workflows. You can speed up your work by using metadata from one file as a model and importing it into other files. XMP is used to describe and sync metadata stored in different formats, like EXIF, IPTC (IIM), and TIFF, which makes it easier to view and manage.

Using Smart Previews

It can use smaller versions of the original picture called "Smart Previews" when:

o Working with photos in the Develop module (and Quick Develop panel) when the originals are offline, like when they're on a drive that's not plugged in?

o Syncing Lightroom Classic files to the cloud so that Lightroom on mobile devices can view them.

Smart Previews are kept in a different file called Smart Preview.lrdata and are not the same as the previews used in the Library module (in Grid, Loope, Zoom, Survey, and Compare views).

How to Make Smart Previews

On Import

Make Smart Previews when you load new photos into Lightroom. This is the best way to do it. Just click on the button on the right that says **"Build Smart Previews."** (Look at the picture above.)

Images Already in the Catalog

Pick out the pictures you want to turn into Smart Previews from the ones that are already in your library, then go to the Library drop-down choice.

Pick **"Previews"** and then **"Build Smart Previews"** from that menu.

To get to a specific picture, click on the **"Original Photo"** box that's right below the bar. After you do that, a box will pop up asking if you want to make a Smart Preview:

When you work on a lot of pictures at once, the teasers may take a while to load.

But once they're made, you can edit, change the information, export, or print them without having the originals on hand.

Managing Smart Previews

Smart Previews are pretty much the only thing you need to do after setting them up. You can still view how much room they're taking up and delete them if your laptop runs out of space.

To find out how much space your Smart Previews are using, go to Catalog Settings > File Handling.

You can then monitor the amount of space your Smart Preview file is using.

Deleting Smart Previews from photographs you are no longer working with is the easiest approach to get rid of them if they are taking up too much space.

It is almost the same to do this with a single image as it is to create one.

You should click on the **"Original + Smart Preview"** line. Following that, a window will appear asking whether you want to remove the Smart Preview.

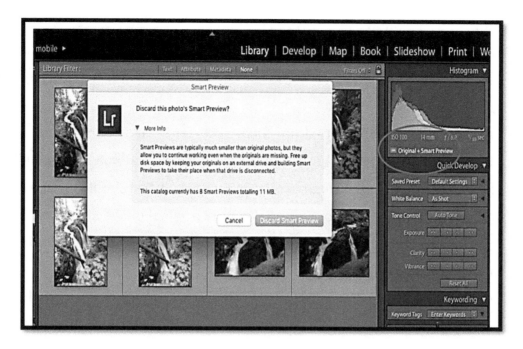

In Grid view, select a group of photos, then go to the Library drop-down option. There, click "Previews" and then "Get Rid of Smart Previews."

How to tell Lightroom to only use Smart Previews

As we already said, you can tell Lightroom to only work with Smart Previews, even if you still have the originals (i.e., your external hard drive with the photos is still connected).

There is a drop-down button in Lightroom that says "Preferences." Click on that to do this. You can then click on the "Performance" tab. There is a box for changing pictures. Check "Use Smart Previews" instead of "Originals."

Use Smart Previews by going to **Lightroom > Preferences > Performance**

After that, you'll need to restart Lightroom.

Limitations of using Smart Previews

When working with Lightroom's Smart Previews, it's important to be aware of their limitations, particularly if you frequently use Photoshop or perform tasks like HDR and panorama merges.

1. **Compatibility with Photoshop:** Smart Previews cannot be sent directly to Photoshop or used with plugins. To edit your photos in Photoshop, you'll need to work with the original source files. In Lightroom, you should go to the menu and select "Edit In > Photoshop" to open the original image in Photoshop.

2. **HDR and Panorama Merges:** Smart Previews also cannot be used for merging photos into HDR (High Dynamic Range) or creating panoramas. For these tasks, you'll need access to the original source files. If your workflow involves a lot of HDR or panorama work, Smart Previews might not be sufficient for your needs.

3. **Quality and Adjustments:** The 1:1 preview generated from a Smart Preview differs from the 1:1 view of the original RAW file, especially when it comes to detailed adjustments like sharpening and noise reduction. Smart Previews are lower resolution compared to the full-sized RAW files. Once you have access to the original file again, it's a good idea to review and adjust any sharpening or noise reduction changes, as they might not appear as accurate in the Smart Preview.

If you mainly edit within Lightroom and don't often use Photoshop or perform HDR merges, Smart Previews can be a useful tool for efficient editing and workflow management. However, if your work involves these advanced tasks, you might need to rely more on the original files to ensure the best quality and accuracy in your edits.

CHAPTER FOUR

UTILIZING THE NEW FEATURES

Remove distractions in a photo with Generative Remove

To successfully remove distractions in a picture, use the Generative AI option in the Remove tool. With this new tool in Lightroom Classic, you can easily get rid of things like cars, signs, poles, and more that you don't want in your photos, even if the background is complicated.

1. In the **Develop module**, go to **Remove** and then pick **Generative AI**.

2. Use a brush to remove the item. To pick very precisely, change the brush size and the overlay's opacity.

3. After moving your brush over the item, use the Refine tools to pick out the following:

    o **Add**—Fix the selection by adding a brush.

    o **Subtract**: Take away parts of the selections that you don't want.

In Mask Refinement, you can change the size of the brush.

4. Adobe Firefly is used by Lightroom Classic to give you three different version options. To develop three new versions, you can also choose Refresh.

5. Pick as many as you need:

   o **Tool Overlay:** When you move your mouse over a picture, you can view the pins. It also lets you choose when to show the pins of the spots you've removed when you move your mouse over a picture.

   o **Visualize Spots:** This tool helps you see where you want to pick something so you can make a good choice. In some situations, it shows a layer with a lot of contrast.

Tip:

- If you don't want the mask adjustment to open immediately, hold down Cmd (Mac) or Ctrl (Windows) as you move the mouse over a new area to brush it.

- Press the Escape key to hide the shape of the spot or to deselect it without changing the tool layer.

- To get the best results, make sure to include the shadows of the items you want to remove.

Object Aware in Lightroom Classic

You can use Object Aware to find an object in the brushed area. This helps you make an exact pick when you want to keep as many scene details as possible.

Note:

- You can only use Object Aware with Content-Aware Remove and Generative Remove. You can't use it with Heal or Clone.

- When the Generative AI box is not checked, Content-Aware Remove is used.

- For Content-Aware Remove, hold down Cmd (Mac) or Ctrl (Windows) and drag a spot on the picture to select it.

Go to the **Develop module** and choose **Remove > Object Aware**.

2. Use a brush to remove the item. To make a precise pick, change the brush size and the overlay's opacity.

3. The Refine settings let you choose the following things after you've chosen an object:

   o **Add**—Fix the pick by adding a brush.

   o **Subtract**: Take away parts of the selections that you don't want.

In the Refine menu, you can change the Overlay color and the size of the brush.

4. When you use Generative AI along with Object Aware, it can look at the object, automatically choose it, and then remove it with Adobe Firefly for the best results.

5. Click "**Reset**" to undo the changes you made.

    Find the Provide Feedback on Generative Remove button and let us know what you think about the Generative AI Early Access feature.

Lens Blur in Lightroom Classic

1. In the Develop module, go to Lens Blur and click on Apply.
2. Pick which of the Bokeh effects that you want to use.
3. Change how the sliders are set;

Blur Amount: To change how strong the blur effect is

Boost: This lets you change how strong the chosen Bokeh effect is.

Focus Range: This lets you change the depth at which you want the blur to appear. To change the effect's range, hold down and drag the slider box from either side to make it bigger or smaller. Alternatively, you can click on the **Subject Focus button** to have AI set the focus area for you. You can also click on the **Point/Area Focus** button and drag a box around the subject to set the focus range by hand.

4. Check the box next to **Visualize Depth** to view a depth map of the image's key areas in a cool and warm tone.

5. Choose **Brush Refinement** to change the depth map. To do this, select **Focus** and then brush over the areas you want to keep in focus. To blur out unwanted areas, select Blur. The Amount, Size, Feather, and Flow buttons let you narrow down the choices.

Lens Blur works with pictures that already have a depth map, like. HEIC files.

Blur Background Adaptive presets

Lens Blur can be added to a picture with just one click by going to Presets > Adaptive: Blur Background. Use the default amount tool to change how strong the blur is. You can pick from the following presets to make your picture look the way you want it to:

- Subtle
- Strong
- Circle
- Bubble
- Geometric
- Ring
- Swirl

To remove the effect, click **Reset Blur**.

Click the plus sign in the Presets tab, then pick Lens Blur and any other setting you want to add, and click Create. This will make your own Lens Blur preset.

Note: Blur Background Adaptive Presets uses AI to find the subject and scan the scene in your picture to blur it.

Batch copy-paste Lens Blur settings

1. Pick out the picture that you want to copy after applying the Lens Blur.
2. Choose Lens Blur and Focus on Subject if you want Lightroom to find the subject of every picture for you. Then, choose Copy. If Focus on Subject isn't chosen, the focus settings from the source picture will be used.
3. Choose a picture or several photos to which you want to apply the settings, then press "Paste" to do so.

Previous, Sync, and Auto Sync in Lens Blur

If you have more than one picture chosen in the filmstrip, the sync buttons at the bottom of the right panel will change. If only one photo is chosen, the Previous button lets you copy and paste all of the settings from the photo that was chosen before to the photo that is currently chosen on the filmstrip.

If you have more than one picture chosen, the Sync button lets you pick which settings to copy from the current photo to the other photos that are also selected. When changes are made to one photo, Auto Sync instantly makes changes to other photos that you have chosen. That's it! The Sync button is now the Auto Sync button. Press Ctrl (Windows) or Command (Mac OS).

Filter by Exported Images

To sort the pictures, go to Library > Attribute. In the library filter panel, you can now choose between the exported images icon and the non-exported images icon to sort the files by whether they have been exported or not. The chosen filter option is also shown by an export state icon on the filmstrip.

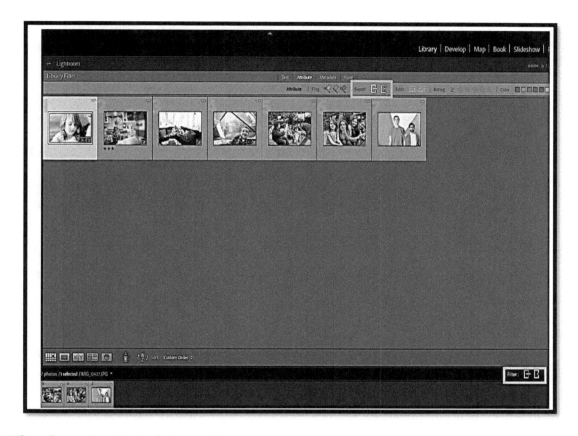

Filter by using Metadata options

From any page, go to **Library > Metadata** and choose Exported Files from the drop-down menu. The section will now allow you to filter images based on

- **Exported Files**
- **Not Exported Files**

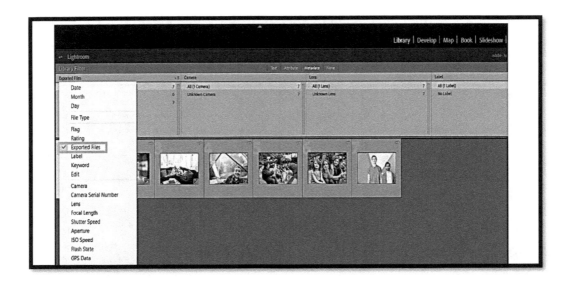

Tip: The date of the last export can be found in the image's information panel. Select the picture, then click **Customize** in the Metadata area of the image to make this choice available. Find the "**Basic Info**" section and click on the "**Last Exported Date**" link in the pop-up.

Filter by editing a Smart Collection

1. To edit a collection, go to **Library > Collections > Smart Collection** and pick out the collection you want to change.

2. Click the collection and then choose Edit Smart Collection from the menu that comes up.

3. Choose "**Exported**" from the drop-down box. By choosing the schedule of exported photos, you can further filter the results down.

4. To filter the collection, click Save.

Filter by creating a Smart Collection

1. Go to **Library > Collections > the plus sign (+) icon > Make a Smart Collection**.

2. Click on "**Rules**" and then "**Exported**." Then, pick the timeline.

3.   Click on "Create" to make a Smart Collection with exported pictures based on the period you chose.

Note: To change the export state of a picture, right-click on one or more images, folders, or collections and choose "**Reset Export Status**." The move above can't be undone.

CHAPTER FIVE

BASIC PHOTO ADJUSTMENTS

Understanding the Develop Module

The Develop module has a toolbar and two sets of panels for watching and editing photos. You can see previews of, save and choose changes you've made to a picture on the left with the Navigator, Presets, Snapshots, History, and Collections panels.

For making global and local changes to a picture, use the tools and panels on the right. The menu has buttons that let you do things like zoom in and out, switch between **"Before" and "After" views**, and play a slideshow on the spot.

Module overview

- The Develop module's Histogram panel may be used to measure color tones and alter the image's tonality.

- Below the histogram, EXIF data, and RGB numbers, more information about the photo's Smart Preview state is shown.

- You can fix red eyes, remove dust and spots, crop and straighten photos, and change certain parts of a picture using the tools in the tool strip.

- You can change the photo's white balance, color intensity, tonal scale, and HDR edits with the main tools in the **Basic panel**.

- For fine-tuning your tone changes, the **Tone Curve panel** has a Histogram. Along with the curve tweaks, Tone Curve also has a Refine Sat. tool that lets you change the color saturation.

- Tools for color adjustment are located in the **Color Mixer panel**. When you hold down the Alt or Option key while making an adjustment to the Point Color or Mixer sliders, only the current hue will be shown in color. All other hues will be shown in grayscale for better visualization.

- The **Color Grading panel** changes the color of black-and-white photos or adds effects to color photos.

- You can change the brightness and get rid of noise in the **Detail panel**.

- You can easily blur any picture with the Lens Blur panel. If you use Adobe Sensei to make a depth map of the picture, the result can blur the background or the foreground.

- In the **Lens Corrections** panel, you can fix chromatic distortion and lens vignetting that are caused by the lens.

- The **Transform panel** lets you fix the issues with the lines going across and down.

- You can add a film-grain effect to a picture and give an edited photo a vignette in the Effects panel.

- The **Calibration panel** allows you to make changes to your camera's basic calibration settings.

Customize the order of Develop panels

You can move the Develop panels to the right of the area around to make your own custom Develop panel menu. You can also pick whether to show or hide the panels.

Do the following to modify the Develop panel menu:

1. Right-click (**Windows**) or control-click (Mac) on any panel's title.
2. From the choice that comes up, choose Customize Develop Panel.
3. When the **Customize Develop Panel** box appears, drag the panel names in the order you want them to appear.
4. Press "**Save**."

   Uncheck the box next to the name of any panel you want to hide. Check the box next to the name of a secret panel to show it. To return to original order, click **Default Order**.

5. When you open the Confirm dialog box again, the Develop panels will be in the new order.

Views in the Develop module

Reference View

In the Develop module, the Reference View is a 2-Up view that lets you put a Reference photo next to an Active photo that can be edited. For editing a picture to make it look like a different picture, this view is helpful. To give you some examples:

- o   Creating presets that match the look of a picture.
- o   Figuring out how consistent the white balance is in pictures.
- o   Make sure that the image properties are equal for all the photos you want to use in a plan or show.
- o   Making small changes to the camera matching profiles so that they look like JPG files made by the camera.

Step 1: Launch Reference View

From both the **Develop and Library** modules, you can open Reference View.

To open **Reference View** from the Library module, do the following:

1. Click on the picture you want to edit in the Grid view or Loupe view.

2. Do any of these things:

- o   Press the **Shift+R** keys or choose **Photo > Open in Reference View** from the menu bar.
- o   Right-click on a picture and pick "Open in Reference View" from the menu that comes up.

Do these things to open Reference View from the Develop module:

3. Once you have a photo chosen, click the icon in the toolbar.

You can edit the picture you chose because it is now in the Active window in Reference View.

Step 2: Select a reference photo

- To make a picture from the Filmstrip the reference photo, drag and drop it into the Reference window in Reference View.

You can also use the grid in the Library module or the Loupe view in the Develop module to set a reference photo. To do this, right-click on a picture and select Set As Reference Photo from the menu that appears.

Do any of these things to change the Reference Photo while you're in Reference View:

- Right-click on a picture in the Filmstrip and choose "Set As Reference Photo" from the menu that comes up.

- Drag and drop a new image into the Reference window.

- Navigate to the Library section. From the option that opens, choose "Set As Reference Photo" when you right-click on an image in the grid.

The Reference picture and the Active photo are shown next to each other on the screen by default in Reference View. In Reference View, do any of the following to change the view to Top/Bottom:

- To change between **Reference View - Left/Right and Reference View - Top/Bottom**, tap the ⊟⊟ button in the menu.

- From the pop-up menu, pick **Reference View - Top/Bottom**.

Step 3: Edit the Active photo

Now, you can use the tools and panels on the right to edit the Active photo so that it looks and has the same qualities as the Reference picture.

While changing a picture in Reference View, press the "" key to see the Before view of your Active photo. In the Active window of Lightroom Classic, the old version of your picture is shown. In the top left area of the Active window, the word "Active (Before)" shows up.

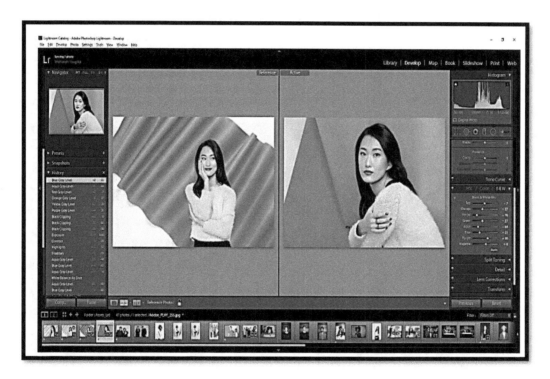

While in Reference View, do any of the following to change the Live Photo:

- Pick out a different picture in the Filmstrip.
- Pull a new picture into the Active window.
- In the toolbar, click the Reference picture lock icon. Then, go to the Library module and pick out a new picture. From the menu bar, choose Photo > Open in Reference View.

Step 4: Exit Reference View

Do any of these things to leave Reference view:

- Press the D key or the Loupe button in the toolbar to stay in the Develop module.

- Press the G or E key or click Library in the Module choice to go back to the Library module.

Edit Photos in Lightroom Classic

Editing Photos in the Lightroom Develop Module

Lightroom has many different modules. We will only talk about the two most popular ones here. These are the **Develop Module** and the **Library Module.**

You can look through your pictures in the Library module and choose which ones you want to edit after Lightroom imports them. You can open a picture in the Develop module by pressing the D key after you have chosen it to edit.

The panel on the right of your screen needs to be open for this module. Click the triangle in the middle of the left side or press the f8 key to open it if it's not already open. The tools you will use to start editing your shot are in this panel.

Using the Histogram in the Develop Module

There is a graph at the top. This is helpful for editing because it lets you see a picture of the tones in your picture. There is a small triangle at the top of the graph on each side. If you move your mouse over or click on these, they will show you where the highlights and shadows get clipped. When dark or light areas are marked, they are clipped and lose detail in those areas.

I made the colors brighter in this case to show the red area where there is cutting.

Cropping in Lightroom Classic

In Lightroom, there is a group of six buttons below the graph. The only one I'll talk about here is the one for the cropping and fixing tool.

The window frame behind the figure shows that my picture is off. To fix this, I can choose the crop and straighten tool and click and drag a corner of the box to make it straight. A grid will show up over the picture when you click on the button. The grid gets bigger when you click and drag a corner, which lets you line up the picture more exactly.

To crop your picture even more, click and drag the handles on any side of it once it's straight.

One thing I like about this kind of fixing is that as you turn the picture, it automatically cuts off any parts of the frame that go beyond the image. If it didn't do this, as you move the picture, the corners might show up as empty squares.

Adjusting Sliders in the Basic Panel

Lightroom Classic's Basic Panel has all the tools you need to make the light and color in your photos look good. Very often, this is the only panel you will need to work with. This is especially true if your photos were well exposed.

I'm going to talk about every bit of the Basic Panel here.

Treatment

You can make your picture look like either a color or a black-and-white shot.

When you click on Black and White, the picture changes to black and white and the Vibrance and Saturation settings become gray.

White Balance

There are different tools in this sub-panel that you can use to change the white balance of your photos.

There is a neutral tone in your picture that you can click on with the eyedropper to fix the white balance. This might make the white balance better, but it might not.

There is also a drop-down button here that lets you pick a white balance setting.

Most of the time, I leave my camera's white balance on auto. I only change it when I'm taking pictures in strange lighting. When it's sunny, I like how the auto white balance setting on my camera works.

The yellow and blue glass behind my subject makes this picture more difficult to understand. The light on the left side of her face comes from a window that is open to her right. The color looks a little too warm, so I moved the Temp slider toward the blue side to cool it down a bit.

Tone Sliders

The tone range in your picture can be adjusted using the following set of tools. Although there is an option to have the changes made automatically, I prefer to control each slider by hand. When I hit the "**Auto**" button in this case, you can see that it didn't do anything amazing.

Most of the time, I begin with the Blacks setting. This is a question of taste. In some parts of most of my shots, I like a pure black tone.

Key Tip

I will go back and forth between the different sliders as I work on this panel. I don't just set one and forget about it. During the editing process, I often go back and change how scales are set.

In this case, clicking the squares in the top corners of the histogram window can be useful. This shows you where any cutting might happen as you move your tools. I click the little handle and then move with my mouse wheel to work with a scale. I feel like I have better control this way than when I click and pull the slider handle.

I'll move the Shadows slider after I move the Blacks tool. Often, making the blacks darker also changes the shadows. To make the shadows a little less dark, I move the Shadows tool to the right.

I have not changed the exposure scale for this picture because it already has a good brightness. The Contrast has been raised a little. Because of this, there is now more black clipping, so I will move the Blacks slider back to the middle.

The next thing I need to do is fix the clipped highlights in the window behind my subject. Moving the Highlights tool to the left until the red-cutting highlights go away is all that's needed.

The Whites scale doesn't need to be changed for this picture. If I have to make an adjustment to the Whites, I do so carefully. This is because moving this tool even slightly to the left can make whites look gray and muddy.

Presence Sliders

Adobe calls the next sub-panel "Presence." These are tools that let you change things about photos that don't have to do with tone.

There are three sliders in the first group. They are called ***Texture, Clarity, and Dehaze***. All of these change the contrast in your shots in slightly different ways. When you edit your pictures, moving any of these sliders to the left lowers the contrast between features and textures. The contrast can be raised by moving a tool to the right.

Texture, Clarity, and Sharpening can be hard to tell apart (I'll talk more about this in a moment). It's important to try different things because the way you use these sliders together can have very different effects on different photos. Basically, I like using the Texture tool to make skin tones look better. Moving it a little to the left has made my model's skin look even smoother than it did before.

More changes can be made to brightness values with the Clarity tool. This tool works best when used on pictures of things other than people whose skin you want to smooth.

The Dehaze tool lets you change how much haze is in your picture. If there is scattered light that makes it look foggy, or if you want to add a foggy look, this is the tool to use. In this picture, I don't need it. This style works great for scenes that include a view in the distance. Adding blur to a picture can sometimes make it look like a dream. The brightness of a picture can also be changed with this tool.

Vibrance and Saturation

You can change how bright the colors are in a picture by moving the Vibrance and Saturation buttons. The Vibrance scale changes the colors that are the most intense. The Saturation scale changes how bright all of an image's colors are. When you use the Vibrance tool on pictures of people, it doesn't usually change the skin tones. It's risky to change the strength of color in skin tones. Changing someone's skin tone can make them look sick.

That's all there is to know about changing photos in Lightroom Classic's Basic Panel.

Other Adobe Lightroom Classic Panels

There is a whole collection of other panels below the Basic Panel that let you make a lot of different changes to your picture. If you took pictures in well-lit situations and with the right exposure, you probably won't need to change any of the settings in these other panels. This depends on the type of shooting you do.

The Detail Panel

In the Detail Panel, you can see the exceptions. A lot of photographers are tempted to use Sharpening when they edit in Lightroom. Noise Reduction is the other one. Both should be used carefully and in moderation since too much use can ruin a picture when editing it.

I don't think it's possible to improve a picture that isn't in focus when changing it in Lightroom, Photoshop, or any other program. You need to make your pictures sharp right in the camera. You should do this for good shooting practice. It can help to use the sharpening tool in Lightroom when editing a picture that is a little soft. This is the kind of blur that comes from a cheap lens.

It can also happen with some zoom lenses, which might not make pictures that are really sharp all the way through the zoom range. In the same way, some lenses can become soft when you use the largest or smallest apertures. If the picture is this soft, slowly moving the sharpness sliders can make it better.

If you are editing pictures, you can get rid of noise that was caused by a high ISO setting in the Noise Reduction screen. These help get rid of or lessen extra noise in the music. This is most often seen when there isn't much light. If you change the Luminance and Color choices, you can get good results. Be careful not to move them too far to the right. It will make you look less serious if you do it too often.

I've barely cut down on the noise in this example shot. Setting the Luminance and Color to the same amount most of the time when I change them.

Key Tip

When you're editing in Lightroom, press the Z key to get a better look at the changes. If you use the switch in the upper left corner of any panel, you can turn off and on the changes that you made, so you can see the difference between what was there before and after.

Tone Curve

Compared to the RGB color profile, the tone curve lets you change the highlights, lights, darks, and shadows even more based on light. In other words, this tool lets you change the tones of the red, blue, green, or the whole RGB curve. If you use the linear point curve or move the points across the plane, this tool lets you change the color of the whole picture.

HSL/Color

The next tool is the HSL/Color block. It lets you change the color, brightness, and intensity of red, orange, yellow, green, aqua, blue, purple, and magenta in the picture.

You should only use this when none of the other tools in develop mode are working right. It's the best way to get the color scheme you want.

It's best to use this tool last, after making all the other changes to the light and the edits, because changing one color too much could ruin the effect.

Split Toning

Split fading lets you change the color of the highlights and shadows in a picture. You can use the color bar or the box next to highlights and shadows to pick a color. Once you've chosen the color, you can change the brightness by moving the bar to the right or left.

You can use the middle balance bar to make the highlights and shadows look great together. It will look even if you put it in the middle. When you move it to the left, the dark tint stands out more. When you move it to the right, the highlights stand out more.

Lens Correction

Lens Correction lets you fix any problems that your lens has caused. Lightroom will show you the lens you want in the make, model, and description boxes if it knows what lens you want. If you check the "**Remove Chromatic Aberration**" or "**Profile Correction**" box, the picture will be fixed right away. This will clear up any blurriness or blocks. But you can also make these changes in the manual area. Lightroom will make changes for you in the profile setting.

Transform

Utilizing the Transform tool, you can change both the width and height of your picture. If you have Lightroom, you can use the auto, guided, level, vertical, and full presets. But they don't always work well. You can always use the straightening tool if not.

You can also change the picture in this setting, which gives you options like size, orientation, sale, x offset, and y offset. Some pictures might not need these changes, but it's best to try them all and see which ones work best for you.

Effects

With the Effects feature, you can make effects that are only available on that camera. You can change the center, roundness, feather, and highlights here to make the vignetting (the black shadows around a picture) stronger. In the effects area, you can also add grain to your pictures to make them look like they were taken on film. You can change the strength, size, and number of bars by moving them left or right.

Exporting Your Finished Images

All of the changes in Adobe Lightroom Classic are non-destructive. In other words, your original RAW files are not changed. As you work, the changes you make are like adding layers on top of the RAW picture. When you use Lightroom, these changes are saved automatically as you work.

Exporting your picture is the next thing you should do after changing it. To do this, right-click on the picture and pick **Export > Export** from the menu that comes up. You can also go to the top menu and choose **File > Export**. On a PC, hold down Ctrl+Shift+E. On a Mac, hold down Cmd+Shift+E.

In this case, it opens the Export window. You can pick where and how to send your pictures from here. Here, the most important things to keep in mind are:

- Export Location

- File Settings
- Image Sizing

You can pick where to save your pictures by picking a folder and, if you want, a subfolder.

From the drop-down menu further down, you can choose the type of picture file you want to send. You might need to make additional changes depending on your choice. I want to save my picture as a JPEG, so I also need to choose Quality and Color Space.

After that, if you want, Lightroom can change the size of your pictures. This is very helpful when you want to save pictures that you will later share on the internet. It's possible to limit the size and quality. When I use a picture on the internet, I usually keep it to 1500x1500 pixels and 72 pixels per inch. This will make the file small enough to upload quickly and keep the file size acceptable.

CHAPTER SIX

BLACK AND WHITE PHOTOGRAPHY

It takes intuition and care to edit black-and-white shots. You can make your work stand out with a few simple black-and-white editing tips.

These tips will help you get the most out of your black-and-white editing sessions, whether you want to make your photos look more subtle or dramatic.

Choose the Right Editing Software

Let us take a look at some well-known editing software and plug-ins before we start with post-processing. For each digital shooter, there is software that works best for them. Before you start taking black-and-white pictures, you should make sure you know how to use a few apps.

There are some of these that are general editing tools. Some were made just for black and white photographers, giving them a bigger range of tools to choose from.

Once you choose an editor, there is no right or wrong answer. You can try out different choices before you buy anything from most of these sites because they all offer free trials.

Adobe Lightroom & Photoshop

You can improve both color and black-and-white photos with a lot of different tools in Lightroom and Photoshop. You can use tools and adjustment brushes in Lightroom to make any picture stand out.

There are even more editing tools in Photoshop that are great for creative work, repainting, and other tasks. Just one adjustment layer is all you need to turn your photos black and white and make them look great.

Adobe Camera RAW

Adobe Camera RAW works with RAW files. If you mostly take in RAW, this tool will make it easy to turn and edit your photos.

This tool isn't just for black and white photographers, but it can be useful for anyone who needs to convert and edit RAW files a lot.

Nik Silver Efex

Nik Silver Efex is a plug-in made by DxO for black and white photographers who want to be in charge of their work. This is a good choice for people who already have Photoshop and Lightroom. There are straight picture editing tools in these programs.

Dynamic Brightness, Amplify Blacks, and Structure are some of the plug-in's adjustment options. This plug-in might be a good choice for you if you want a full editing experience.

Exposure X7

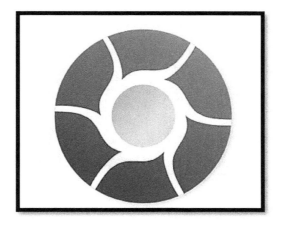

Exposure X7 can be used as a stand-alone tool or as a plug-in for Photoshop or Lightroom. This program, like the first two, is made for all types of photographers and has a number of tools for black-and-white photos.

The editing effects and layers in this tool are what make it stand out. To give your black-and-white pictures a stylish look, you can add artistic blur and texture.

How to Edit Black and White Photos

After you've shared your pictures, go to the Develop module and start editing them.

Convert to Black and White

If you are working with color pictures, you need to convert them to black and white. There are 4 ways to go about this:

- **Use a saturation slider**. Move the saturation all the way to -100. *Know this*: After this, you won't have many changing options. This method can be used if you only want to make a few simple changes to your photos before turning them into black and white.

- Click on **Black & White**, which is at the top of the Basic panel next to Color. This will give you more ways to edit in the future.

- In the Basic Panel, click on **Color** next to Profile and choose **Monochrome**.

- You should use black-and-white filters. This kind of filter is called an action in Photoshop CC. They are known as presets in Lightroom. With filters, it's easy to turn pictures black and white and give them a stylish look.

Use Adjustment Sliders

You might notice that something is missing when you use the saturation scale to turn your pictures black and white. A black-and-white picture might not look as interesting or vivid as its color counterpart if no adjustment is made.

With the aid of adjustment tools, you can easily fix this by changing the black and white tones. A very important part of editing in black and white is these settings.

There is a panel in Lightroom called "B&W" that has these color sliders. If you move the Saturation scale to -100, you won't be able to see this panel.

Some colors in your black-and-white pictures will get darker if you move the bars to the left. If you move them to the right, the colors that go with those sliders will get lighter. This is a good way to make your photos look better overall by adding more contrast and depth to the shadows.

You have a black-and-white picture of a ladybug curled up on a leaf. Moving the Red slider to the left and the Green slider to the right will make the colors stand out more. The ladybug will get darker and the leaf will get brighter. Turn it around and try it the other way around to make the bugs lighter and the leaves darker. It depends on how you shoot.

Create Contrast

Go to the Basic panel after you're done improving your black-and-white picture. You can make small changes to your picture with the tools in this panel.

You need to add contrast to your black-and-white picture for it to stand out. The contrast slider can be moved to the right to do this. It will be interesting if you do this in a sneaky way.

You can also raise the contrast by making the highlights brighter and the blacks darker. You can also fine-tune your picture with the Tone Curve tool, which is right under the Basic panel.

Differentiate Between Texture, Clarity, and Dehaze

You can quickly make your black-and-white pictures better with the texture, brightness, and dehaze tools. Even though they do the same thing, they are different in some ways.

- **Texture:** This will increase the difference between the various levels of detail in your photographs. It won't make noise in your black-and-white shots like the sharpening tool in the Details panel does. It will make the 3D effect look very clear.
- **Clarity:** The clarity scale only brings out the mid-tones. So, you'll be able to make photos that don't have much depth look balanced and clear.
- **Dehaze:** This tool is great for pictures that don't have enough deep shadows. This could be caused by fog, haze, or smoke in black and white scenery picture taking. Remove the haze from your pictures by moving the tool to the right.

If you move the bars to the right, all of these results will happen. The opposite will happen if you drag them to the left.

In order to give your work the look of soft black-and-white photos, move the clarity or texture tool to the left. If you want your pictures to look foggy, move the dehaze button to the left.

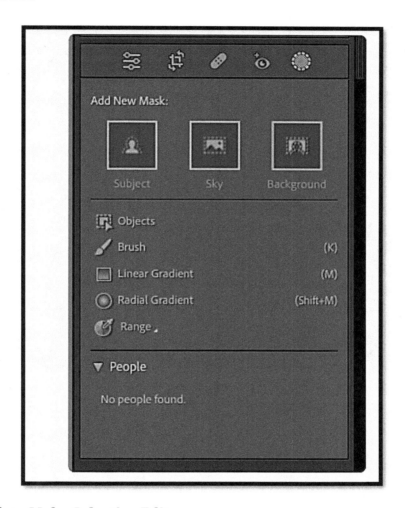

Use a Brush to Make Selective Edits

What if you only want your main subject to stand out? What if you only want to make the model's eyes stand out and not change anything else in the picture? The masking tool can be used to draw attention to a certain part of your black-and-white picture.

You can find a set of 5 icons in the **Develop module**, just above the **Basic panel**. Click on the last icon, which looks like a circle with dots around it. Press **Brush**.

Use the buttons at the top of the panel to change the size of the brush. Feather should be set to 100. Putting this on will give your brush a soft edge that will make your selected cuts look natural.

You can change which sliders you want to use in your picture. Move the highlights tool to the right to add bright spots to some parts of your picture. You can choose between the sharpness and texture settings to make the eyes of your model look better.

Then, use a brush to change the places you want. If the result is too strong, move the buttons around some more. To close the brush panel, click on the circle button again when you're done.

Create an Atmosphere Using Colours

Once you're pleased with all the changes you've made, you can focus on giving your picture a certain mood. You can try out different color effects or give your photos a blur.

This step is not required, but it can help you develop your own style as a black-and-white shooter that is unique.

Get to the Color Grading panel by scrolling down. Colors can be added to the mid-tones, shadows, and highlights of your picture here. You can change the color by dragging the circle in the middle of the wheel. The color effect is stronger the farther away you are from the circle's center.

If you want a simple look, a small amount of color will do to make the black and white look good together. Most of the time, color grading black and white pictures makes them look old. That's an interesting result, but it might not work with all styles.

Common Black and White Photography Editing Mistakes

You might go too far if you edit a black-and-white picture for too long. People who edit black-and-white photos often make the mistake of over-processing them.

Don't make these mistakes when editing your black-and-white photos. They will make the process much easier and result in beautiful photos every time.

Editing JPEG Files

You shouldn't do this on the day of the shoot. You can't make as many changes to JPEG files, even though they are small.

But RAW files are bigger and don't have any compression. They will give you more artistic freedom after you edit them.

Don't worry too much if you can't shoot in RAW. For better gear, make sure it can shoot RAW files if you ever get the chance. When you have the chance to edit raw black-and-white photos, you'll notice a big change in how you work!

Too Much Contrast

There are different amounts of editing that need to be done on each black-and-white picture. You might want to move the contrast tool all the way to the right if you have a set of dull black-and-white photos with a lot of bland gray areas. Most of the time, that won't lead to pictures that look good.

Lightroom has a lot of different ways to boost contrast. With the highlights and whites tools, you can make beautiful black and white highlights. With the shadows and blacks settings, you can make shadows that are very dark and pure black.

You can make your whole picture look better with these adjustment tools if you use them correctly.

Too Much Clarity or Texture

Being clear and having depth can help a simple black-and-white picture stand out. Watch out when you use them because they can change parts of your picture. If you move the scales slowly to the right, you might not notice how off your black-and-white picture looks.

Making it a habit to go back and forth with any changing tool will help you make sure that your changes aren't too big. (Unless you want that look!) Return the bar to 0 if something doesn't look right. If the first picture looks better, go back and make small changes.

Using Presets for Black and White Photography

1. **Choose a photo to change to black and white**

    In the Library module grid, choose a color picture. To open the chosen picture in the Develop module, click Develop in the Module Picker at the top of the screen or press the D key.

2. **Apply a black-and-white preset**

After using a setting to convert the image to black and white, we'll look at how to adjust the black-and-white treatment. Click on the Presets panel's title bar on the left side of the Develop module to open it. If you click on the B&W area in the Presets panel, a list of black-and-white presets will show up.

Moving your mouse over the black-and-white presets will show you a taste of how each one will look in your picture. To use one of the presets in this area on the picture, click on it. We picked **B&W High Contrast** for this case. If you change your mind, you can use a different preset on top of this one, or you can press the **"Reset"** button to go back to the first picture and use a different preset there.

3. **Open the Basic panel**

It's time to see how the effect can be customized for a specific picture now that a pre-set black-and-white effect has been applied. Get to the right side of the

124

Develop module and open the Basic adjustment panel. It's clear that in the setting we used a black and white image and changed the Whites and Blacks sliders to make the contrast stronger.

4.   **Customize with manual adjustments**

It still looks like this picture is too bright. To make the picture a little darker, move the Exposure scale in the Basic panel to about -0.60. To give the picture more punch, move the Clarity scale to about +25. This will increase the contrast in the middle tones.

5. **Adjust the black-and-white mix**

Sliders that let you change how the colors in the original picture are turned into black and white can be found in the black-and-white panel

Note: In Lightroom Classic, you can only see the Black & White panel if you have already turned a shot black and white.

You can change the amount of grayscale brightness for each color in the original picture using this panel. To make the sky and sea look less blue, move the Blue scale to about -20. If you move the red scale, the dark bars on the lifeguard tower will get darker or lighter.

Different black-and-white presets and manual changes can help you get the exact black-and-white look you want.

CHAPTER SEVEN

SAVING AND EXPORTING PHOTOS

Exporting Photos from Lightroom

Here are the steps to export photos from Lightroom, including detail settings for both Lightroom and Lightroom Classic, as well as a part just for Lightroom Mobile.

After you're done changing your picture(s), go to **File > Export (Shift+E in Lightroom, Ctrl+E** in Lightroom Classic). There's also a share button in the upper right corner of your Lightroom window.

1. **Lightroom CC:**

    1. On the right side of the program, your export settings will appear. You'll also need to click on "**Custom Settings"** if you use the "**Share**" button.

    2. You can now pick the options you want, such as the file type, size, watermark, and more complicated name and metadata choices.

    3. Pick the file type you want to send pictures in Lightroom to get the best quality:

        o   JPEG for web/digital

        o   JPEG XL / AVIF for HDR displays

        o   JPEG/TIFF for print

        o   DNG for RAW files (best quality overall, but incompatible with many editing software)

    4. If you can, set the Quality level to 100% and choose the right **Color Space** settings for your file under "**More Options**." For web/digital, choose **sRGB**, for print, choose **AdobeRGB**, and for HDR media, choose **sRBG**.

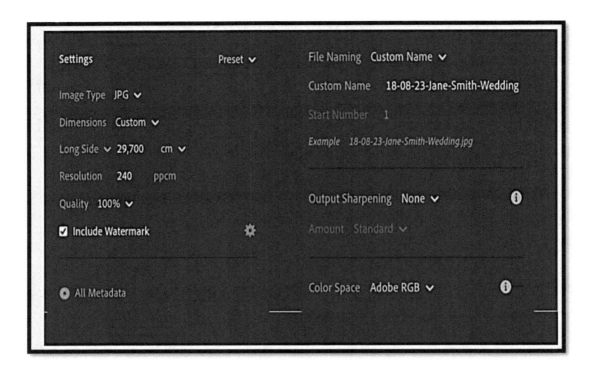

5.   The following settings are the best for exporting TIFF files, except for Output Sharpening, which depends on what you want to do with the picture. This menu lets you choose the type of paper you want to use when you're editing to print. Professional photographers, on the other hand, say that you should improve your picture by hand instead of using this built-in feature.

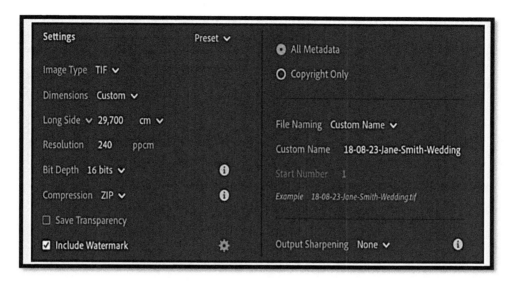

Note: TIFF vs. JPEG

Because JPEG and TIFF files use very different ways to reduce data, JPEG files are much smaller than TIFF files. Lossy compression is what JPEG does. You may have heard of it. It makes it easy to store jpg files, but some of the image info is lost, which hurts the picture. People save or screencap pictures and then share them online, where they are recompressed, which creates lossy compression effects. This is also why many JPGs online lose their quality over time.

The Tag Image File Format (TIFF) uses perfect compression to keep the quality of the images. However, this makes the files much bigger and harder to share online. Because the file is so good, TIFFs are great for keeping because they don't have any artifacts. Also, TIFFs can contain transparent picture parts, just like PNGs and GIFs.

To sum up, JPEGs are great for sharing online as long as there are no obvious compression artifacts. TIFFs, on the other hand, are great for backups, especially for pictures with transparent parts, as well as for more digital editing.

2.   **Lightroom Classic:**

   1.   If you click Export in Lightroom Classic, the export menu will appear with more detailed settings than in the cloud version of Lightroom.

   2.   Lightroom Classic has the same file name, picture sizing, sharpening, information, and watermarking settings as the basic version above.

   3.   To get the best quality, go to File Settings and choose the file type you want. This is similar to how Lightroom CC works:

      o   JPEG/PNG for web/digital

      o   TIFF for print

      o   PSD for further editing in Photoshop

      o   DNG for RAW files (best quality overall, but incompatible with many editing software)

      o   Any format for HDR displays (but not DNG). Lightroom Classic, not Lightroom CC, lets you use HDR color spaces for any file format. Good settings for HDR files can be seen here:

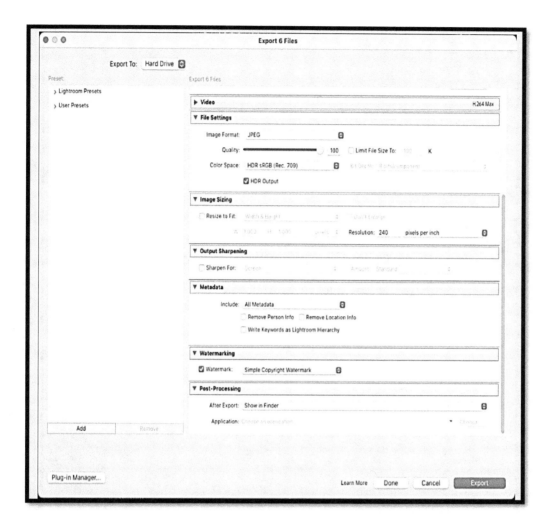

4.   If you can, set the Quality level to 100% and choose the right **Color Space** settings for your file under "**More Options**." For web/digital, choose sRGB, for print, choose ProPhoto RGB, and for HDR media, choose sRBG.

5.   You can choose the color space for TIFF files in Lightroom Classic, but not in Lightroom CC at this time. This is how your Lightroom settings should look if you want to print:

▼ File Settings				
Image Format:	TIFF			
Compression:	ZIP		Save Transparency	
Color Space:	Adobe RGB (1998)		Bit Depth: 8 bits/component	
	HDR Output			

▼ Image Sizing				
Resize to Fit:	Width & Height		Don't Enlarge	
	W: 1.000 H: 1.000	pixels	Resolution: 240	pixels per inch

▼ Output Sharpening

Sharpen For: Screen   Amount: Standard

▼ Metadata

Include: All Metadata

☑ Remove Person Info ☑ Remove Location Info

☐ Write Keywords as Lightroom Hierarchy

▼ Watermarking

☑ Watermark: Simple Copyright Watermark

▼ Post-Processing

After Export: Show in Finder

Application: Choose an application...   ▼ Choose...

3.   Lightroom Mobile:

Photographers are using Lightroom Mobile more and more. Even though editing is a little slower on mobile than on the PC, Lightroom Mobile has almost all of Lightroom CC's features and lets you edit on the go from your phone. That being said, these are the best Lightroom Mobile export settings:

1.   Go to the top right part of your app and tap on the Share button. It's between the Help button and the Cloud button.

2.   The next screen will show up:

3.   Tap on **Save copy to device** to save the picture to your phone.

4.   Tap on Share to send the picture to a different app. Before you share, you can also choose to add a border. This is a fun choice if you have a quick camera that can connect to Bluetooth devices.

5.   Tap on Export as to get to the advanced export settings. This brings up a screen that has settings that are a lot like the PC version of Lightroom.

6.   To send in the best quality in Adobe Lightroom Mobile, choose the file type you want, just like in the CC version of Lightroom:

     o   JPEG for web/digital

     o   JXL / AVIF for HDR displays

     o   JPEG/TIFF for print

○　　　　DNG for RAW files (best quality overall, but incompatible with many editing software)

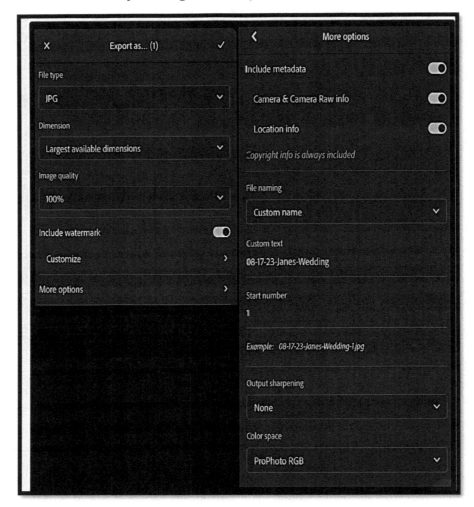

Note: ProPhoto RGB vs Adobe RGB

Putting ProPhotoRGB and Adobe RGB next to each other is the best way to show how they are different:

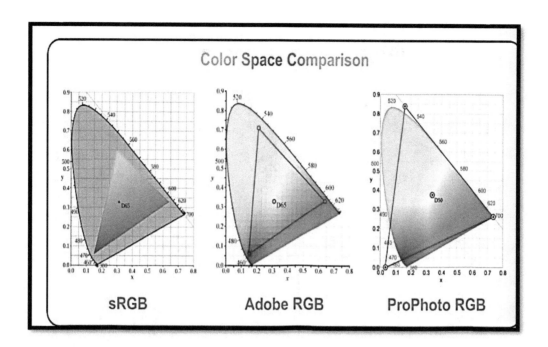

Color Space Comparison

sRGB   Adobe RGB   ProPhoto RGB

You can see that sRGB, the most common color setting on the web, doesn't show nearly as much color as the human eye. Overall, Adobe RGB shows more colors than sRGB, but it leaves out some important ones that are in sRGB.

This is still a better color mode for printing. As a result, ProPhoto RGB is one of the best color modes for editing but a terrible one for exporting because the file size grows so big and most computers won't show ProPhoto properly, making colors look dull and customers unhappy.

7.   When exporting to TIFF, Lightroom Mobile is more like Lightroom Classic than Lightroom CC. You can choose both the Bit Depth and the Color Space. LZW compression at 16 bits is actually only available in Lightroom Mobile (CC and Classic* both remove it). If you want to print from Lightroom Mobile, these are the best settings I found:

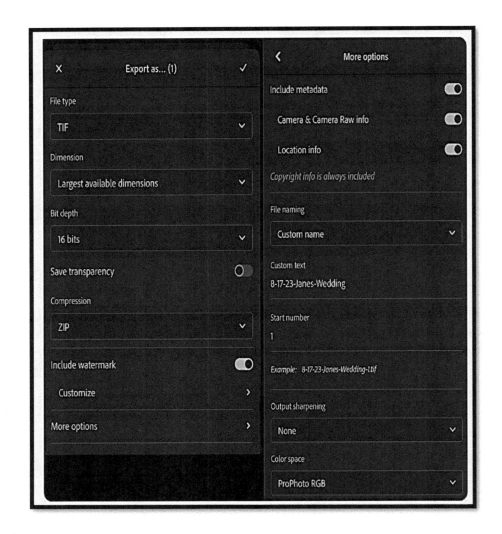

Note: 16-bit export choices were removed from earlier versions of Lightroom because they increased file size for no apparent reason unless you were working in Pro Photo.

Things to Keep in Mind when Exporting Photos Lightroom & Lightroom Classic

When you use the export tool, here are some helpful tips:

1.   You can export using the same settings in both PC versions of Lightroom. Just click on **File > Export with Previous**.

2. You can use presets in all versions of Lightroom. You can save your best presets from the web or make your own, and then open them in the Lightroom version you like.

3. You can send more than one picture at once in all versions of Lightroom. You only need to pick out the ones you want to send.

4. You can add tools to Lightroom Classic to push photos directly to Adobe Stock, Flickr, or other sites.

5. You can add photos to your portfolio for free in both Lightroom CC and Lightroom Classic. You can also make a portfolio in Lightroom Classic (File > Export as Catalog).

6. Additionally, Lightroom Mobile lets you make an Edit Replay, which is a useful tool for people who make and sell presets and for sharing short vertical videos on TikTok, Instagram Reels, and YouTube Shorts.

Using Export Presets

When you use export presets, you can quickly send photos to common places. For instance, you can use a Lightroom Classic setting to send JPEG files that are good for emailing to friends or clients.

Export photos using presets

1. Pick out the pictures you want to send out. Click the **Export button** or go to **File > Export With Preset.**

2. Pick a **preset**. The following export presets are already built into Lightroom Classic:

   o **Burn Full-Sized JPEGs:** This option saves pictures as JPEGs that have been changed to sRGB and are tagged with that color space. The resolution is 240 pixels per inch, and the quality is the best. This setting saves the exported files to the Files On CD/DVD location chosen at the top of the Export dialog box. The files are saved in a directory called Lightroom Classic Burned Exports.

- o **Export To DNG:** This option sends pictures in the DNG file format. This setting doesn't tell you what to do after clicking **Export**, so you can choose a folder to send the files to.

- o **For Email:** This opens a message box where you can email the pictures to someone.

- o **For Email (Hard Drive):** Saves pictures as sRGB JPEG files on your hard drive. Photos that are exported can only be 640 pixels wide or tall, have a density of 72 pixels per inch, and are of average quality. Lightroom Classic shows the pictures in the Explorer (Windows) or the Finder (Mac OS) when it's done. After clicking Export, pick the folder where you want to save the file.

Save export settings as presets

1. Choose the export settings you want to save in the Export text box.
2. Click the "**Add**" button at the bottom of the "**Preset**" panel on the left side of the text box.
3. In the New Preset box, tell it what you want to call it in the Preset Name box and click Create.

Saving Photos in Various Formats

Saving to the Lightroom Catalog

For some reason, Lightroom saves your pictures in the Lightroom Catalog instead of on your computer's files. This means that the data you changed about the picture stays with it after you save it to the Lightroom Catalog. The shop is the only way to get to the new picture. If you open the changed picture file in a different app, you won't be able to tell the difference.

This also means that if you delete the catalog, the edit data for the pictures in it will be removed too, but the pictures themselves will still be in your files. When you're done editing a picture, it's important to save it as a different file.

Saving Changes As XMP files

This is another way to save your Lightroom edits: save each picture with an XMP file. To do this, go to **Edit > Catalog Settings** on a Windows computer or **Lightroom Classic > Catalog Settings** on a Mac computer.

There are several tabs at the top of the Catalog Settings window that let you change settings. Go to the Metadata tab.

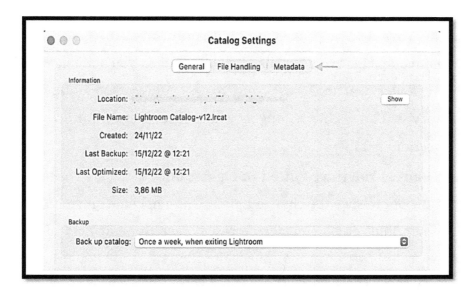

If the box next to Automatically write changes into XMP is already checked, leave it there. Otherwise, you're already saving your edits as XMP files.

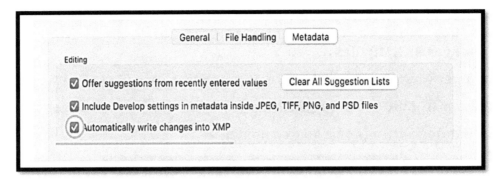

Now, when you go to the root folder, you'll see different XMP files next to the picture files. There is an XMP file that holds the changes you make to a picture when you edit it. This is helpful if you need to access those changes from other libraries.

But this method usually makes a lot of XMP files, especially if you edit a lot of shots at once. If you're working on a computer other than the one you usually use, you should only save changes as XMP files. If not, it's probably easier and takes up less room to just back up your collection often.

Understanding How Adobe Photoshop Lightroom Saves Images

The Adobe Photoshop Lightroom works with the cloud, so you don't need to keep files. Instead, any changes you make are sent to the Adobe cloud immediately. Your changing history will be visible as long as you're logged into your account and your internet connection is stable.

How To Save Photos You Have Edited In Lightroom

However, if you want to save the changed picture as a new file on your computer, you should use either TIFF or JPEG. Lightroom will save the edit data instantly to the catalog. There are a few things that affect the file type you should use to save the picture.

Saving As TIFF

Find the picture or pictures you want to save as a TIFF file in either the Library or Develop module. Then, go to **File > Export**.

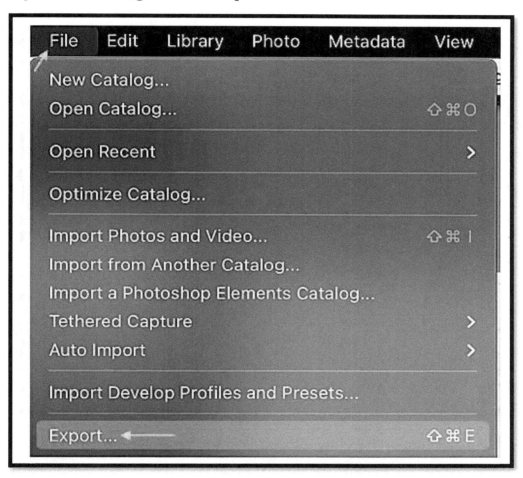

This is when the Export Window shows up. You can give your file a name and choose where to send it here.

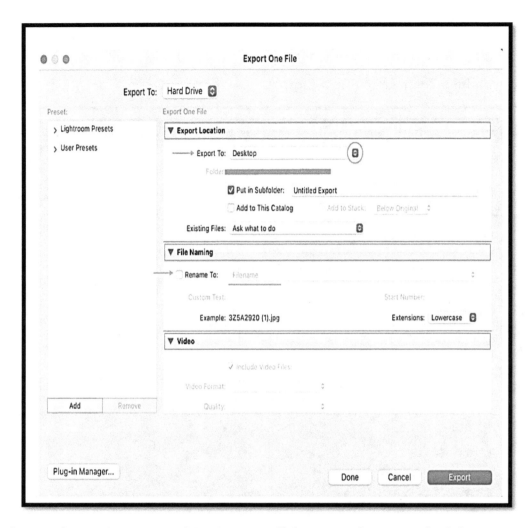

The last and most important thing is to scroll down until you see the File Settings tab. It will open. Click the drop-down menu next to **Image Format**. Pick out **TIFF** from the list of options.

When you click **Export**, the picture will be saved to your hard drive as a TIFF file.

When you export your pictures as a TIFF file, the adjustment you made stays with the file. This means that when you open a TIFF file again in Lightroom, you will be able to see and edit all of the edits.

But because they are so big, this isn't the best way to store or share a lot of TIFF files. It's good for things you might need later. If you work with TIFF files a lot, you'll need a lot of room.

Saving As JPEG

You could also save your picture as a JPEG. This will keep the size the same while the raw data is compressed and the edited data is baked into the picture. You won't be able to get to the edit data to make changes again, but the file will be a lot smaller and easier to share.

Go to **File > Export** to save your picture as a JPEG.

Name your picture and choose a place to save it.

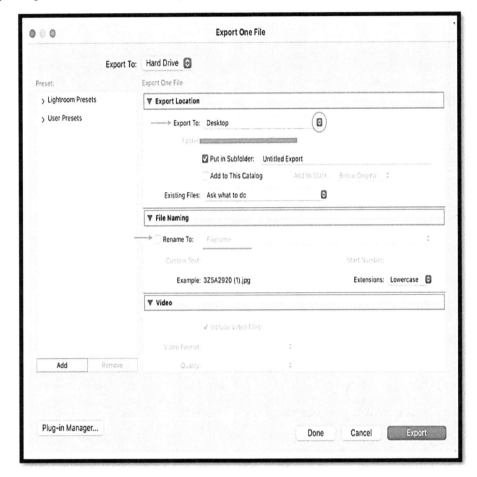

After that, scroll down until you see File Settings. Find the JPEG file in the menu next to Image file and click on it. It may already be chosen.

When you click **Export**, your picture will be sent as a JPEG.

You can be sure that your photos are saved the way you want them to be saved now that you know the different ways Lightroom will save them automatically and how to change the save settings to your advantage.

Watermarking Photos

Creating a Text Watermark in Lightroom

We are going to show you how to make a text stamp in Lightroom. It's possible to get to the watermark feature in Lightroom by going to **"Edit->Edit Watermarks"** (**Lightroom->Edit Watermarks** on a Mac) or from the Export window. I usually get to it through the export window, which you can get to by going to *File > Export* or hitting **CTRL+SHIFT+E**:

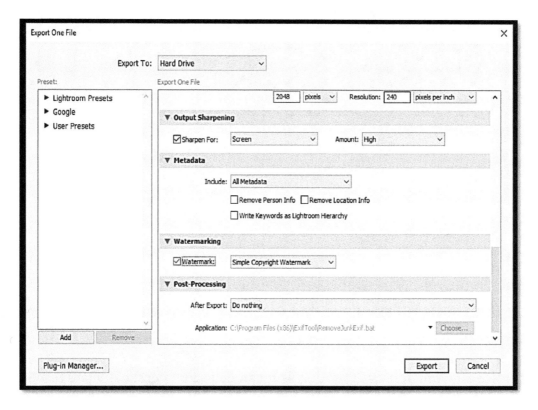

Scroll down until you see "**Watermarking**." Next, check the box next to "**Watermark**:" and then pick "**Edit Watermarks**..." from the menu that will appear. This is what the "**Watermark Editor**" will look like when it comes up:

It's very simple and easy to use the logo maker. In the bottom left corner, you type the text. On the right side of the window, you can change the style. Allow us to begin typing the text. Put the copyright symbol (copy-paste it from here – © or press ALT + 0169 on PC / OPT + G on Mac) first, then put your name afterward. Under "**Text Options**" on the right side of the screen, pick the font you want to use.

You can use any font you want as long as it can be read. I personally like the "Myriad Web Pro" font. Pick the style and orientation, then pick the word color. If you want to use a color in a word stamp, I think you should keep it white. There are some settings for Shadow that should work fine, but if you want to change how the shadows look, you can do that here. Now go to "Watermark Effects" and scroll down:

As I've already said, you don't want the copyright marking to be completely clear, so it's best to make it only partially see-through. For me, 50% visibility works best, but you can try anything from 30% to 80% and see what you like. The best size to stay with is "Proportional," not "Fit" or "Fill." A 10% cut works well most of the time. Change the amount to a bigger number if your copyright text looks too small.

The next step is to choose an "Anchor" point, which is where your copyright will be. It is best to keep it in the top left/right and bottom left/right corners, as I said before. Start in the upper left spot. Don't forget that our goal is to make 4 watermarks in 4 different places. After that, click "Save." The "New Preset" window will appear:

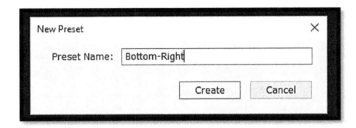

There should be a useful name for it that makes it clear where the type of marking is. As you can see above, I named mine "**Bottom-Right**." When you click "**Create**," you'll be taken back to the Export screen.

Now do the job three more times and make three more watermarks for "**Top-Left,**" "**Top-Right,**" **and "Bottom-Left.**" Your "Watermarking" drop-down should look like this at the end:

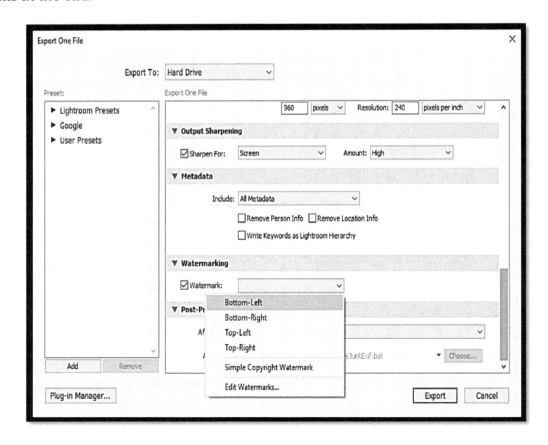

How are you going to use the word watermarks now that you have them? In Lightroom, just pick out a bunch of shots, open the export window, choose a label, and click "Export." That's all!

In general, this is how I do it:

1. Select all photos to be extracted in Lightroom.
2. Press CTRL+SHIFT+E or CMD+SHIFT+E to open the Lightroom Export window.
3. Select the "Bottom-Right" watermark (this works best for most pictures).
4. Click on "Export."
5. Once the pictures have been extracted, look through each one and mark the ones where the brand doesn't look good or can't be seen.
6. Pick out the pictures that need a new watermark. Open the export window again and choose a new spot for the watermark.
7. Click "**Export**" again, and then delete the old picture.

You may need to do steps 5–7 more than once to get the watermarks in the right place. That's all there is to it. Now let us talk about logos on visual watermarks.

Creating a Graphic Watermark in Lightroom

Now let's talk about the cool stuff: using Lightroom to add a graphic tag with your name to photos. The word watermark will never look as good as a graphic brand, no matter how good you make it look. But to do this, you'll need a clear file type of your brand or company name, like PNG or GIF. We can't save your logo as a JPEG because JPEG doesn't allow transparency.

You should have the original logo in vector/EPS file if you had a professional develop it. There may also be a clear PNG or GIF file in the same folder. If you can't find one, it's easy to turn your logo into a PNG file as long as you have the original file.

Because we're going to make your logo partly see-through, the picture should be white instead of black. To quickly change things in Photoshop, just press CTRL+I or CMD+I to flip the colors of the logo:

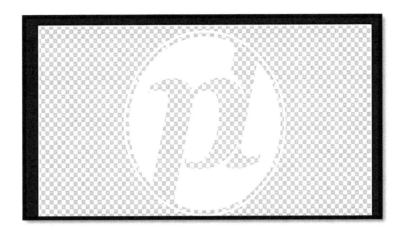

To send the picture out of Photoshop, go to "File" > "Save for Web & Devices" > "PNG-8" in the drop-down menu at the top. Check the box next to "Transparency," as shown below:

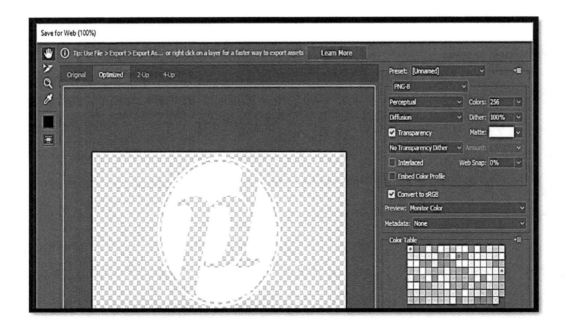

Now that the picture is ready, you can use it in Lightroom. Also, make sure the image you use is at least 250 pixels big. What if you make your logo too small? Lightroom will have to make it bigger for big photos. This will make your image look bad when you send it. And if you use a PNG picture with a lot of detail, Lightroom will make it smaller before you send it.

Here are some shots to choose. To open the Export window box in Lightroom, press CTRL+SHIFT+E. To edit watermarks, go to the drop-down menu and select "Edit Watermarks..." Make sure the box next to "Watermark:" is checked. There will be a new window called "Watermark Editor":

In the upper right part of the window, we need to choose "Graphic" if we want to use a graphic logo. Scroll down to "Image Options," click "Choose," and then find the logo you saved earlier. As soon as you pick a picture, the logo will appear on the left side of your photo sample. The "Text Options" are now grayed out as well. When you get to "Watermark Effects," scroll down:

As with the word marking, you need to choose the right opacity. For me, 50–60% works well. Keep the size "Proportional," and a size of 10-15% works well most of the time. You can change the "Inset" numbers in "Horizontal" and "Vertical" to move your name up, down, and left and right if it's too close to the edge.

In this case, I set both the horizontal and vertical inset numbers to 1. This made the name a little farther from the window's edge. Pick one of the Anchor points again (start with Bottom-Right) and give the Preset a new name, like "Bottom-Right Logo."

To change the Watermark, open it again, move the Anchor to the bottom left, click Save, and name it "Bottom-Left Logo." Do the same thing for the top left and top right. When you're done, you should have four watermarks in four different places.

Now try exporting a few pictures and see how you like the end result:

1. Select all photos to be extracted in Lightroom.
2. Press **CTRL+SHIFT+E or CMD+SHIFT+E** to open the Lightroom Export window.
3. Select the "**Bottom-Right**" graph watermark (this works best for most photos).
4. Click on "**Export**."
5. Once the pictures have been extracted, look through each one and mark the ones where the brand doesn't look good or can't be seen.
6. Pick out the pictures that need a new watermark. Open the export window again and choose a new spot for the watermark.
7. Click "**Export**" again, and then delete the old picture.

The good news is that the above method works for both horizontal and vertical pictures, so you don't have to split the vertical sections. If all four sides are very bright and the white logo doesn't work, make a black clear logo and add more watermarks. It will look great to stamp very bright photos with the black logo that is only 50% see-through.

CHAPTER EIGHT

ADVANCED LIBRARY MANAGEMENT

Part 2: Intermediate Techniques

Using the Map Module

Lightroom read the GPS information that was contained in the chosen photo file and found its location automatically. A yellow pin shows where the photo was taken. From the zoom level, you might be able to see how many pictures are at that spot on the pin. To view previews of the photos taken at that location, click on the pin.

You can use the View Menu to show the Map Info layer and Map Key that explains how the colored pins on the map work if you can't see them in the top right corner of the map. The image you see on your screen may be different from this one depending on the map style and zoom level you chose the last time you used the Map module.

These are the steps:

1. To hide the Map Key, press the "x" button in the top right corner or select "Show Map Key" in the View menu. Tap the map twice to get a better look at the pin. The left panel has an overall map that stays zoomed out even when you zoom in on the main map view. It has buttons to lock pins and load GPS tracklogs, as well as a Zoom tool and a Map Style menu. It's down below the map view. In the Metadata panel on the right, you can see the location info that is built in. The map can be moved around in the main view. This will make a certain spot bigger. If you hold down the Option or Alt key and drag the mouse, you can move the main map view.

2. Press the Zoom In (+) button several times. It's to the right of the scale in the Toolbar. From the Map Style menu, pick one of the six styles at a time. Place names, like Teatro Juarez, can be found near the first pin in other styles. You can use the Location Filter bar above the map to only see pictures taken in places that can be seen or to filter out photos that have been tagged or not.

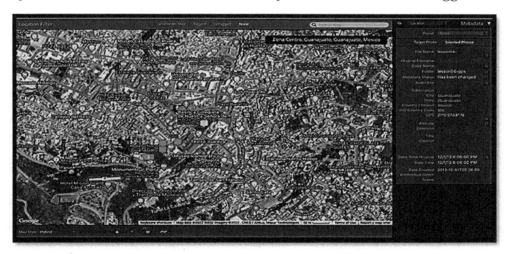

3. In the Location Filter bar, click on each of the four filters one at a time. Then, look at how the pictures in the Filmstrip change. When a picture has a GPS location, a location marker badge appears in the Grid view of the Filmstrip and

Library module. For Map view, click on the location marker tag on a photo in the Grid view or the Filmstrip of the Library module to go to where the picture is.

Geotagging photos taken without GPS data

Even if your camera doesn't record GPS data, the Map module makes it easier to tag your pictures with places on a map. These are the steps:

1. In the Filmstrip list, click on items 1 and 2. These pictures don't have any GPS data built into them.

2. In the Location Filter bar's search box, type "Ladera de San Miguel, Guanajuato" and press **Return or Enter**.

TIP: To see if a picture in the Library has GPS metadata, go to the Metadata panel, select the Location metadata set, and look for values in the GPS field. The map has been changed, and a Search Result sign shows where the new position is.

3. There is an X button to the right of the text search box in the Location Filter bar that you can click to remove the Search Result marking.

4. Click on the spot on the map and choose "**Add GPS Coordinates to Selected Photos**."

5. Select None by going to **Edit > Select None**. Move the mouse over the map marker pin to see a peek at the pictures that were taken there. When you click on the marking pin, you can see the pictures that are connected to that spot. You can move through the other pictures that are linked to this place by clicking on the white arrows on the sides of the preview thumbnail. To close the preview, click anywhere outside of it.

6. Click on the pin on the map and choose "Create Collection." Type "Ladera San Miguel" as the name of the new collection, then clear the list of choices, and click "Create." You can see the new collection in the Collections panel, which makes it easy to move the pictures to it.

Saving map locations

A collection of favorite places can be saved in the Saved Locations panel, making it easier to find and arrange photos that go with them. You can save a map location to cover a group of places you went or to mark a single spot you used for a client's picture shoot.

These are the steps:

1. If you're not in your folder yet, click on the Recent Sources menu at the top of the Filmstrip and choose it. Change the map view so it looks like the picture.

2. If necessary, make the Saved Locations panel on the left bigger, and then press the Create New Preset button to the right of the title.

3. In the New Location box, type Zona Centro as the name of the place. Change the Radius number to Meters, type 20 into the field that's there, and then click "**Create**."

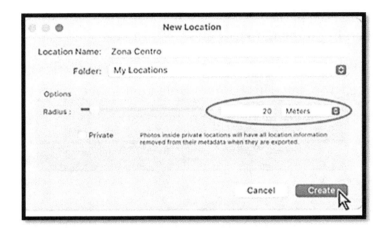

It will show up in the Saved Locations panel, along with your new item. There are four tagged pictures within the given radius (the white circle). The map shows a saved location with a gray pin in the middle that can be moved and another pin on the edge that can be used to change the radius of the first pin.

You can edit a location by clicking on it in the Saved Locations panel. The circle location overlay will then appear. There are two different ways to add pictures to a saved spot to make it look better.

One way is to drag the pictures from the Filmstrip to the Saved Locations panel's entry for the place. You can also pick out the photos in the Filmstrip and click the box next to the place name in the panel.

To get to a saved spot on the map, move your mouse over its name in the panel for saved spots and then press the white arrow to the right. As soon as you want to change a saved address, just right-click on it and select address Options. After giving your pictures places, the different filters and search options make it easy to look through your library.

4.   To get to the Library module, click on Library in the list of modules.

Working with Keywords Hierarchies

Groups of keywords make up hierarchical search results. Giving you an example is the best way to show you. Here's one based on where it is.

North America > United States > New York State > New York City

This is how the keywords are put in order in a hierarchy:

Continent > Country > State > City

It takes a lot of time and work to set up keyword groups. It might be easier to use Keyword sets instead of keyword groups when you're using personal keywords. Keyword structures, on the other hand, can save you a lot of work if you post your pictures to photo-sharing sites or stock libraries, or if you think you might in the future.

How to create a keyword hierarchy by adding keywords

Key word groups can be made in Lightroom in two different ways. The first way is to add new keywords to the Keyword List page. This is how to add the keywords you want to use to Lightroom if you haven't already:

1. Click the plus sign in the Keyword List panel to add a new keyword. For this keyword and all the ones you add in the next steps, make sure that the boxes next to Include on Export and Export Containing Keywords are checked (see below). If you need to, you can also add synonyms (don't forget to check the Export Synonyms box). I'm adding the keyword "North America" to this case.

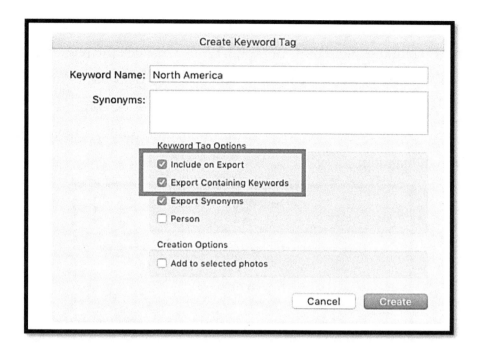

2. The new keyword you made is added to the list of keywords in the Keyword List panel by Lightroom. Select **Create Keyword Tag Inside "(keyword)"** when you right-click on it.

It's also possible to right-click on the keyword and choose "Put New Keywords Inside This Keyword" from the menu that comes up. When you click the plus sign, Lightroom will now add any new keywords you make to the keyword structure immediately.

3. Make a new keyword and, if necessary, add some substitutes. In this case, I replaced the keyword "America" with some popular ones, one of which was in a foreign language.

4. You can do this again and again to add as many levels of hierarchical keywords as you need.

How to create a keyword hierarchy with your current keywords

Here's the second way to set up a keyword structure. You can use it if you have already put the keywords you want to use in a certain order on some of your photos. At this point, you can click and drag them to make an order.

Let's stick with our example: let's say you have the following keywords listed one after the other in the Keyword List panel and want to arrange them in an order. They are on this list by letter.

o America

- o   North America
- o   New York City
- o   New York State

This is the hierarchy you want to achieve.

To do this, you would need to click and drag New York City onto New York State, then New York State onto the United States, and finally the United States onto North America.

The Keywording panel

Lightroom now adds all the keywords above "New York City" to a picture, like "New York State," "United States," and "North America," along with any synonyms, like "America," "United States of America," and "Los Estados Unidos."

Let's check out the Keywording panel again.

Make sure the Keyword Tags options are set to Enter Keywords. There is only one keyword tag that can be seen: New York City.

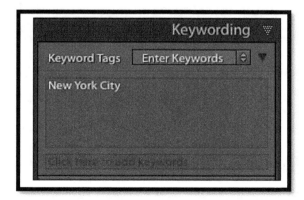

With the Keyword Tags options set to Keywords and Keywords That Contain Keywords. There are four keyword tags that can be seen: New York City and the three tags above it in the order.

As long as the Keyword Tags option is set to "Will Export." And now you can see even more keyword tags: New York City, the keywords that come before it in the order, and any words that are similar to those keywords.

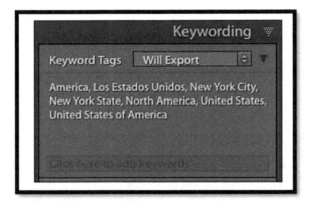

Adding top-level headers to your hierarchical keywords

Are you still with me? Stop and take a deep breath if you need to. This is likely the hardest lesson on keywords. One more thing for you to see.

We're going to add a new keyword this time, but it will only be used for order. I'll show you how it works.

1. To begin, click the **+ sign** in the Keyword List panel.

2. Put an underscore in front of and behind your new keyword (see below). This is where I put the keyword "Geography." Click the Create button after making sure that all the boxes are not checked.

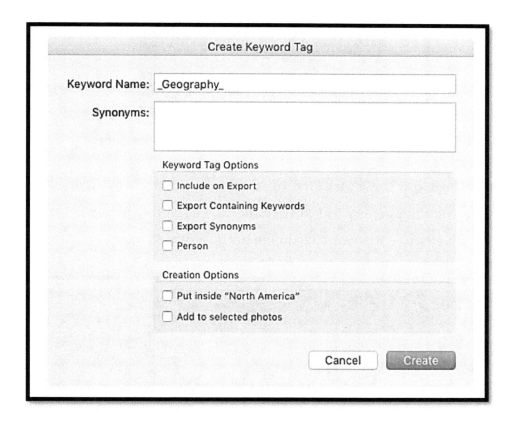

3. I'm going to move the "North America" keyword tag over to "_Geography_" now. This is how it looks.

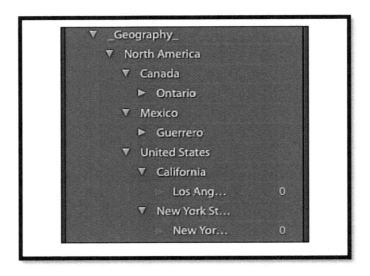

Let's add the keyword "New York City" to a picture and then check out the Keywording panel to see what happened. You can see the change in this picture of the Keyword Tags field with all three Keyword Tag menu options turned on.

Here you can see that the keyword tag "_Geography_" shows up under "Keywords" and "Containing Keywords," but not under "Will Export."

What does this mean? The "_Geography_" keyword tag is only used for organization. It's there as a header so that you can put all the keyword structures that are important below it. The underscore makes sure that it shows up near the top of your list of keywords (only keywords with numbers appear above it, in order). The most important thing is that it won't show up in the list of keywords that are exported with the picture. It is not a descriptive keyword; it is a useful one.

Downsides of using keyword hierarchies

1. **Keyword hierarchies are not preserved when you export your photos.** They won't show up in other apps or when you bring the picture back into Lightroom after exporting it.

2. **Keyword hierarchies are Catalog specific.** When you join Catalogs that don't have the same keyword structure, things can get messy. If you ever combine Catalogs, remember this important point.

Managing Multiple Catalogs

You can keep your albums the same and still save your photos in a few different ways. Get rid of the pictures you don't want to keep first. To choose a picture, just move your mouse over it. There will be a sample when it's done.

Make a folder called "Images" and put all of your pictures in it. After that, you can move them to the "Images" folder. If you have a lot of photos, this might not be the best option for you. You could also make a new album and put the pictures you want to keep in it. Pick up Lightroom and go to the Lightroom Catalog tab. Click on the + sign at the bottom of the box. In the window box, choose the photos you want to "resave." Next, you can add these photos to a new Lightroom collection and name it whatever you want.

Organizing the Lightroom Catalog Using New Folder & Library Folders

You can make good use of your time by organizing your Lightroom catalog well. Most of the time, you can't avoid editing pictures; it's often important to make your work better. The organization and user-friendliness of an app can be seen in how easy it is to use and navigate.

It's too bad that Lightroom is the best choice for photo processing because it has so many tools and features for handling and organizing your work. You can easily arrange your photos with LUTs, layers, and the new Photoshop Preferences panel.

Organizing photos through folders and categories provides a more efficient way to quickly find what you need.

1. **Begin by cleaning out your Lightroom catalog.**

   Lightroom has a lot of settings and options that you might not need or that aren't right for you when you first open it. There are some of these options in the "Customize" menu and some at the very bottom of the window. Every once in a while, cleaning out your catalog is a good way to get rid of things you don't need and focus on the parts you use the most. If copies are found, they are easy to get rid of and add back the right way. It's okay to get rid of things that are broken or no longer useful.

   From the choice that shows up on the screen, pick Lightroom. Next, go to **Library > Preferences > Advanced** and select "**Clear Catalog**." Finally, close the Catalog. If you are using an older version of Lightroom, go to Preferences - Advanced and check the "Clear Catalog" box. This will make the "**Remove Catalog**" choice work. After that, close the catalog.

   In the Library window, the "Feedback" button is on the left side of the list bar. It will open the Lightroom Preferences window if you click on it. When you click the "Clear Catalog" button on the Lightroom Toolbar (the white menu button), go to the bottom of the window and click the "Clear Catalog" tab. This will quickly clean up your catalog.

2. **Create a New Folder and Additional Folders**

   Now that you have cleaned out your catalog, you can start putting folders for different areas in order. Start with the "Explorer" tab on the left. To make a new folder, click the gray menu button that says "New Folder" and then "Add Folder." Once the folder is made, pick it from the menu at the top and click "Add Folder" from the menu at the bottom.

That's all there is to making new folders in Lightroom! To quickly choose a color from the Color Picker panel, you might want to use the Color Picker Toolbar, which is at the bottom of the window and is the dark gray tool bar on the far left. Pick out the Color Palette you like, then right-click on the picture and pick "Use Palette."

3. **Organize Your Photos**

    The "Settings" tab is now open. We will quickly work on a few folders to make it easy to find the pictures we need and put them in the right place. You can find these folders in your Library, which is on the right side, below the window's bottom. With these folders, you can organize your pictures in a second level.

    - The usual folder on your hard drive is at the **first level**.
    - **Level Two:** Pictures from your Lightroom library and folders. You'll probably use these photos, like ones you've already edited or ones that fit into certain groups, like parties, cars, or sports.
    - **Third Level:** Pictures from various folders like "Library," "Favorites," "Photos to Use," and more.
    - Lightroom's **fourth level** has all the other photos, like those in your camera roll and RAW files.

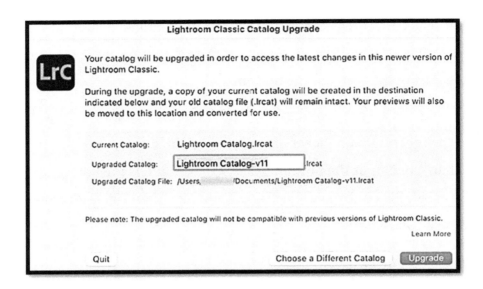

Click "File" in the bottom right part of the window to open the File Palette. It will show you all of your pictures and help you put them in the right folders. From the gray menu button, choose "New Folder" and then "Create New Folder." The "Photos to Use" folder will help you organize all the photos you will be working on in Lightroom.

Once you click "OK," wait for the icon to turn green, and then click "OK" again to confirm that the new folder was made. With the "Photos to Use" folder now in the right column, below your usual picture folder, you can add more photos to it. You can find your picture in the "Photos to Use" folder by selecting "Photos from Catalog" (the gray menu icon) and then "Edit Folder."

This will open an editing window that looks like the one in the "Explorer" tab. Choose "Edit Subfolder" from the gray menu, then click "Select Folder." Make sure that this path has a folder called "Photos to Use" in it. Press "OK" when you're done. Every picture you've taken will be in the folder you get. If you want to say more about each picture before you edit them, you might want to add an "About" note. The top of Lightroom's window has a list of options. Choose "Main" and then "New Folder."

A folder for the photos you want to edit will be created here. To show you what I mean, let's make a folder called "Photos of Walking Dogs." Once you're done making the folder, press the "OK" button.

Drag and drop the pictures from folders to move them. When selecting a picture in Lightroom, it's simple to see all the pictures you've already changed. If you tap on a picture, you can see all of its editing choices.

If you pick them all, you can quickly move the photos you've already changed to the "Photos to Use" folder. This is very useful when working with a folder full of pictures. After making a second level of folders for "Photos to Use," all that's left to do is hit "**Save**" to add the new folder for editing photos below the main folder for photos.

Avoid Multiple Catalogs, Merge Them as One

How do I mix several Lightroom Catalogs? This is a question that photographers get asked a lot. Since Lightroom 3, there has been a new tool called Merge. It is easy to join various Lightroom Catalogs, and you don't need any help or knowledge beforehand. The exact steps needed to combine several Lightroom Catalogs into one will be covered in this part.

It's important to know how Lightroom works before you try to merge several Lightroom Catalogs into one.

1. **Merge Settings**

   You should first change the settings in Lightroom that let you merge shots. You have a few options, but it's important to pick the best one for you. These are the ones you will use most often, but you can also use the other two. You can change the Merge Settings to how you want them. It's possible that the Merge Settings could use some presets. You can move on to the next steps once you're done with that one. In the Merge Settings, split the Content Order, choose all of your options, and turn it on. These are the settings that need to be changed. Right now, the Preferences part doesn't matter.

2. **Editing Lightroom Catalogs**

   Before we start combining, let's take a look at the different kinds of collections. Here is a short picture that shows the different types of Lightroom Catalogs: How can one effectively handle the different types of catalogs? Compared to your earlier merge settings, this job will take longer since there are four different types of catalogs. Here are the different kinds of Lightroom Catalogs in case you haven't done enough research:

   Comprehensive Lightroom Catalog

   All of your photos are in one place with a thorough catalog, which makes it easy to look through many pictures.

   Library Catalog

   A Library directory puts all of your pictures in a library-like layout, similar to a full directory. Go to **Edit > Library > Add New Library** to make a new library. A different catalog might not always be needed, but it's better to have it in this Catalog so everything is in one place.

Unordered Catalog

These types of Lightroom catalogs are the most popular ones. They hold pictures taken in different places. If you merge albums with another Lightroom user, you can choose the order of the pictures.

Featured Collection Catalog

This type of portfolio is like showing off a collection on Instagram, where you can put your photos in a certain spot. Following picking a certain book type, it's simple to add your pictures to the right spot. This method is often chosen by people who want to keep and show off their pictures.

It's too much to have four different kinds of brochures. How do you make it so that these publications blend together? Easy. There is a way to make it happen.

3. **Merge Settings**

The settings need to be changed so that one of the four different stores can be merged into one. For putting pictures together, Lightroom has a lot of settings. You can change some settings after picking the type of Catalog to join. We will only change two of those settings in this case.

The "**Open In Develop module**" setting is now called "**Merge Master**," and it makes it easy to join the picture and the catalog. Lightroom calls this setting "**Local Merge**." To find it, open Lightroom Classic and look to the right. It's going to change the second setting. This is a better way to put the picture and the book together. Let's talk about how to change the "Merge with Other Locs" setting.

4. **Merge Settings: Local Merge**

Before merging the picture and the catalog, Lightroom will show you all the possible Locs that you can add. It will show you a list of places you can go if you have a "Local Merge" book with pictures from another "**Local Merging**" catalog.

5. **Merge with other locs**

Make sure that the "Show Proxies" choice is off in our "Local Merge" catalog before joining with it. Go to "Properties" and then click on "View" to get to the store. In the list, find the "**Proxies**" tab and uncheck "Show Proxies." This will keep any pictures in our "Local Merge" catalog from being copied. To turn off "Show Proxies" in the catalog, go to the catalog and uncheck "**Proxies**." That's fine, but we want to combine the picture with the "Organize Changes" catalog.

In order to do that, we need to click on that exact spot. Let's talk about "Select Locs for Merge." This will show you a list of folders where you can join the picture. The picture needs to be merged only in two folders: "Organize Changes" and "Merge with Other Locs." Pick out the "Merge with Other Locs" folder to start. Look at the list of all the Locs. On the far left is a folder called "Merge with Other Locs." You can add pictures from other catalogs to the "Organize Changes" catalog by clicking on "Merge with Other Locs."

Sync Lightroom Classic with Lightroom Ecosystem

Sync your photos to access them anywhere

When you connect your computer's Lightroom Classic to the Lightroom Ecosystem, you can share important picture collections with Lightroom for mobile, Lightroom on the web, and the PC cloud-based Lightroom app. This is a great way to:

- Bring important pictures to show off to family and friends.
- Sort through and edit pictures whenever you have time.
- Post pictures from your phone to Instagram and other social networks
- These pictures should be used in your Adobe Portfolio.

Note: To share pictures between all of your devices, you need to join Creative Cloud or try it out for free.

1. **Enable syncing on your computer**

    Make sure you can connect to the Internet and start Lightroom Classic on your home computer. If asked, enter your Adobe ID and password on the Sign In screen. Then click Sign In.

    There is a **Cloud Sync** button in the top right part of Lightroom Classic. After clicking that button, click **Start Syncing**.

    Keep in mind that you can only link one Lightroom Classic file to the Lightroom Ecosystem at a time. The pictures you shared in Lightroom Classic will be added to the new catalog if you switch between catalogs while they are still being synced.

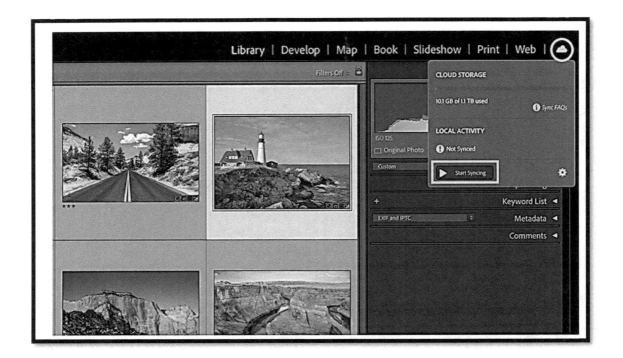

2. **Sync existing photo collections**

You can pick which photos from Lightroom Classic on your PC are linked by picking groups of photos you already have or want to add. You need to put each picture you want to sync in its own group.

Open the Collections panel and click the plus sign to the left of a collection to add a sync icon with two points. The collection will be in sync now. In the upper right part of the thumbnails, there will be a sync icon when the pictures are joined.

Note: A collection is like a picture playlist. Picture can be in more than one group, like a song can be in more than one set.

3. **Create new synced collections**

There is a plus sign (+) in the Collections panel that you can click to make a new collection and share it. Check the box next to Sync with Lightroom in the Create Collection window, then click Create. You can drag pictures onto the name of the collection in the Collections panel to add them.

4. Access your synced collections on mobile

On a phone or tablet, open Lightroom. Tap Sign in and enter the same Adobe ID you used to sign in on your computer if you aren't already logged in.

When you sync your collections from Lightroom Classic on your PC to the Lightroom app on your phone, they show up as albums. How long this takes will depend on how fast your internet is and how many photos are being shared.

5. **Sync photos from mobile to your computer**

Your computer's Lightroom Classic will automatically sync with any photos or groups you add to the Lightroom Ecosystem on your mobile devices or through Lightroom on the web. Any pictures you add to Lightroom on your computer will also be synced with Lightroom Classic.

In Lightroom Classic on your PC, you can view these pictures in the From Lightroom collection set. Synced pictures also show up in the Catalog panel in the All Synced Photographs collection. They can also be found on your desktop under the name of your device in the Folders panel in Lightroom Classic, or in a folder you choose in Preferences > Lightroom Sync > Location.

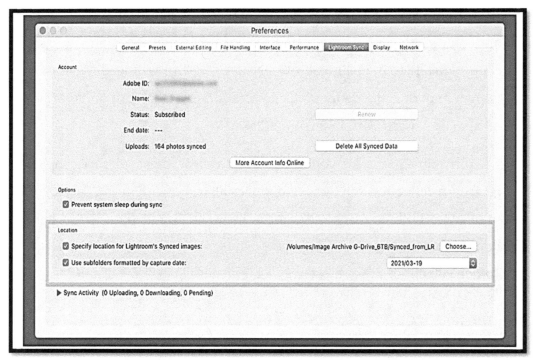

6. **Sync edits across the Lightroom Ecosystem**

Any changes you make to photos that are synced from Lightroom Classic on your computer are instantly made to all of your other devices and Lightroom.com.

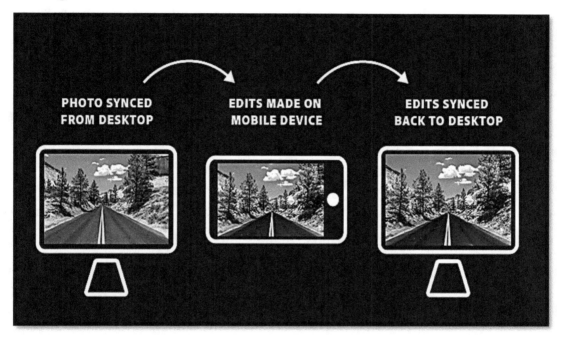

CHAPTER NINE

CREATIVE DEVELOP TECHNIQUES

Tone Curve Adjustments

To improve contrast, lighting, and color in your pictures, the Tone Curve is one of the best tools you can use. But unlike tools that are easier to understand, it makes a lot of photographers, especially new ones, confused.

Based on tone and color, this tool separates parts of a picture. It lets you precisely change these parts of a photo, which can help you get any look you want, from the trendy matte look to the classic high contrast of fashion ads.

What Does The Tone Curve Do In Lightroom?

The Tone Curve in Lightroom helps editors target certain exposure levels in a picture, add more color, and make creative looks that are fun and different.

The tool can be found on the right side of the screen in the Develop module, above HSL, and below Basic. It gives you fine control over an image's shadows, highlights, and midtones.

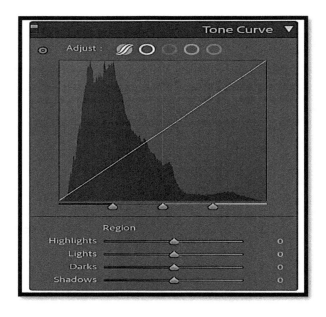

You can change how bright or dark these parts are by pulling the straight line up or down. The name **"Tone Curve"** comes from the way the line curves when it is pulled up and down.

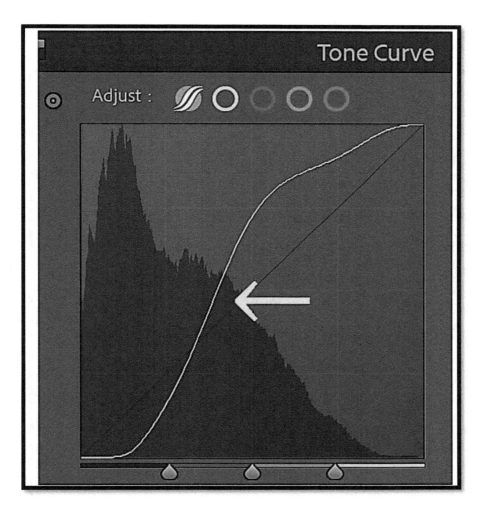

The Tone Curve graph resembles a Histogram in appearance, which may be known to photographers. Your photo's shadows are shown by the "mountains" on the left, its midtones by the ones in the middle, and its highlights by the ones on the right.

To put it simply, the Tone Curve graph (behind the vertical line) is the original image's histogram, which can be used to fix the exposure. If you click and drag on the tone curve, you can change the photo's brightness or contrast. It gets brighter when you pull the straight line up and darker when you pull it down.

To show this, if you pull up the line at the tone curve's shadow point, the shadows will get brighter.

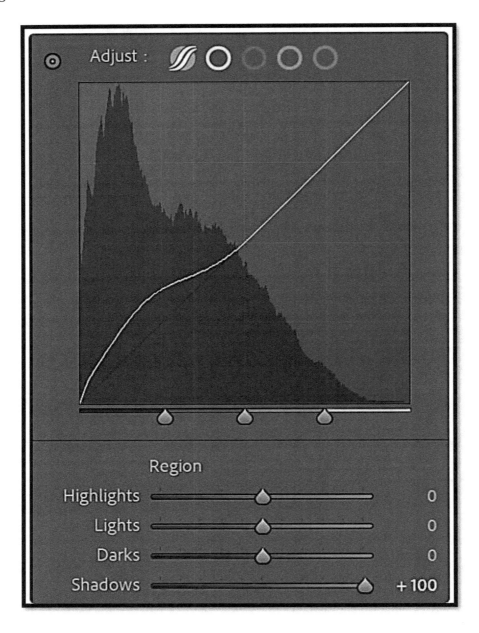

If you pull down the line at the graph's highlight point, on the other hand, the highlights will dim. Although the changes will be applied to your picture, the graph behind the tone curve will not change. This line only shows the histogram of the original picture; it doesn't change when you make changes to it like the histogram above the Basic Panel in Lightroom does.

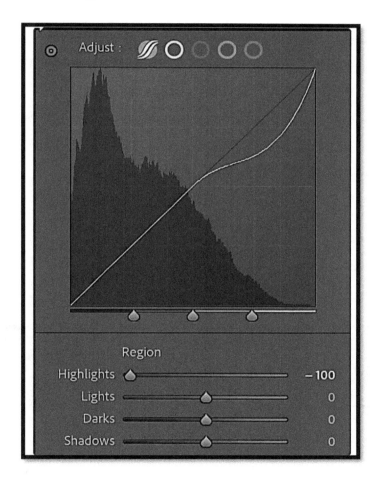

This is why the Tone Curve is a great tool for changing photos. You can make very accurate and detailed changes to your shadows, highlights, and midtones without affecting each other. The shadows and highlights settings in the Basic Panel only let you make some changes to the brightness and contrast. This lets you make even more changes.

At the top of the Tone Curve panel in Lightroom Classic, you'll find five different options for adjusting the Tone Curve. These settings allow you not only to modify the overall Tone Curve but also to control which color channels your adjustments will impact.

The first option is the **Parametric Curve**, also known as the **Region Curve**. This setting is particularly useful for those new to working with the Tone Curve. It provides a simplified approach by allowing you to focus on specific tonal regions of your image:

- **Shadows:** Adjusts the darkest areas of your photo.
- **Darks:** Affects the darker midtones, just above the shadows.
- **Lights:** Modifies the lighter midtones, just below the highlights.
- **Highlights:** Changes the brightest parts of your image.

The Parametric Curve offers a more intuitive way to fine-tune these areas using sliders. This method is ideal for beginners because it breaks down the Tone Curve adjustments into more manageable parts, making it easier to see and understand the impact of your changes.

The Point Curve is the second one. You can add anchor points to your diagonal line to change particular areas, and this will remove the exposure range settings.

The Red, Green, and Blue Curves come next, in that order. You can change the tones of these individual color bands this way. You can use these to get rid of colors that you don't want in an image or to add minor color grading effects to the highlights or shadows.

When To Use The Tone Curve In Lightroom

In Lightroom Classic, the Tone Curve is a powerful tool that works best as a complement to the basic adjustments made in the Basic Panel. After you've set the initial exposure and contrast using the sliders in the Basic Panel—such as the blacks, whites, shadows, and highlights—you can use the Tone Curve to make more precise and nuanced adjustments to brightness and contrast.

For example, the basic sliders in the Basic Panel can adjust overall brightness and contrast but might not allow for fine-tuning specific tonal ranges. The Tone Curve excels in providing this level of control. It lets you target specific parts of the tonal range—shadows, midtones, and highlights—more precisely than the Basic Panel sliders.

Contrast Adjustments: The Tone Curve allows you to adjust contrast selectively. If you want to increase contrast specifically in the highlights and midtones without affecting the shadows, you can do this using the Tone Curve's anchor points. This level of control is difficult to achieve with the Basic Panel sliders alone.

Color Adjustments: Beyond contrast, the Tone Curve also lets you adjust color balance with precision. Each color channel (Red, Green, Blue) can be adjusted independently. For example, if your shadows have an unwanted yellow cast, you can use the Blue color channel to add blue specifically to the shadows, leaving the midtones and highlights unaffected. This targeted adjustment helps correct color casts and balance the overall look of your photo.

Fixing Color Casts: To correct color casts, you can add the opposite color using the Tone Curve's color channels. For instance, if your image has a green cast, you can add magenta to the Green channel to counterbalance it. This adjustment is precise and helps in achieving more accurate and pleasing color representation in your image.

You can also use the colors to make creative changes, like giving your scenery pictures a moody green look.

Region Curve VS Point Curve

The Parametric (Region), Point, Red, Green, and Blue Tone Curves are the five available curves, as was already stated. When you choose the first choice, "Parametric Curve," you'll find the Region Curve.

Region Curve

The Tone Curve editing panel is split into two parts in the Region Curve view. The top part has a histogram chart with a vertical line, and the bottom part has four sliders with the word "Region" at the top of each one. Without the use of anchor points, you can edit your Tone Curve using these settings.

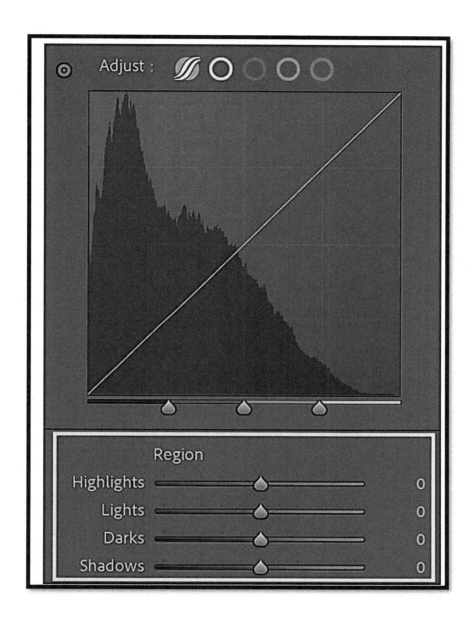

The vertical line changes to show the change when you move any of the buttons in the Region box.

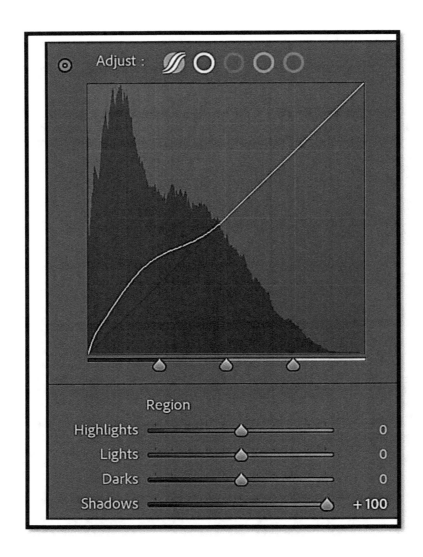

For beginners or people who want a slightly more general adjustment, the Region Curve is the best tool to use. The Region Curve also sets a cap on how much the curve can be changed.

This helps you make a modest adjustment to the exposure so you don't go too far and ruin the picture. When you work in the Region Curve, Lightroom tells you how far your curve can be changed while still keeping the brightness tones.

This choice might not let you make the adjustments you want, though, based on what you need in an edit. That means the Point Curve will work instead.

Point Curve

You can make a much more complex adjustment called the Point Curve that lets you set anchor points that you can then move around separately from the vertical line.

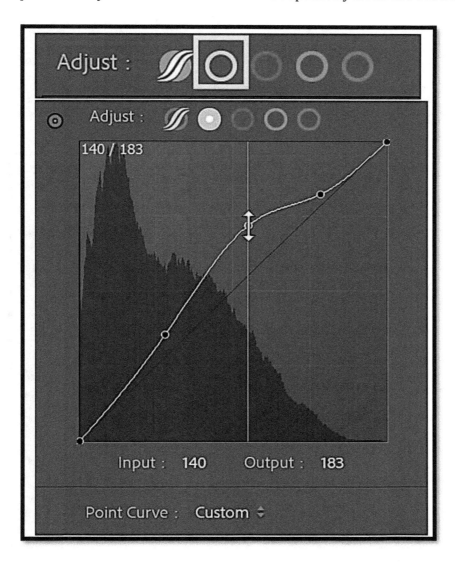

You can add anchor points to the Point Curve by clicking on different parts of the vertical line and putting a point there. After that, you can move this point up and down. You are free to move as much of the point as you want.

Moving this curve up will make your picture brighter, and moving it down will make it darker. Better and more precise changes can be made with this than with the Region Curve's limited adjustments.

There are a few settings at the bottom of the Point Curve that make it easier to make changes. When you pick either **Medium Contrast** or **Strong Contrast**, points are drawn right away. Most of the time, linear is used because it doesn't draw any points.

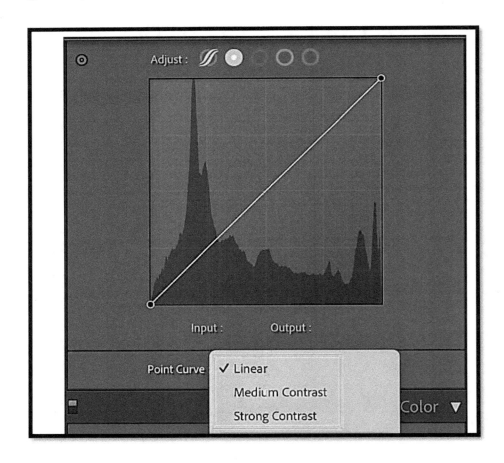

There are good things about both the Region Curve and the Point Curve. When I have to choose which one to use, I think about both my own tastes and the purpose of my edit. Because it is so simple and accurate to make changes to brightness and tone, I tend to use the Region Curve more frequently.

But the Point Curve gives me a lot more options when I want to add something extra to my shots. Overall, there is no right or wrong answer. Try each one out to see which one you like best. It's better to start with the Region Curve for most people who are new to it.

Red, Green, and Blue Tone Curve Channels Explained

The Region Curve and the Point Curve both work on an image's tones. The Red, Green, or Blue Tone Curve, on the other hand, only works on one of those three color channels.

You can change the color channel's tones by pulling the straight line either toward the color (upwards) or away from it to the color that goes with it (downwards). Similar to the Point Curve, you can add points to the vertical line to make your changes extremely precise.

Remember that adding a point to the shadow area and moving it up or down will only change the color in the shadow area, just like with tint tweaks.

As an example, moving the Blue Curve up in the middle of the curve will make the whole picture bluer, including the highlights, midtones, and shadows, because the curve always goes up from the line.

This is a great way to remove color casts, even out the colors, or give a picture a moody look.

How To Edit The Tone Curve In Lightroom

It might seem hard to use the Tone Curve to edit a picture, but it's not! Remember that the histogram is split into two parts: light and dark. This will make using this powerful editing tool much easier.

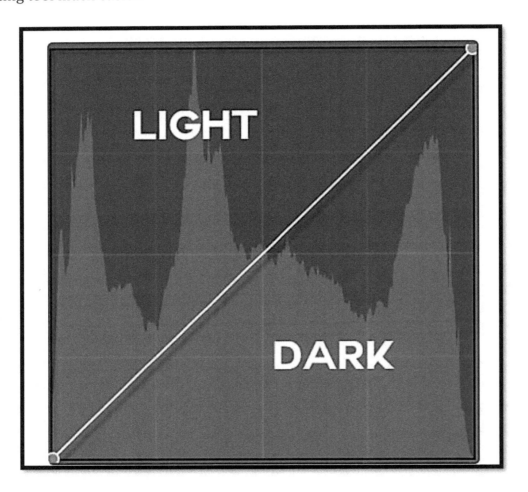

Use the Region sliders if you only want to make small tweaks to your picture and don't want to change the exposure.

Use the Point Curve if your picture needs something more important. A more general adjustment is made by adding one point, but a more detailed adjustment is made by adding many points. Most of the time, two or three anchor points along a curve are enough, but the case below shows how crazy you can get.

What you want to do with the picture you are changing and how you use the Tone Curve will determine how much you use it. You can learn how to use a tool quickly by playing with it. Just keep in mind that pictures do start to look too edited after a while, so try not to go too far and lose quality.

Using The Tone Selector

With the Tone Selector tool, you can focus on certain changes in tone in a certain part of your picture. If you feel like you can't quite focus on a part of your picture, this will help.

The Tone Selector is shown as a small dot on the far left side of the Tone Curve panel, next to the word "Adjust." Press this and then move the mouse to the picture you want to change.

Move the mouse to the tone you want to change, click and hold it, and then slide that tone up (to make it lighter) or down (to make it darker). Based on the exposure range you chose for your picture, Lightroom will add a fixed point to the Tone Curve on its own.

Tone Curve Editing Examples In Lightroom

These are some very popular ways to edit with the Tone Curve.

Matte Contrast

In the camera world right now, the matte look is in style. Matte pictures don't have much contrast, and they almost look like they have a texture that goes across the whole screen. The idea for this type of editing came from matte prints in photography. In these prints, the sheet is rough so the picture doesn't have as much contrast when it's printed.

The black point needs to be raised so that it looks more like gray than black. This is the key to smooth contrast. It's easy to grab the black point and lift it with the Point Curve to add matte contrast. This is because you are making the darkest parts of a picture look brighter all of a sudden.

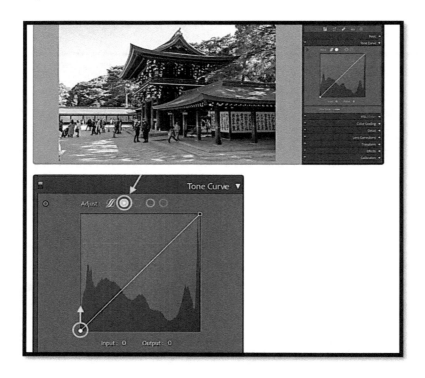

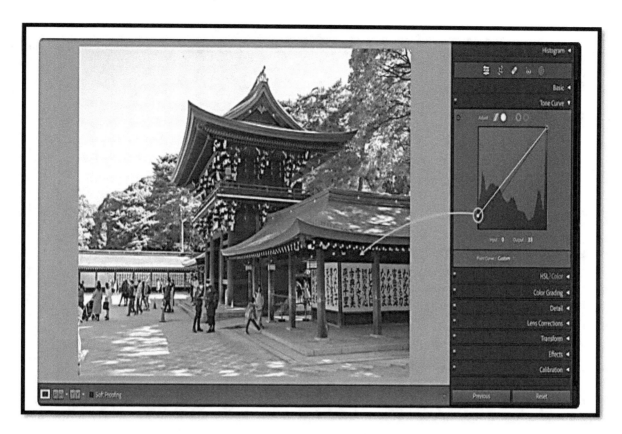

High Contrast (S Curve)

To make a look with a lot of contrast, your Tone Curve will look like the letter S. With the shadows pulled down and the highlights pulled up, you can make the picture stand out more. As was already said, the end result will look like the letter S. It's more contrasty when you go to the extremes and make your curve look more like a real S.

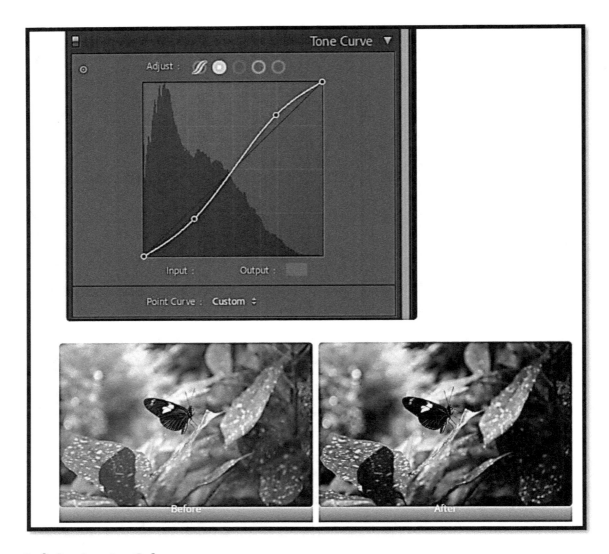

Soft Contrast + Color

Soft contrast is a small S curve that lets you keep the contrast pretty low. Take your shadows and pull them down a bit, then take your highlights and pull them up a bit. This will make a S curve that is softer.

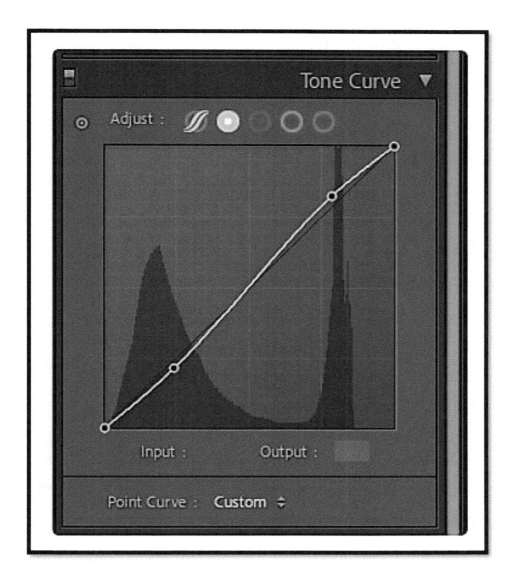

Once you're done, you can go to the color channels and make changes to make the colors look good. There is a yellow tint to my picture, so I can make the shadows bluer. I'll put a control point on the line at the top so the highlights don't change, but I want to keep some of the yellow tints in the highlights.

Creating Tone Curve Presets In Lightroom

One of the best things about Adobe Lightroom is that you can save settings as "presets." But most people think of presets as covering the whole editing panel. The Tone Curve, on the other hand, lets you save a special kind of setting. This setting only changes the Tone Curve and nothing else!

When you use the Point Curve choice, you can save Tone Curve presets. When changing in Point Curve, after you add points and move them up and down, the button next to "point curve" will change to "custom." Click on "custom," then press "**Save**," and give your preset any name you want.

You can get to this setting the next time you press the Point Curve dropdown menu.

Tones Curve is a powerful tool that can help you make your photos look better in more creative ways than just the Basic Panel. At first, it might be hard to get, but after a while, it will be your favorite Lightroom tool!

Color Grading

When you change an image's global properties to give it a certain look or feel, you are color-grading it. It's a personal and style-based process that can include a lot of different changes, but in general, it means changing how the picture's highlights, shadows, and midtones look. This lets the shooter set a tone or mood and make the viewer feel a certain way.

Any adjustment to an image's style could be regarded as color grading in a strict sense. You can change the color by using the HSL/Color panel or by changing the tone curve.

Most editors, though, mean the way a certain tint is added to the shadows, highlights, and midtones when they talk about color grading.

One common way to change the color of things in movies is to make the midtones more orange and the edges blue. In both movies and pictures, this makes them feel more powerful and like they belong in a movie theater.

Color grading vs split toning

In earlier versions of Lightroom, the Split Toning tool had its own panel in the Develop module. It has been replaced by the Color Grading tool.

Split Toning lets users change the color of shadows and highlights but not midtones. It was kind of like a beta version of Color Grading. This was helpful, but the fact that midtone changing wasn't included was an annoying flaw that made the tool much less useful.

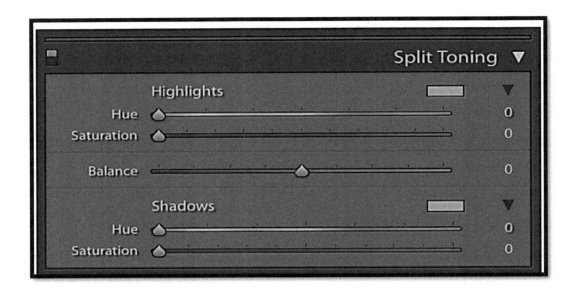

Color Grading does everything that Split Toning does, plus a lot more. The Color Grading tool will preserve all of the changes made to any photos that were changed with Split Toning.

Along with midtone editing, the Color Grading tool adds color wheels instead of linear scales, which are much more useful:

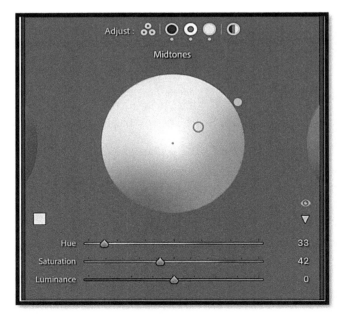

The Lightroom Color Grading tool: A step-by-step guide

The color grading tool has a lot of features, but it's very easy to get to and start using.

Click on the Develop module when you open Lightroom.

This is all there is to it. Just open the Color Grading panel on the right.

In the middle of the Lightroom Color Grading panel are three color wheels. At the top are a row of icons, and at the bottom are two scales. There are three color wheels. Each one lets you change the brightness of the midtones, shadows, and highlights.

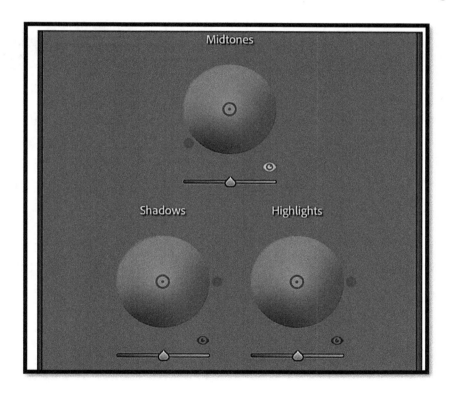

You can see the edit being made to your picture right away by clicking and dragging on any of the color wheels. Move the slider around to change the color grade's saturation. As you do this, keep in mind that the slider's position around the circle changes the color grade's hue.

If you only want to change the brightness, you can click and drag the inner circle. The outer circle will change the color. If you are using a different color wheel, you can use the scale at the bottom to change the general brightness of the midtones, shadows, or highlights.

If you only want to change the color, hold down the Ctrl or MD key and press the Shift key.

To temporarily disable the tint adjustment in Lightroom Classic, you can click and hold the eye icon, which is located just below and to the right of the color wheel. This will temporarily remove the tint effect, allowing you to view your image without the applied color grading. When you release the mouse button, the adjustment will be reapplied, making it easy to toggle between the edited and unedited versions for comparison.

If you want to reset the tint adjustment entirely, double-click anywhere within the color wheel. This action will revert the color wheel to its original state, removing any previous adjustments and giving you a fresh start to make new color grading changes.

Within the Color Grading panel, you'll find two important sliders: the Blending slider and the Balance slider.

- **Blending Slider:** This slider controls how the color adjustments to the midtones, shadows, and highlights blend together. By adjusting the Blending slider, you can either smooth out the transitions between these tonal areas or keep them more distinct. This helps in fine-tuning the overall harmony of your color grading, allowing you to achieve a balanced look or emphasize certain tones depending on your creative vision.

- **Balance Slider:** The Balance slider allows you to adjust the overall emphasis between highlights and shadows. Moving the Balance slider above 0 will make the changes in the highlights more prominent, while moving it below 0 will make the shadow adjustments stand out more. This tool is especially useful when you want to create a specific mood in your image, such as making the scene brighter or giving it a darker, more dramatic feel.

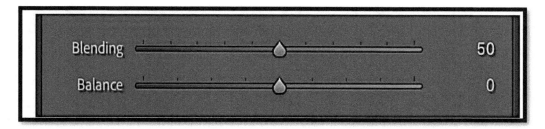

To keep your shadows, midtones, and highlights separate, move Blending to the left. To make your changes mix into one another, move Blending to the right. To make your shadow changes apply to a larger area of the picture, move Balance to the left. To make your highlight changes stand out more, swipe it to the right. Or, don't do anything with these buttons. You should be fine.

If you look closely at the top of the Color Grading panel, you will see a row of round icons that don't look right. Each one looks like a circle with a different pattern of shading. The first one looks like an alien hieroglyph. These let you change between the Color Grading panel's different styles.

All three editing tools are shown at once in the first button, which has three small rings around it: Highlights, Midtones, and Shadows. You can change one setting at a time with the others. The last icon is a general adjustment for Hue, Saturation, and Luminance.

With these buttons, you can change between changing highlights, shadows, and midtones all at once or one at a time. The last circle has a world adjustment for Hue, Saturation, and Luminance.

If you want to make even smaller changes, you can click on one of the buttons that shows a bigger version of any of the three adjustment factors. With better power over how your edits are applied, this can help you choose your adjustments with pinpoint accuracy.

How to use the Color Grading tool for great results

When it comes to using the Color Grading panel in Lightroom Classic, there's no single "correct" method. The beauty of this tool lies in its flexibility, allowing you to shape your images according to your personal style and creative vision. Just like any other tool in Lightroom, the key is to experiment and see how different adjustments impact the final look of your photos.

If you're new to color grading and unsure where to start, let's walk through a simple edit together. This will give you a hands-on understanding of how you can use the Color Grading panel to enhance your images.

When there are a lot of different tones in a scene like the one above, I like to start by editing the shadows. Instead of using the "all-in-one" adjustment choice that shows all three circles, I like to edit each value separately using the larger circles. I like how this gives me fine-grained control.

First, you should change the Luminance slider. Moving it to the left will make the darkest parts of the picture even darker, and moving it to the right will make them lighter. In this case, I'm going to lower the brightness to make the shadows stand out more.

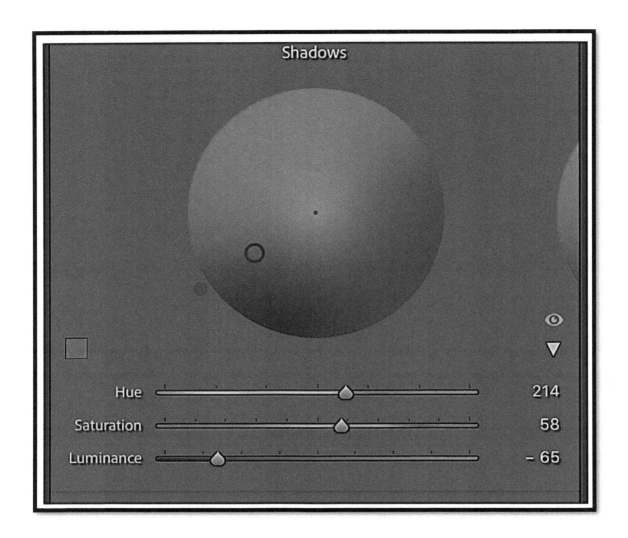

Then, click and drag on the color wheel to give the shadows a green tint. This will start to make the picture look more like a movie. With only the shadows changed, your picture might look a little off, but once you change the highlights and midtones, it will look good.

Next, click on **Highlights** and use the **Luminance** tool to change how light or dark the brightest parts of the shot are. Before making any color edits, some people prefer to change the **Luminance**.

Once you're satisfied with the brightness, the next step is to enhance the color contrast by adding a complementary color. In this case, you can click on the color wheel to introduce a touch of orange into your highlights. Orange is opposite teal on the color wheel, and this combination is popular in photography because it creates a striking contrast.

By applying orange to the brightest areas of your image, you'll make those highlights pop against the cooler, teal-toned shadows or midtones. This contrast not only draws attention to the lighter parts of the image but also gives your photo a more dynamic and visually engaging look.

The use of teal and orange is a classic color grading technique, especially in cinematic photography, because it adds depth and dimension to the image. The warm orange tones in the highlights create a natural separation from the cooler teal tones in the shadows, which can make the subject stand out more clearly.

As you adjust the color, keep an eye on the overall balance to ensure that the effect enhances your image without overwhelming it. This approach will help you achieve a polished and professional look in your photos.

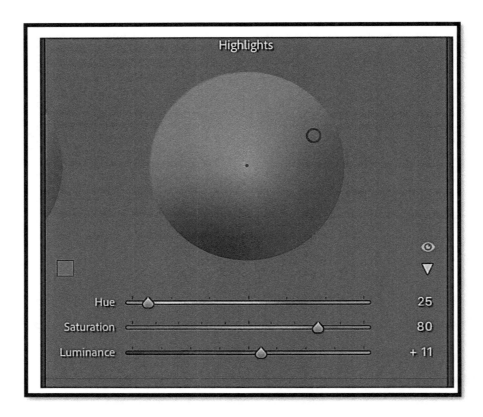

The example picture is beginning to take shape at this point. A bit of green in the shadows and orange in the highlights give it a rougher, more cinematic feel than the original.

Going to the Midtones wheel after editing the highlights and shadows will let you change how warm or cool your picture feels altogether. The Midtones wheel doesn't change the look of the brightest or darkest parts of your picture; it changes the look of everything in between.

With midtone adjustments, you can change how warm or cool your whole picture looks. To make your picture warmer, move the Luminance scale and then, click and drag the dot to orange or red. To make it cooler, move it to blue.

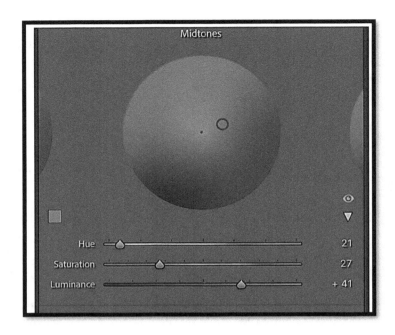

Right now, the picture is almost done, and you can see the end result below. Compared to the first one, this one sounds very different and dull.

Changes have been made to the shadows, highlights, and midtones. The picture isn't quite finished yet, though.

The Blending and Balance settings need to be adjusted after the shadows, highlights, and midtones have been edited.

As I already said, blending is the measure of how much each of the three factors stays in its own band. Its default number is 50, which makes the color grade pretty smooth generally.

If you move the slider for blending to the left, your changes to the shadows and highlights will only affect the darkest and lightest parts of the shot, respectively. When the balance is 0, each edit stays in its own lane and doesn't change the picture as a whole.

Also, moving the Balance scale to the right will make the gap between each tone area bigger. Most of the time, the effect is pretty minor, but if you use it carefully, you can see it.

After editing the shadows, highlights, and midtones, the blending was set to 0. The path is where you can see the change the most.

With the Balance tool, you can change how much of the picture is blacks and how much is highlights. The adjustment you made to the shadows will be applied to a larger portion of the image if you move the tool to the left. When you move the tool to the right, the highlight changes are also affected.

Once you've added a tint to the shadows, move the Balance tool to the left to make that tint cover more of the picture. Similarly, move the Balance tool to the right if you want the highlight adjustment to work on more than just the brightest parts.

It is now -54 in balance. There is now a lot more of the rest of the picture that is colored green from the shadows.

Tips and tricks for Lightroom color grading

When color grading, it's important to understand that there is no one right answer. Don't see color grading as a quest to find the best way to change your picture. Instead, see it as a gateway to endless options that you can use however you like.

You can click on the color wheels and try different things on your own to learn more about color grading. Since Lightroom doesn't delete files, you can always go back to an earlier version of a picture. Between now and then, you might think of a new way to edit your photos that you had not thought of before.

For now, here are some tips that will help you get better at color grading:

- Before diving into Lightroom's Color Grading tool, it's essential to ensure your image has a balanced brightness. The Basic panel is your go-to for making initial adjustments to highlights and shadows, setting a solid foundation for further color grading.

- When working with shadows, you can add depth and richness by introducing cooler tones like green, blue, or purple. These colors tend to enhance the moodiness of the darker areas, making them appear fuller and more nuanced. On the other hand, applying warmer tones like yellow, orange, or red to the shadows can create a striking contrast against the highlights, drawing attention to the interplay between light and dark in your photo.

- For midtones, subtlety is key. Adjust them gently to ensure they complement both the highlights and shadows without overpowering them. The midtones should act as a bridge, harmonizing the overall color palette rather than competing with the other elements of your image.

- The Blending slider is a crucial tool for fine-tuning how your graded colors transition and interact. Small adjustments here can significantly impact the smoothness and cohesion of your color grading, helping you achieve a more polished look.

- To see how your changes are affecting the image, you can quickly toggle between the before and after views by clicking the eye button next to any of the color wheels. This feature allows you to assess the impact of your edits in real time, ensuring you're on the right track.

Split Toning

The split-toning panel is one of the easiest and most useful post-processing tools in Lightroom. The split-toning tool is tucked away between the HSL and Detail sidebars, so most photographers don't use it very often. Why should it be that way? Lightroom already has a lot of ways to change an image's colors, from tint to intensity, so adding another one doesn't seem necessary. But split-toning is actually a lot more useful than it might seem at first, and even more useful than some photographers think it is.

Both split-toned and single-tone changes are very easy to make in Lightroom's split-toning tool. You can choose between highlight hue, shadow hue, highlight saturation, shadow saturation, and balance. Take a look at this picture:

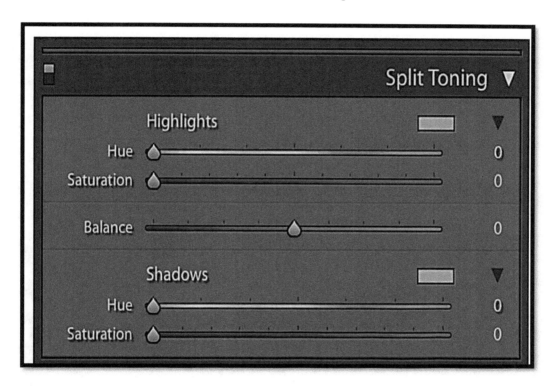

It's not too hard to figure out what these five changes do, so I invite you to try them out on your own photos. Lightroom lets you get a full split-tone effect by separating the highlights and shadow changes. This means that dark and light parts of the photo can be colored differently.

With the saturation adjustment, you can change how toned a picture is. A very strong color will be added with high saturation, while a tone will be added with low saturation. A blue "hue" will give your photos a blue tone. The **"hue"** options control the real color that you add.

Balance is the hardest choice, but it's still very simple to use. Basically, balance lets you choose which levels of brightness are shadows and which levels are highlights. If you move the balance tool all the way to the right, the photo will have highlights everywhere. If you move it all the way to the left, the picture will have shadows everywhere. You can make much more precise split-tone changes with the balance tool, as shown below.

The "Balance" setting is set to zero in this picture. If you look closely, you can see that the sky and road are orange-red, and the grass is purple-blue.

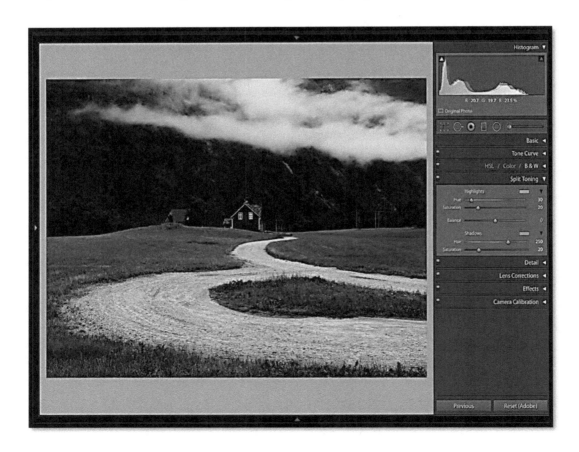

It looks like the balance slider is set to +100 here. This means that Lightroom sees every color in the picture as a highlight, which is why it turns the whole picture orange-red.

This picture shows what the picture looks like when "Balance" is set to -100. Here you can see that Lightroom now sees the whole picture as a shadow, which makes everything blue-purple.

There are two more things about Lightroom's split-tone panel that are worth talking about. In the first place, look at the small square below, which is near the words "Highlights" and "Shadows":

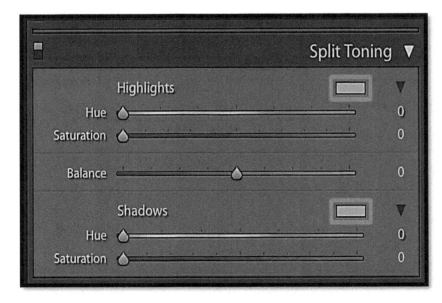

There is a cool adjustment menu that isn't clear at first glance if you click on these. There is a wide range of colors you can choose from with this choice. It blends the "Saturation" and "Hue" options into one adjustment (see below). You can't do anything new with the color tester, but it might help you see the changes you make more clearly. It all comes down to which way is easier for you.

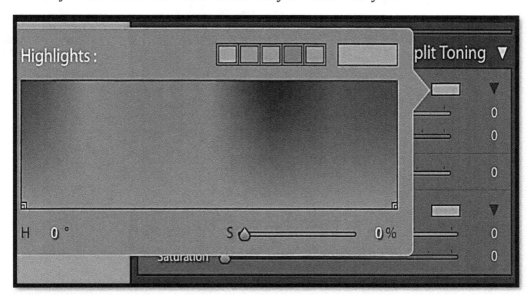

Lastly, there is a "hidden" feature in the Split-Tone panel that lets you see exactly which tone you are adding to the shadows or the highlights. To do this, hold down the "alt" key (or "option" on a Mac) and move the "hue" or "balance" buttons. You will see a high-saturation version of your changes right away! This makes it much simpler to determine which colors you are adding to a picture, especially if your changes are small.

Tinting Color Photographs

Making these changes to a black-and-white picture is the classic and most well-known method of splitting-tone your photos. Indeed, all of the pictures I've added so far have been black and white because split-tone changes stand out more clearly in those types of pictures. But it's just as easy to change color photos in Lightroom.

Why do you want to do this? It depends on what's going on. When it comes to changing the colors of your photos, Lightroom has a lot of options. The most famous is the "Basic" panel's color temperature adjustment. Of course, there are times when split-toning is better. Take a look at this picture:

The picture above makes me happy, but I think the highlights should be brighter (more yellow-gold). They are already too blue for my taste. Only the colors need adjustment; the rest of the picture is exactly how I want it to. In this case, I could change the color temperature, but it would make the rest of the picture look bad. Look below:

This above adjustment changed the color of the highlights, which was great, but it made the colors look bad everywhere else. The tree stem stands out as being way too red. Instead, a split-tone adjustment to only the highlights is a much better way to warm up the picture, as shown below:

In the version above, I changed the highlights to a gold color by giving them a hue of 37 and a brightness of 40. In order to make sure that this adjustment only affects the strongest highlights, I also used a balance setting of -62. Keep in mind that the edges are now a lot more yellow, but the tree stems are still the same color.

Adding yellow-gold colors to an image's highlights is the most common split-toning adjustment, which can be seen in this picture. That being said, it is very usual to change the shadows to look a little blue, which is not something I did with this picture. Of course, these are just broad statements, but they reflect how we see the world: dark areas are blue, and bright areas are gold.

Split-toning is clearly a useful tool for some pictures. Other changes might have produced the same outcome, but the split-tone panel was definitely the easiest to use for the picture above. But you should avoid split-toning in some situations, like when the color temperature scale works much better. In the next part, I'll talk about those scenarios.

When to Avoid

The split-toning worked much better in the redwoods picture above than the color temperature adjustment. Since color temperature doesn't give as many adjustment choices, split-toning adjustments would theoretically be better for color temperature slider changes most of the time. But this isn't really true in real life.

Color temperature uses a different method than split-toning and one that works better with big changes. Look at the picture below, which comes straight from the camera:

I don't like how cool (blue) this picture is, so I need to move the colors toward orange to make it better. I can do one of these two things. To begin, I could use the split-toning adjustment to turn both the dark and highlight hues orange. I can also change the temperature of the color in the "Basic" tab. The color temperature adjustment is better in this case. Look at the pictures below. The "Before" picture was fixed with split-toning, while the "After" picture was fixed with color temperature.

These two choices are both better than the first one. But I like the one that was changed with color temperature better. Pay close attention to the highlights near the bottom left of the picture. This area still has good contrast and detail after the color temperature adjustment. The split-toned version, on the other hand, looks faded and flat. You might like the worn look, which is fine, but I like the version with more contrast better. At the very least, they are very different from each other, and those differences won't always help split-toning.

To put it simply, split-toning makes the picture less detailed in its highlights and shadows as you make the changes more extreme. That's normal; split-toning is meant to give your photos personality, not (usually) fix the white balance. Still, it can do two things for some shots. You can change the "white balance" with the split-toning tool if you want a styled shot, but I don't think it's a good idea if you want the most realistic picture.

Lightroom Detail Panel – Sharpening

There is a very powerful editing tool in Lightroom. It is in the Develop module, in the "Detail" panel. It works a lot like Photoshop's "Unsharp Mask" tool, but it's better because you can improve your pictures in more ways. Before I found Lightroom, I had to sharpen every picture in Photoshop, which was painful, took a long time, and was damaging (you can't undo changes you make to an image in Photoshop). Lightroom doesn't change pictures like Photoshop does; changes are saved in either a separate file or the image headers, based on the type of file. If I mess up or want to go back to the original picture, I can use the past panel to reset the image to its original state or undo any changes I've made. Another time-saver, especially when working with thousands of photos, is the ability to define custom settings on pictures while they are being imported.

Sharpening Settings

Giving examples is always a better way to explain something. First, open a sample picture in Lightroom. Then, do the following:

1. To access the Develop module, press the "D" key on your computer or click "Develop" in the upper right panel.
2. To view your photo at 100%, left-click it. Before making any changes to the sharpening, I strongly suggest that you view your photos at full size (100%).
3. Lightroom's right panel should be opened up and scrolled down until you reach "Detail."

This is what the detail panel will look like:

There are four types of sliders on the Sharpening Tool:

1. **Amount** – How much editing you want to do to a picture is called "amount." Zero means that the picture is not sharpened at all. You will see more clarity as the number goes up. The noise will also get worse if you sharpen too much. Most of the time, I leave the number at 50 for my images, but based on the image and noise level, I can sometimes raise or lower it.

2. **Radius** – In terms of radius, this is the size of the cutting area around the edges. If you leave the number at 1.0, Lightroom will sharpen the edges by more than 1 pixel. If you set the radius to 3.0, the sharpening will be spread

out over three pixels around the edge, making the lines wider and more "shadowy." It's best to keep the radius number below 1.5, which is what I do most of the time.

3. **Detail** – The "detail" tool, as its name suggests, lets you change how much the edges of the picture are sharpened. A low value, like 0, only makes big edges sharper. A high value, like 100, makes all edges sharper, no matter how small they are. If you leave the detail setting at "0" on a picture of a bird, for example, only the edges of the thick feathers will get sharper. On the other hand, if you use a number above 50, even the smaller feathers will stand out and get sharper. When I move the detail scale, I try to keep it below 50. This is because higher numbers tend to make a lot more noise.

4. **Masking** – Masking is the most useful and flexible feature. It works like Photoshop's mask tool to hide areas that don't need to be improved. The "Amount" and "Detail" settings will add extra noise around your objects. This tool will get rid of it. It's not very useful for pictures with too many lines and too many details, but it's great for pictures where the subject is separate from the background. It works best when the background is soft and not very clear. Take a look at these samples.

By using all of these settings together, you can improve your pictures without much work and cut your work time by a huge amount. Here is a real picture that we can use to learn how to improve it in Lightroom.

The Option/Alt Key

This had to have its own heading so you wouldn't miss it. If you're using a Mac, press the Option key. If you're using a PC, press the Alt key. Seeing how sharpening changes your pictures is one of the hardest parts of the process. Sure, watching the picture at 100% helps, but Lightroom users often get lost when they play around with tools like radius, detail, and masking since small changes might not be noticeable when looking at the picture. That's when the Alt/Option key comes in handy. On your keyboard, press the Option or Alt key. Then, use the mouse to move the bar from left to right to choose from the four settings. This is what you'll see:

And this is what the picture looks like when I move the "Radius" scale and press the Alt key. This makes it very clear to me how the radius will change my picture. You can see that the radius around the edges is too thick at the highest setting of "3.0," which makes the picture look strange and casts dark shadows around the subject. If we hold down the Control or Alt key and move the Amount and Detail scales, we can also see the effects on a gray background. This gives us a good idea of how the setting will change the picture.

Using the Option or Alt key changes how the "Masking" tool works in a small way. As I already said, the masking tool is used to keep the smooth parts of the image the same while sharpening only the edges. By changing the slider from 0 to the right, we can change where the lines begin. When the value is "0," no masking is applied to the picture, so the whole thing is sharpened. The sky is a smooth background, so sharpening will add noise to it, even if there wasn't much noise there to begin with. As you move the scale, the following things take place:

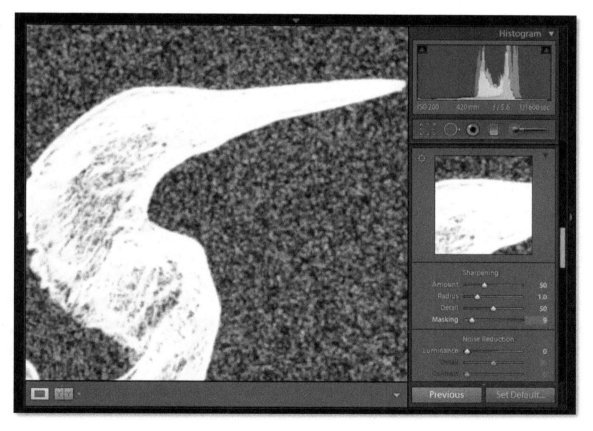

You can see that there is a lot of grain in both the bird and the background. In other words, sharpening is done to all of those places. Take a look at this picture:

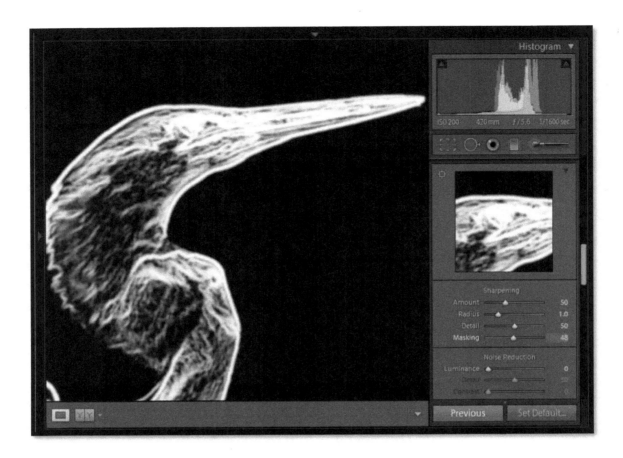

The dust or grain in the sky went away as I moved to the right, leaving only the bird in the picture. Basically, this tells Lightroom to only sharpen the bird and leave the rest of the picture alone. This is a great way to improve only certain parts of a picture without changing the whole thing.

Sharpening Example

To show this, let's look at a real case. Get the full-size version of the picture below on your computer, then bring it into Lightroom:

1. To get to the Develop module in Lightroom, press the "D" button. Open the right toolbar and scroll down until you see "**Detail**". This will take you to the Develop module.

2. Press and hold the Option or Alt key and slide the Amount bar to about 75. Look at how the background gets a little less clear when the number goes above 50. If you move it all the way to 100, you'll hear a lot of noise in the background. When you're done, press and hold the Option or Alt key and go back to 75.

3. As you hold down the Option or Alt key, move the Radius scale from 1.0 to 3.0. Take note of how thick the edges get around the bird. Let go of the Alt or Option key and look at how bad the lines look in color. To return the Radius to 1.0, move the scale or type "1" on the right side.

4. Press and hold the Alt or Option key and move the bar to 75. Take note of the background sounds and edges that are brighter.

5. The last step is to hold down the Option or Alt key and move the Masking tool from 0 to 50. Keep in mind that you can only see the bird and the tree; the background should be black.

6. If you look at the end result and press the "" key a few times, you can see how the picture looked before and after you sharpened it. If you press the "Y" button, you can see the "Before" and "After" pictures in two different windows. You can also turn Sharpening on or off with the switch on the "Detail" panel.

See what's different between these "before" and "after" pictures:

What about Output Sharpening?

A lot of Lightroom users don't understand what the Output Sharpening tool in the Export window does. Should it be used after a picture has already been sharpened? I suggest that you turn off Output Sharpening during the export process if you want to keep the image's original size. If you are adjusting the picture to fit on the web, I suggest keeping it checked and applying the Screen/Standard amount of sharpening.

Images lose some of their sharpness when they are shrunk in Lightroom, but it doesn't hurt to make them a little sharper. But when you use Output Sharpening, it doesn't use the same settings you used in the Develop Module. Instead, it just makes the whole picture a little sharper.

Lightroom Detail Panel: Noise Reduction

Photos can get two different kinds of noise.

Luminance noise changes the color of a pixel but not its brightness. In the dark, you can see more of what it looks like, which are black and white dots.

The picture below (zoomed in to 1:1) has brightness noise. I took away some of the darkness to make it more visible.

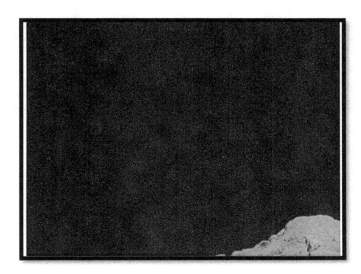

The manual Noise Reduction sliders in Lightroom Classic make it hard to get rid of luminance noise. I'll show you some examples of how much better the new Denoise tool is below.

What is color noise?

Color noise changes the pixels' color but not their brightness. It mostly looks like bright dots in the dark.

The picture I showed you above was taken with color noise reduction turned off. The color noise can now be seen too.

Zoom and noise reduction

When you view your picture at a 1:1 zoom, you can really see how the noise reduction sliders work in Lightroom Classic.

You can do that in two ways.

The first is in the Detail panel. At the top, there is a preview square with a 1:1 zoom. To show or hide the preview square, click the triangle on the right. To see a different part of the picture, click and drag on the square.

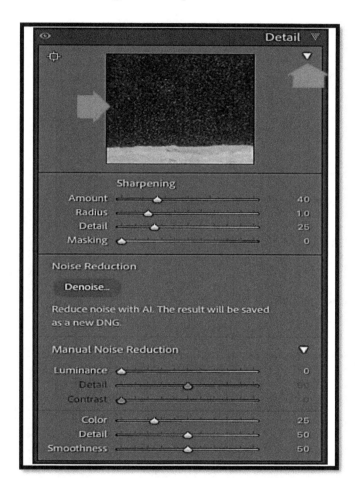

Lightroom Classic shows an exclamation mark at the top of the Detail panel if the preview box is hidden and you aren't looking at the picture at 100%. To set Zoom to 1:1, click the button.

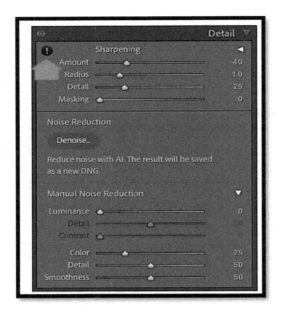

Denoise or Manual Noise Reduction?

Before the Denoise tool was added, Lightroom Classic already had a number of sliders you could use to make your shots less noisy. These have been moved by Adobe to the bottom of the Detail panel, next to Manual Noise Reduction.

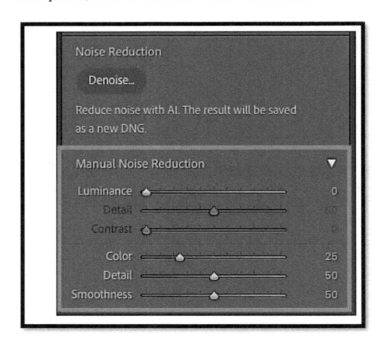

Now you have to decide whether to use the new Denoise tool or the Manual Noise Reduction sliders.

Here are some good things about using the buttons by hand:

- They can open any kind of file, even JPEG and TIFF ones. It can only work with Raw files.

- Quicker than you think. How long the Denoise tool takes to work depends on how old and powerful your computer is. It could be thirty seconds, ten minutes, or even longer.

The biggest problem with Manual Noise Reduction is that it makes the picture less detailed when Luminance Noise Reduction is used. You can't get rid of brightness noise without making the shot less sharp. That's why Luminance Noise Reduction is set to 0 by default. That's also why AI-based tools like Denoise work so well: they don't have this problem.

So, this is why using Denoise is a good idea:

- Noise is a much better tool for getting rid of noise, including brightness noise, without losing any detail.

The disadvantages of using Denoise are:

- The procedure takes longer (30 seconds to 10 minutes or more for each picture, based on your computer's specs). Because of this, it can't be used to process more than a few pictures at once.

- It makes a new DNG file that is up to four times bigger than the original Raw file, so you need more room to store it.

- Denoise can only be used on photos that are in the Raw or DNG format. Even though Adobe hopes to add support for JPEG and TIFF files, it's not yet available during this writing.

With all of its flaws, I love the Denoise tool. The reason for this is shown below. At a show, I took this picture with ISO 12,800.

You can see the difference between the original picture (on the left) and the new one (on the right) that was made with Denoise and the Manual Noise Reduction settings. You can see the whole screen because I only showed you a small part of it. The end product is great.

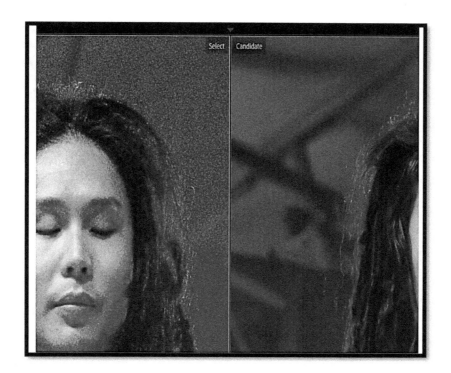

So, because of the time it takes to process, I think you should choose each shot individually whether to use Denoise or Manual Noise Reduction. If you want to get the most out of shots that were taken at high ISOs and have noise that you can see, use Denoise. As you can see, the wait was worth it. In some pictures, you should use the buttons by hand instead.

How to use Manual Noise Reduction in Lightroom Classic

Here are the steps you need to follow to use the hand sliders. We'll look at lowering brightness and color noise in Lightroom Classic one at a time since they each have their own sliders.

Luminance Noise Reduction Sliders

It is important to know that Luminance Noise Reduction will remove details from the shot before you touch the Luminance tool.

There's a good chance you've seen that JPEGs from cell phones taken in low light look a bit blurred. That's how brightness noise reduction works.

In order to avoid this, the brightness noise reduction setting is set to zero by default. It's best to leave it there most of the time.

But if you do use it, slowly raise the amount. Instead of 30 or 60, begin by setting the scale to 5 or 10.

Luminance noise reduction can take away some detail. You can get it back by moving the Detail tool. Slide the Contrast bar to add back any contrast that was lost.

The images below show a sample window part of a photo that has brightness noise at 1:1 zoom. The settings for Luminance 0 and Luminance 20 are very different in how soft they are.

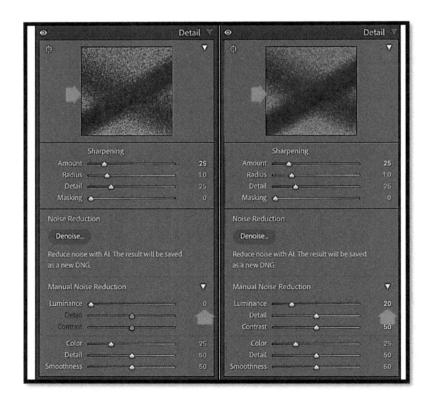

Color noise reduction sliders

The Color slider cuts down on color noise. It does the same thing by slightly blurring the picture.

For the Color slider, the usual setting is 25. This setting might have color noise. If it does, move the bar to the right until it goes away.

The detail that was lost during the process is brought back by the Detail scale. The setting that comes with it is 50.

The Smoothness tool reduces noise created by the Color and Detail sliders. The influence is so subtle that one must go a considerable distance to see a difference. The setting is 50 just how it was previously.

Here's one more illustration. When color noise reduction is adjusted between 0 and 100, the same picture is shown.

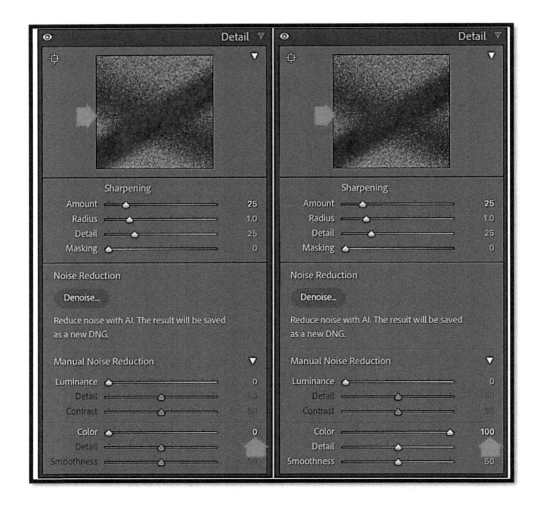

When it comes to color noise reduction, you want to find the sweet spot where the bar is as far to the left as it can go and still completely remove all color noise.

Using the Histogram for Adjustments

A histogram is a graph that displays the exposure level of your image. You can see how bright or dark each tone is. The "hills and mountains" display the midtones, highlights, and shadows. Additionally, Lightroom's histogram displays the percentage of each primary color (or colors) in a tone. Another thing that the histogram displays is clipping. This occurs at the extremes of the shadow and/or highlight spectrums, when information or detail is lost.

The Lightroom Classic Location

Lightroom Classic's Library and Develop modules both have this capability. It is located in the Library Module at the top of the right panel, above Quick Develop. Press the arrow button located in the center of the right side of the program screen if you are unable to view this panel immediately.

The Develop module's graph remains in the same location, but it is now visible above the Basic tab. If the hidden panel on the right is not visible, tap the arrow symbol again.

How To Read the Histogram In Lightroom

The histogram is not as difficult to understand as it may seem at first. Your White people are on the right, and your Black people are on the left. Compared to the highlights, the whites are paler.

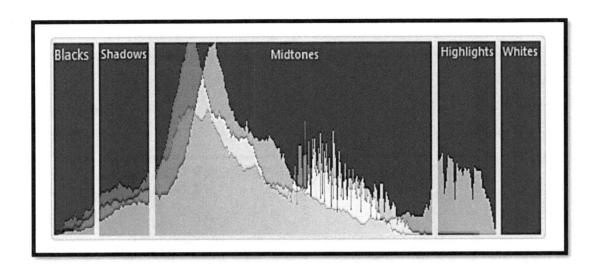

The number of shadows, highlights, and mid-tones in a picture is shown by the "mountains'" peaks and slopes.

The picture is too dark if there are a lot of high points on the left side of the screen. There are not many mid-tones or highlights in your picture. Here is an example of a picture that is too dark and causes the histogram to be skewed to the left:

A picture that is too bright, on the other hand, would have a histogram that is off to the right. So, this means that the picture has a lot of bright tones.

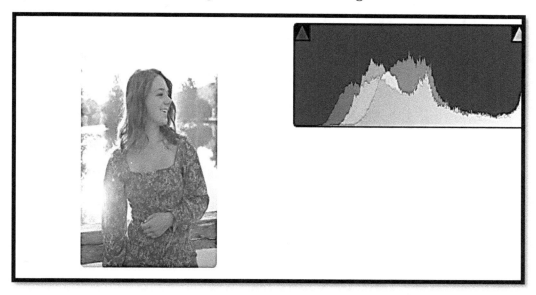

If a picture doesn't have enough contrast, the histogram won't have any peaks and valleys in the blacks or highlights (on the far left and right sides of the screen). The mid-tones will have the high points.

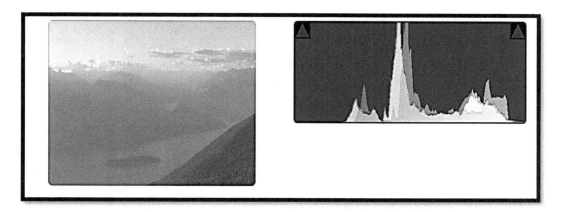

A picture with good or even exposure will have a group of mountains that go across the whole histogram, mostly in the middle.

The Histogram And Color

It is also evident that the histograms have colorful "mountains." The primary hues shown are blue, green, and red. Where they combine, magenta, cyan, and yellow may be found. In the dark, everything comes together. This indicates the percentage of that hue or colors in that tone. One illustration would be the abundance of blues in this image's Highlights section.

The Histogram And Clipping

Additionally, the graph displays a tone issue known as "Clipping." Clipping occurs when detail or information vanishes at the extremes of the highlight and/or shadow ranges. If your shadows are clipped, it signifies that you are losing information in the darkest area of your image. In the same manner, if any hues are missing from your photo, it's overexposed.

An arrow symbol on either side of the screen indicates when your highlights or shadows are clipped. The line on the left becomes gray when your shadows or highlights are removed, and the same thing happens on the right when they are removed.

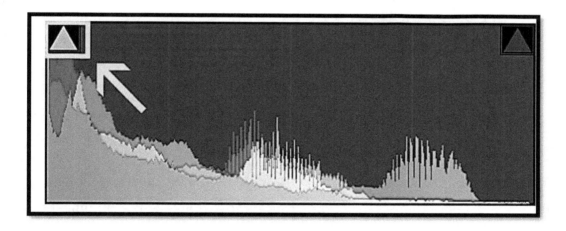

Editing Your Photos Using The Histogram In Lightroom
Step 1: Observe The Histogram to See Where the Tonal Issues Are

Open the histogram for the image you have. You may make your picture's tones seem better by using the histogram. The histogram also helps with editing by keeping you from making too many adjustments that lead to blown highlights or gloomy shadows.

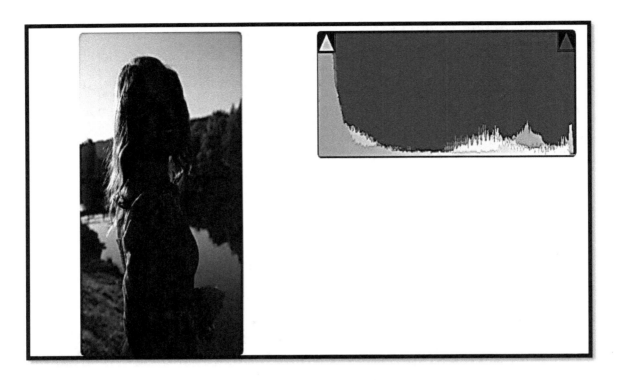

It looks like this picture is very dark because there are too many blacks and shadows. The marked dark line on the left side shows where the clipping is.

Step 2: Locate The Basics Tab and Adjust The Exposure Slider

To lighten the image, I'll choose the Basics tab and drag the Exposure tool to the right. I adjust the tool until there is no longer any darkness along the left clipping line.

However, when I adjusted the exposure slider to the right, more highlights and whites emerged. Consequently, my whites and highlights deteriorated even if my shadows were corrected since the histogram's right-hand arrow now displays cutting.

Step 3: Make Individual Adjustments Based On The Histogram Information

To fix this, I lowered the Whites and Highlights settings until the lines stopped showing clipping.

Following this action, my histogram indicated that both of the arrows were a light gray hue, indicating that my image was now properly exposed and that there was no longer any cutting.

When To Not Follow The Histogram In Photo Editing

Still, you don't have to follow the chart. For that reason, it should be seen as more of a guide, advice, or reference. Following the histogram exactly won't always help you, like when you're editing in a Light and Airy style, making changes to outdoor sunset photos, or editing photos taken at night.

For instance, the way I would edit this picture doesn't match up with what the histogram tells me.

This is what my edit would look like on a histogram, showing that I didn't fix the shadow clipping. But I left it that way because I thought the shadows made the picture look better.

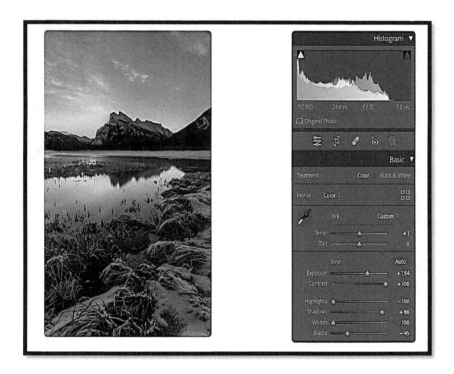

When editing, it's not just about what a computer graph says; it's also about what you think looks good. Use your best judgment.

Using The Histogram Clipping Warnings In Lightroom To Improve Your Exposure

The location of the clipping may be seen directly in the image by using the Lightroom histogram. The image brightens to indicate the precise location where the highlights are removed as you move your mouse over the cutting arrow on the right. Highlights are cut in red, while shades are clipped in blue.

The cutting highlights (or shadows) will stay visible even after you move the mouse. All you have to do is click on the arrow.

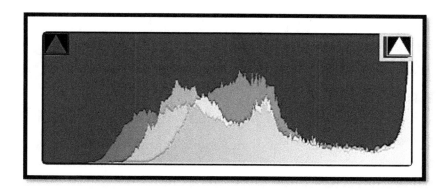

The bright red or blue will either disappear (because you've resolved the clipping issue) or intensify as you make adjustments to your image (because you're causing clipping to occur). You may gauge the progress of your change with the aid of these editing notifications.

In addition, clipping warnings come in rather handy for those who want to print the image they are editing. Clipped highlights and shadows will not print effectively due to the lack of detail.

CHAPTER TEN

LOCAL ADJUSTMENTS AND MASKING

The Lightroom Brush Tool

The Lightroom Brush tool, which is also called the Adjustment Brush tool, lets you "paint" on your picture like a real pen. Moreover, changes are made where the Brush touches.

It means that the Brush tool is made for precise edits. It is used to make changes to specific areas of the frame rather than to the full picture. You can use Lightroom's sliders to change the whole picture, which is also known as a "global edit."

Keep in mind that you can edit a picture in a variety of ways using the Brush tool. With a brush, you can:

- Make changes to the brightness
- Make the white balance different
- Change the amount of contrast
- Change the blur, sharpness, and roughness
- Change the noise and sharpness
- Change the color
- And more!

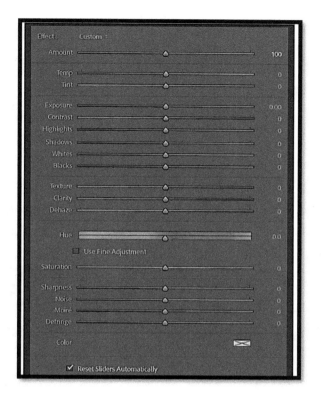

With the Brush tool, you can choose which Lightroom adjustments to make, but not all of them. For example, you can't add color grading to certain parts of a picture with the Brush tool, and you also can't make specific color calibration changes.

When is the Brush tool useful?

While editing some parts of a picture with the Brush tool, it leaves other parts alone. This can help you if you want to:

- Make background objects less bright or dark
- Lighten or fill up your major subject
- Dodge and burn to make things look more three-dimensional
- Sharpen only certain parts of the picture
- Soften only certain parts of the picture
- Darken parts of the sky

It's amazing how well this 3D-printed 35mm camera turned out.

The Brush tool can be used for almost anything, and you can often get great results just by trying different things. One use for the Brush would be to warm up only the sky. You could also use the Brush to change the color of a flower or make the eyes stand out in a picture.

How to use the Brush tool in Lightroom: step by step

It's pretty easy to use the Brush tool. To begin, open a picture in the Lightroom Develop module and then select Mask:

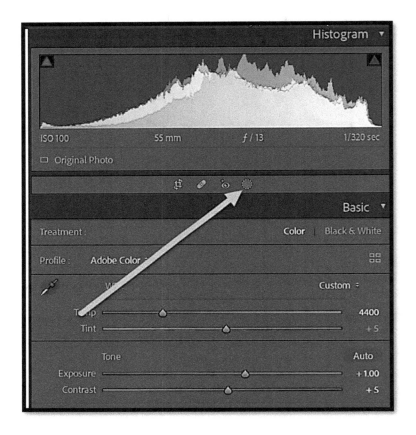

There are many choices in the dropdown menu, such as Linear Gradient and Radial Gradient. However, you should choose Brush:

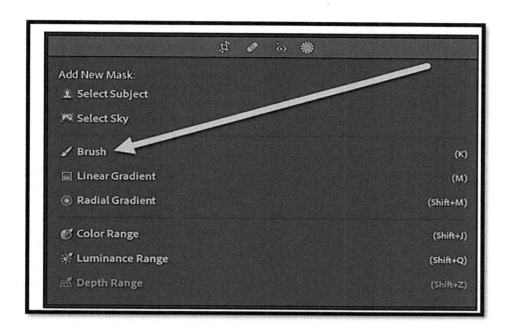

You'll see the Lightroom Brush panel pop up, and your mouse will change into two circles with a "+" inside each one:

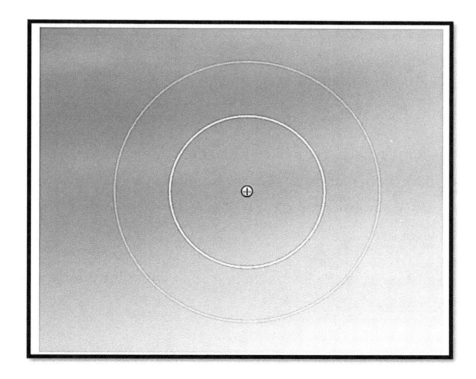

You can change the Brush's Size, Feather, Flow, and Density at the top of the Brush panel. The Size slider changes how big or small the Brush is, and the Feather slider changes how soft or hard the edges of the Brush are. The Flow slider sets how much of the editing effect is added to each stroke, and the Density slider lowers the editing effect as a whole.

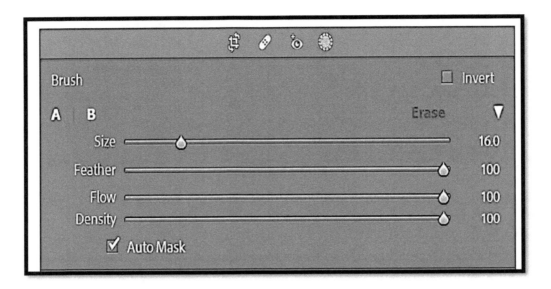

(Set the Feather to 100 and the Flow below 50 for very light changes. Keep the Feather low and the Flow high for heavy effects.)

You can edit with the tools that are below the Brush properties. Even though these sliders work like normal Lightroom sliders, they will only show up where you paint with your Brush. Feel free to change the buttons however you want. Then paint over the parts you want to change.

If you make a mistake, click the "**Erase**" button or press the "**Alt" or "Opt"** key and go over the places you messed up.

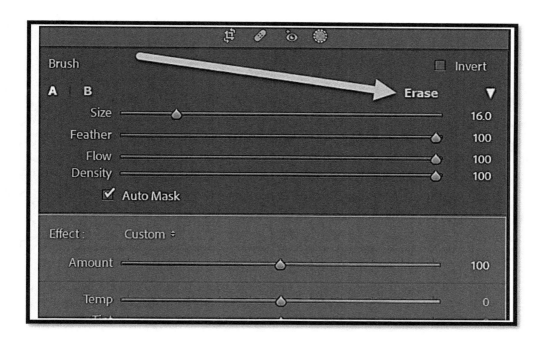

When you are done using a Brush, click the "**Done**" button at the bottom of the screen. You can then edit your picture as usual. You can choose Masking again and then click on your Brush edit in the Masking panel if you later decide you want to change your brushwork. You'll be taken to your Brush panel, where you can make any necessary adjustments to the sliders or paint on the picture. All of your previous changes will still be there.

You can also make more Brushes; just click the plus sign in the Masking panel, choose Brush, and then proceed as described above!

5 tips for Outstanding Brush tool results

Let's look at some tips and tricks to improve your changes now that you know how to use Brushes:

1.   **Use the A/B option to alternate between different Brush versions**

Every time you choose a new Brush or Brush Mask, you can make two different forms of that Brush: an A version and a B version.

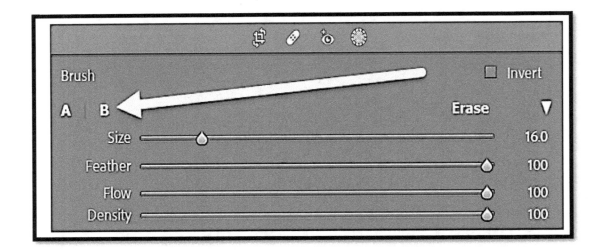

These versions of the Brush don't change the editing tools; instead, they let you make two separate Brushes with two separate sets of features.

From what I've seen, this A/B Brush option is incredibly helpful. I simply build an A Brush and a B Brush and switch between them as I work because I frequently need more than one Brush to make the necessary changes.

As a pro tip, press the slash key (/) to switch between the two forms of Brush.

To edit the little features in my picture, for example, I might make one small Brush with sharp edges. I might also make one big Brush with soft edges to work on bigger things.

I changed the background in this next picture with a big Brush and the flower leaves with a small Brush:

2. **Create custom Brush presets**

   When you use brush presets, you can save changing effects to use later. You can speed up your work with them if you keep making the same Brush changes.

   These are the basic Brush presets that come with Lightroom. To get to them, click the Effect flyout menu. There is a preset to smooth skin, a preset to whiten teeth, and a preset to make eyes look better.

   But if you want to make your own presets, which I really think you should do! – just make a Brush and move the sliders around. Choose **Save Current Settings as New Preset** from the Effect flyout menu.

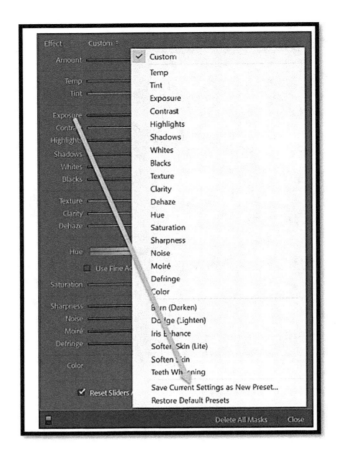

You can choose to give your setting a name. All you have to do is click "**Create**."

For instance, I frequently like to brush in some sharpness while lowering the noise, so I made a custom setting that raised the Sharpness slider and lowered the Noise slider. There are also custom presets for teeth whitening and smoothing the skin that are not in Lightroom's settings. This way, I can switch to the Brushes whenever I need to, without having to set up the sliders all over again.

3. **Use a Brush to add color to your photos**

    Enjoy this cool trick if you want to make your photos look better by editing them in creative ways.

    Make a Brush and then pick a color:

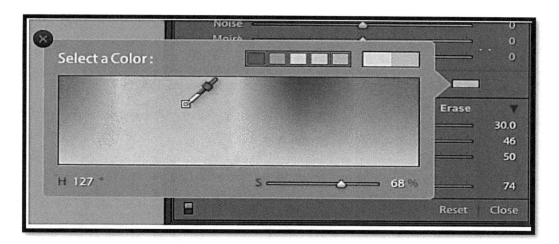

And use the paintbrush to paint right on your picture!

If you want a lifelike effect, I suggest that you keep the color intensity low. To do this, choose a color menu area near the bottom. Trying out different colors is a good idea, so pick out a few colors with different amounts of intensity and see what you think!

I used this method to give the baby's face a small splash of color:

You can use it on a much bigger scale, too, like to change the color of flower leaves or make the eyes of a picture subject look very different.

4. **Use Auto Mask to restrict the Brush to specific areas**

    The fact that the Adjustment Brush tool only comes in one shape—a circle—is one of the most annoying aspects of it.

    When you're changing pictures that have sharp edges and lines, this can be a little tricky. How do you make sure that your Brush changes only affect a certain area?

    There it is: the Auto Mask tool! If you check the "**Auto Mask**" box, Lightroom will try to find the edges and keep the Brush strokes from going off the sides. You can use it a lot to edit pictures, wildlife, birds, and other photos.

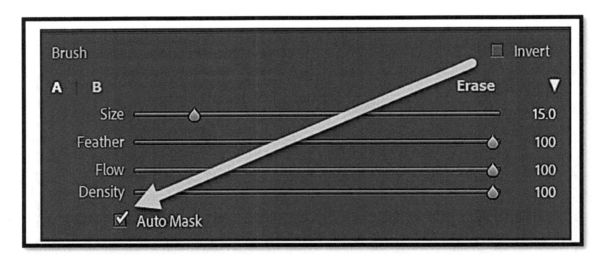

I used Auto Mask on this next picture to keep my Brush changes inside the flower petals:

Take a look at the red layer, which is my brush strokes:

Adjustment Brush

In the Develop module, the Adjustment Brush button is on the far right, below the Histogram, and above the Basic panel. To use it, press the "K" key or click on the button. This will show you the effects that you can choose from.

Take your brush, which is represented by a circle with a plus sign in the middle, and drag it over the parts of your picture that you want to edit after you've chosen your adjustment settings. In the bottom right area of the sample window, click "Done" when you're done.

Seeing Where You've Brushed: Make sure the Lightroom adjustment brush you want to examine is chosen (its pin has a black center) and click the "Show Selected Adjustment Mask Overlay" box next to your picture to see where you've brushed your modifications. All of the picture regions that have been altered with that specific adjustment brush will be highlighted in red as a result.

Changing Brush Size: You can change the brush size in a few different ways:
- Move the tool next to the brush settings.
- Move your mouse's wheel left or right.
- Press the brace keys on the left and right ([]).

Using a New Brush: You will have to "pick up" a new brush every time you want to use a different brush (a different adjustment). Pick **"New"** at the top of the Adjustment Brush panel to do that. You'll see that all of the sliders are still where they were in the last brush. To clear all the scales, double-click **"Effect,"** or use the drop-down menu to choose a new brush setting.

How to Erase: There's a simple workaround if you accidentally brush over an area where you don't want your modification to be. Your brush now has a minus sign on it if you click delete or Option (Mac) or Alt (PC). It will eliminate everything you brush it over. If you want to permanently remove a brush that you have applied to your image, make sure it is highlighted (has a black center pin), then choose **Delete**.

Brush with Color: If you want to bring out a certain color in a picture, you can pick a color from the list at the bottom of the brush panel and use it in your adjustment brush. Adding extra color in this way is a great way to make eyes, scenery, or even certain colors in a picture look better.

Adjustment Brush Presets

Adjustment Brush presets are pre-saved brush settings that enable quick and simple picture adjustment. These Adjustment Brush Presets are accessible via the drop-down button in the Adjustment Panel.

The Graduated Filters

This filter can be used to bring out features in the center, even out the background, recover highlights and shadows in landscapes, and a lot more.

Finding the Graduated Filter

Open up Lightroom Classic and go to the Develop module. On the right side, just below the Histogram, you should see a row of icons. The Graduated Filter is the fourth one from the left. To get to it, press the **M key** on your computer. The buttons will show up after you click in, just like they do in the Basic editing panel.

Using the Graduated Filter

To move the filter in the middle of the picture, you can drag it from either side. That is, from the side, the top, or the bottom. To use the Mask function, press the O key on your computer. This lets you see where the graduated filter gets thinner. If you hold down Shift and press O, you can even change the mask's color.

If you tap **NEW**, you can add more Graduated Filters to your picture. Each new filter adds a pin. Make sure Show Edit Pins is set to Always in the bottom left corner of the picture panel before you click on each pin to edit it.

Editing your filters

You can choose from the different sliders to edit your choices once you have your filter set. This includes things like Highlights, Shadows, Exposure, Contrast, and more that you can use to give your picture more depth and dimension or get back lost highlights and shadows.

Even **Temp, Tint, Hue, and Saturation** can be changed. You can move a slider left and right to change the amount, or you can type in the numbers on the right to change it online. All the sliders are reset to 0 when you double-click Effect. You can also double-click the button to restart just that one.

Using the brush

The brush tool, not the Adjustment Brush tool, is another thing that makes it stand out. It shows up right below the brush icon and is called "**Brush**." This lets you brush different parts of the mask in or out. To choose where you want the mask to show up, press the **Alt key (or Option key** on a Mac) to switch between brush and eraser mode.

Finishing off

In Graduated Filters, once you have the picture you want, just click "**Done**" in the bottom right corner of the picture panel to go back to the main editing panels. By selecting the Edit option in Lightroom's Graduated Filter section, you can go back and edit your photos again.

Radial Filters

One of the easiest ways to add effects to only a part of a picture is to use the radial filter in Lightroom. We'll show you how to use it.

The radial filter in Lightroom makes a small adjustment to a circle in the picture. The different settings and sliders in Lightroom determine whether the edit fits in or makes the image look very different.

Some changes can be made to the tool so that it can do more than just edit things inside or outside of a circle.

The Lightroom radial filter simply adds an effect to a circle in the picture. It's been trimmed so that the rest of the picture stays the same.

The different Lightroom options change what's outside of the original circle when the radial filter is set to its usual settings. You can also use the reverse radial filter Lightroom tool to apply the effect only to that circle.

With the brush and range mask and other tools, the tool can do more than just make a circle or square.

You can use the radial filter to make a lot of different effects. Lightroom has tools that can be used to add or remove vignettes. A more customized background can be added to a picture using the radial filter tool.

You can also use the tool to draw more attention to a part of the picture by making that part sharper or more colorful.

The options are pretty much endless. These can be used to make a spotlight effect, brighten the subject but not the background, "turn on" lights that aren't on in the picture, and a lot more.

The radial filter is the best tool to use if you only want to apply the effect to a circle or oval part of the picture (or to nothing at all).

You should know how the Lightroom radial filter works before you use it. First, the controls for effects only work on the area outside the circle.

That doesn't make sense to many people. With a simple tick, you can flip the filter so that it only affects the circle in the picture.

Second, the radial filter has a lot of the same sliders that you'd find when changing a finished picture, but the effects aren't applied to the whole picture. Finally, Lightroom has some tools that let you change exactly where the effect shows up in the picture.

How to Use the Lightroom Radial Filter Tool

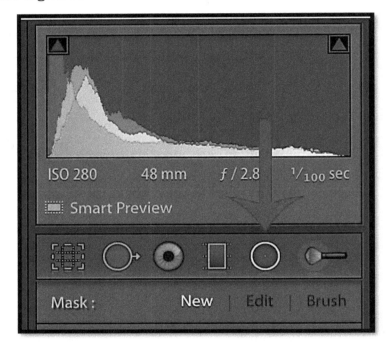

1. **Start by adding the Radial Filter**

   The radial filter tool in Lightroom can be found in the Develop module, in the tool panel right below the histogram.

   As of right now, the fifth tool from the left in Lightroom is the radial filter. It can be found in a simple circle. The healing tool is a circle with an arrow in it. Do not mix up the radial scale with it.

You can also use the computer shortcut to get to the same tool. If you are in the Develop module, press **shift and M**.

When the radial dial is chosen, the cursor changes to a plus sign, which makes a circle around the part of the picture that needs to be changed.

Click in the middle of the area where you want the circle to go. As you hold down the mouse button, move the pointer back to make the circle bigger.

Hold down the shift key while making the circle to get an exactly round one.

2. **Fine-Tune Where the Adjustment Will Be Applied**

It's not set in stone once you let go of the mouse button. Click and hold on the middle dot after making the circle to move the whole thing to a different part of the picture.

To change the size and shape, click on one of the four squares on the circle's edge and drag to change the shape. You can also press the shift key to change the size without changing the shape.

If you hold down the shift key while making the radial filter, a perfect circle will appear. Once the circle is made, pressing the shift key will keep its shape when you change its size, instead of stretching one side.

If you want to see what parts of the picture the tool changes, check the box that says "show selected mask overlay" or press the "O" key to see those parts highlighted in red.

Press shift and O at the same time to change the color of the shortcut. For example, if your picture has a lot of red and the mask is hard to see, you can do this.

When you first click on the circle, the effect will only be on the outside.

That is something you can think about while you edit. You can make the exposure darker if you want to make the picture brighter. You can also flip the mask over if it helps you picture how it changes the inside of the circle.

All you have to do to flip the filter is check the **"invert"** box at the end of the tool.

With feathering, you can change even more about where the effect is applied. The quickness with which the adjustment disappears is controlled by feathering photos, just like with other tools.

There would be no feather to make a clear line between the adjusted and unedited parts. It would look more natural with a big feather.

Use the tool near the end of the radial mask area to change the amount of feathering.

3. **Add in the Effects**

You need to be clever now. With the different sliders, the Lightroom radial filter can be used to make a lot of different effects. You can lighten, darken, add sharpness, change saturation, and more with the settings in the tool area.

From white balance to sharpness, most of Lightroom's sliding tools can be used with the radial filter.

From the drop-down box for effects, you can also choose to use your brush presets. There is a dodge and burn setting in Lightroom that can be used with both brushes and the radial filter.

What you want to change with the tool will determine the precise edits. Slide the exposure bar to the left to add a blur.

You can use more than one scale at a time with this tool. Like, to make a lamp that isn't lit look like it is, you'd use the white balance and exposure tool to give it an orange glow.

Keep in mind that Lightroom is a non-destructive picture editor, so you have nothing to lose by trying out different things. Other than maybe a few minutes of your time. If you double-click on a button, the number will go back to zero.

The size, arrangement, and feathering of the radial filter can also be changed further. Now, to get rid of the whole radial filter, press the delete key while the middle of the filter is chosen.

You can add more than one radial filter too. Not the edit button, but the "new" button at the top of the tool panel.

4. **Optional: Fine-tune with the Range Mask**

The radial filter is best for making effects that are round or oval, but Lightroom has other tools that can be used to make effects that aren't round. With the range mask tool, you can pick a color or brightness to make the effect only show up in that area.

The colors or brightness outside the circle are still subject to Lightroom's adjustment by default. To work inside the circle, use the opposite tool.

The range mask drop-down box is set to off by default. To choose only the colors outside (or inside, if you use reversed), the filter tool chooses colors from it. After that, click on the line tool next to the range mask.

While holding down the shift key, click on as many colors in the picture as you want to include. Only the colors you chose will now be affected by the filter adjustment.

The luminance range mask can also be used. This mask limits the affects based on whether the picture is light or dark. Choose the luminance choice from the range mask drop-down menu. Then, use the range tool to make the range smaller.

Lightroom will leave out the darker parts of the picture if you move the point on the left to the middle. Lightroom will only work on the lighter parts of the picture as you move from left to right.

The smoothness tool lets you change how smoothly the lights and darks fade into each other. Move it to the right for a smoother shift, and to the left for a rougher one.

Just change the dropdown menu back to **"off"** if you change your mind about the range mask effect for some reason.

How to mask in Lightroom Classic (with AI masking)

The ability to hide in Lightroom has been around for a while, but the new AI masking tool has really changed the way photos are edited! Let me show you how to hide in Lightroom Classic so that you can take better portraits.

Masking is a three-step process for editing a portion of an image:

1. **Create** mask – select the part of an image
2. **Refine** the area selection, if necessary
3. **Edit** the selected area

Mask is a word you might not have heard if you have never used Photoshop. If you want to edit only a part of a picture, you can use this feature, which was added in this big update.

Lightroom masking uses AI to make it easy to pick out different parts of a picture to edit. This is because images are made up of many different items and backgrounds.

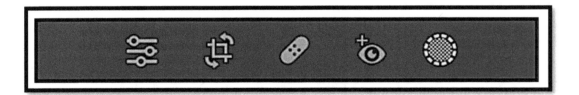

In the Develop Module of Lightroom Classic, the tool strip is shown above. The tools that are being used in a given picture are shown below with marks.

Where's the masking tool in Lightroom?

The histogram is at the top of the Develop Module. Below it is a tool strip, which is a row of buttons that used to be for local adjustment tools. A masking tool button is the last one on the right. Some of the local adjustment tools, like the radial filter, graded filter, and brush tool, have been moved into this tool.

There are three groups of masks under "**Add New Mask**" when you open the masking panel:

- Subject, Sky, Background
- Objects, Brush, Linear Gradient, Radial Gradient, Range
- People

It's not a mistake that you saw that you can choose both the theme and the people. Both kinds of masks are used to hide people in pictures, but they offer different kinds of adjustment options.

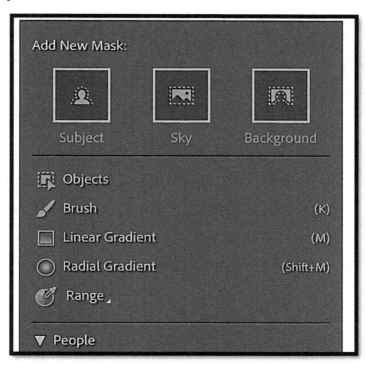

Step 1: Create mask in Lightroom Classic

Make a mask of the place you want to edit first.

- Select the **Develop module**.

- In the toolbar below the histogram, click on the masking button.

- Pick out the mask you want to use.

If you want to go straight to the masking panel in the Develop module, you can press **Shift+W** from anywhere in Lightroom.

The Masks panel will look different if you've already made a mask. To see all the masks, you need to click on **Create New Mask**.

Next, based on what you want to edit, select the appropriate mask type. Lightroom Classic gives us 21 different ways to hide, but not all of them are clear at first glance.

- Click on Range to pick one of the three range masks: light range, color range, or depth range.

- To open the "**Person Mask Options**" panel, click on the triangle next to "**People**." Then choose very specific places, like the whole body, the skin on the face and body, the eyebrows, the sclera, the iris, the pupil, the lips, the teeth, and the hair. I'll say more about this auto-mask feature soon.

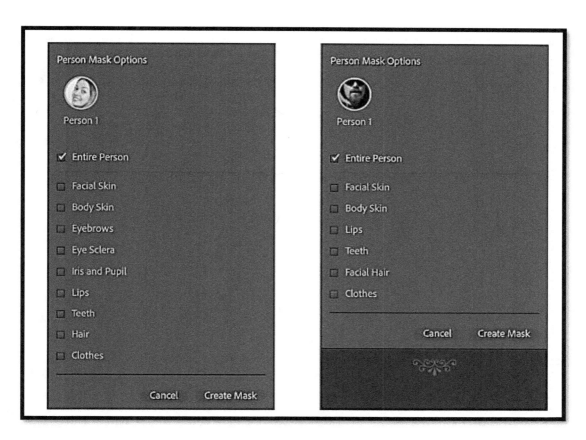

Masking options for Lightroom users. You can see that a feature isn't shown in the list of **Person Mask Options** if it can't be seen in the picture. For example, there is no Facial Hair choice on the right, and there are no Eye options on the left because he is wearing sunglasses.

So, the **21 different masks in Lightroom Classic** are:

1. Select Subject
2. Select Sky
3. Select Background
4. Objects
5. Brush
6. Linear Gradient
7. Radial Gradient

8.   Color Range

9.   Luminance Range

10. Depth Range

11. Entire person

12. Face skin

13. Body skin

14. Eyebrows

15. Eye sclera

16. Iris and pupil

17. Lips

18. Teeth

19. Hair

20. Facial Hair

21. Clothes

In case you didn't believe it, all of these new masking tools in Lightroom are useful, especially for picture photographers! Before we talk about Lightroom masking tools, we'll look at each type of mask.

1.   **Subject mask**

You can use the subject mask to pick more than just people; it can also be used as an auto mask to select things. Now, with just one click, you can correctly choose the subject(s) in your picture.

Under "**Add a new mask**," all you have to do is click "**Subject**."

Lightroom will make a copy of the subject(s) on its own.

2. **Sky mask**

Simply selecting "Sky" under "Add a new mask" will allow you to edit the sky in your shots in a matter of seconds.

Lightroom will make a mask of the sky for you instantly.

3. **Background mask**

For easy background editing in Lightroom, a new masking tool lets you choose the background. Before, choosing the background, we had to first choose the subject and then flip the mask around. It only takes one click now.

Under "Add a new mask," all you have to do is click "Background."

With one click, Lightroom makes a copy of the background, center, and pretty much the whole picture except for the subject.

4. **Objects mask**

Another new auto mask choice is the objects mask, but it's not a one-click fix. Plus there's an extra step, which isn't there when you use Select Subject to select items. In Lightroom Classic, you can use either a brush or click and drag to pick items with the items mask.

To get to the objects panel, click "Objects" next to "Add a new mask." After that:

Choosing an object with a brush, choosing an object with the square click and drag tool, and an object mask, from left to right.

- To pick something, click the brush button and move it over it. You don't have to be very precise when you brush; a rough pass over the item will be enough for the AI to find it and hide it.

OR

- You need to click and drag a square around the thing, even if it has a strange shape. The AI will find the item inside the area and make an object mask.

Brush mask

It used to be called the "local adjustment brush tool" and was in a different spot. It still works, but now it works even better.

To get to the brush tool, click on Brush under "**Add New Mask**." If you're not in the Develop module, you can press K on the keyboard to open the brush tool there.

- Choose the brush size and feather, and make sure the flow is set to 100%.
- Check the Auto Mask box to pick out only the area you need and do not "color over the lines."

Then brush over the area to apply the mask.

To make this easy, press O to bring up the mask layer. In this case, it will be a red overlay.

Color Range mask

Changing the color of a subject's shirt in Lightroom has become a straightforward task, thanks to the color range mask feature. This process involves two simple steps that allow you to precisely select and alter specific colors within your image.

The first step is to create a color range mask. To do this, start by opening the masking panel, where you'll find an option to "Add a new mask." Click on "Range," which will bring up the range mask tool. From the available options, select "Color Range," or you can use the handy keyboard shortcut Shift+J to access it quickly. Once selected, your cursor will change into an eyedropper tool, indicating that you're ready to pick the color you want to target.

With the eyedropper tool, you can click on the area of the image where the color you wish to change is located, in this case, the subject's shirt. The tool will automatically create a mask that isolates this color, making it easy to apply adjustments specifically to this area without affecting the rest of the image.

This method provides a high degree of control, allowing you to make precise color adjustments, whether you're aiming to alter the hue, saturation, or brightness of the selected area. It's an incredibly powerful tool for creative editing, enabling you to change the color of objects within your photos with just a few clicks.

Now you have three ways to use the color range mask, depending on your needs. So, for the next step:

- For a single, solid color, like a blue sky for example, just click on the color to select it
- For a range of colors, click and drag around the area of the color
- To adjust several colors, hold Shift and click up to five different colors to select them

Lightroom will automatically create a color range mask.

Luminance Range mask

Instead of adjusting the brightness of the whole image you can create a luminance mask to adjust specific levels of brightness within the image.

Lightroom chooses an area when you construct a luminance range mask depending on the luminance value (area brightness) you choose. Therefore, you may need to delete some of the masks after using this range mask option.

You also have a couple of options with this type of range mask. So the first step:

- Click "Range" under "Add a new mask" in the masking panel to open up the range mask tool
- Click Luminance Range (or use the keyboard shortcut Shift+Q)
- The cursor becomes an eyedropper tool

Next step, select the area:

- Either click and drag on a small part of the area with the luminance value you want to change
- Or adjust the luminance range slider by dragging the two triangles below the slider to select and increase or decrease the luminance range you want to adjust

As you'll see a little later, Lightroom automatically builds a brightness range mask, which you can then brush out to further adjust the region.

Expert advice: click the "Show Luminance Mask" box under the slider to see the chosen region.

Depth Range mask

With the exception of iPhone photographs, which have depth information enabled, the range mask option will be grayed out when taken with a digital camera.

Even in a busy and challenging image with people wearing helmets, Lightroom could detect and automatically create 4 people masks

People masking in Lightroom

You can access the following nine masks using the People Masking tool. Simply choose "People" to access all of Lightroom's masks for editing a single person, several people, or specific individuals.

In order to produce masks, Lightroom's artificial intelligence can identify several persons in a picture. You may sync the modifications to many photographs at once after using the new auto-mask function to mask and edit each person separately. Photographers of portraits will save a ton of time with this.

Because it's so fast and simple to display processed photographs for selection, I've used it a lot to batch-process images for in-person sales sessions. Once a customer has chosen the photos they like, I then examine them more closely and provide a more thorough edit.

Entire person mask

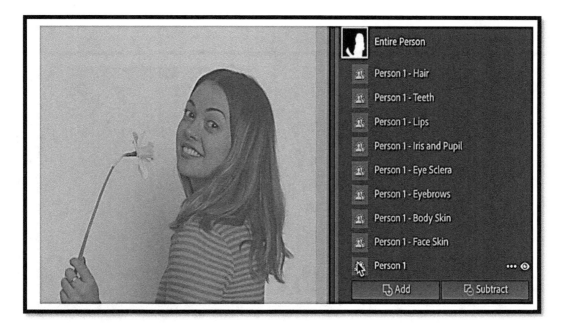

To make adjustments to an entire person, or several people, in an image, open the People masking tool.

- Start by opening the masking panel and selecting "**Add a new mask**." From the options provided, click on "**People**." Lightroom will then analyze the image and identify the individuals within it, presenting their profile pictures for easy selection.

- Next, click on the profile picture of the person or people you want to work with. Lightroom allows you to choose multiple individuals if needed, making it convenient when working with group photos.

- Once you've selected the person or people, the "Person Mask Options" menu will appear. Here, click on "Entire Person" to create a mask that includes the full body of the selected individual(s). This mask will allow you to apply edits to the entire person, giving you the flexibility to enhance or alter specific features, adjust skin tones, or even change the lighting around them.

Face skin mask

To make adjustments to the face skin of the main subject, or several subjects, in an image, open the People masking tool.

- Start by opening the masking panel and selecting "Add a new mask." From the options provided, click on "People."
- Next, click on the profile picture of the person or people you want to work with.
- Once you've selected the person or people, the "Person Mask Options" menu will appear. Here, click on "**Face Skin**".

Body skin mask

- Start by opening the masking panel and selecting "Add a new mask." From the options provided, click on "People."
- Next, click on the profile picture of the person or people you want to work with.

- Once you've selected the person or people, the "Person Mask Options" menu will appear. Here, click on "**Body Skin**".

Eyebrows mask

- Start by opening the masking panel and selecting "Add a new mask." From the options provided, click on "People."
- Next, click on the profile picture of the person or people you want to work with.
- Once you've selected the person or people, the "Person Mask Options" menu will appear. Here, click on "**Eyebrows**".

Eye sclera mask (whites of the eyes)

- Start by opening the masking panel and selecting "Add a new mask." From the options provided, click on "People."
- Next, click on the profile picture of the person or people you want to work with.
- Once you've selected the person or people, the "Person Mask Options" menu will appear. Here, click on "**Eye sclera**".

Pro tip: Lower the saturation to make the whites of the eyes whiter. Avoid brightening them with further exposure since this will give them an artificial, glaringly altered appearance.

Iris and pupil mask

To make adjustments to the iris and pupils of the main subject, or several subjects, in an image, open the People masking tool.

- Start by opening the masking panel and selecting "Add a new mask." From the options provided, click on "People."
- Next, click on the profile picture of the person or people you want to work with.
- Once you've selected the person or people, the "Person Mask Options" menu will appear. Here, click on "**Eye sclera**".

Pro tip: To enhance the iris' detail without overly manipulating the processing, just marginally adjust the shadows and clarity sliders.

Lips mask

To make adjustments to the lips of the main subject, or several subjects, in an image, open the People masking tool.

- Start by opening the masking panel and selecting "Add a new mask." From the options provided, click on "People."
- Next, click on the profile picture of the person or people you want to work with.
- Once you've selected the person or people, the "Person Mask Options" menu will appear. Here, click on "**Lips**".

Teeth mask

To make adjustments to the teeth of the main subject, or several subjects, in an image, open the People masking tool.

- Start by opening the masking panel and selecting "Add a new mask." From the options provided, click on "People."
- Next, click on the profile picture of the person or people you want to work with.
- Once you've selected the person or people, the "Person Mask Options" menu will appear. Here, click on **"Teeth"**.

Lightroom automatically makes a mask of each picked person's teeth so you may whiten each one separately. This will come in handy when batch processing a shot. I'll talk more about it soon.

Pro tip: lower the saturation to whiten teeth. Avoid brightening teeth with more exposure, etc., since this will make your teeth seem unnatural.

Hair mask

To make adjustments to the hair of the main subject, or several subjects, in an image, open the People masking tool.

- Start by opening the masking panel and selecting "Add a new mask." From the options provided, click on "People."
- Next, click on the profile picture of the person or people you want to work with.
- Once you've selected the person or people, the "Person Mask Options" menu will appear. Here, click on **"Hair"**.

Pro tip: To accentuate the texture of hair, particularly black hair, increase the amount of shadow. Additionally, avoid sharpening your hair too much since this might make it seem unhealthy and dry.

A few months after the first Lightroom masking update, the next two persons masks were introduced, along with some further masking capabilities I've previously covered.

Facial hair mask

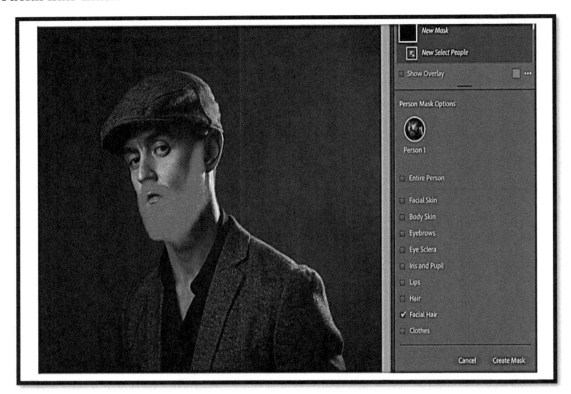

- Start by opening the masking panel and selecting "Add a new mask." From the options provided, click on "People."

- Next, click on the profile picture of the person or people you want to work with.

- Once you've selected the person or people, the "Person Mask Options" menu will appear. Here, click on "**Facial Hair**".

Clothes mask

To make adjustments to the clothes of the main subject, or several subjects, in an image, open the People masking tool.

- Start by opening the masking panel and selecting "Add a new mask." From the options provided, click on "People."

- Next, click on the profile picture of the person or people you want to work with.

- Once you've selected the person or people, the "Person Mask Options" menu will appear. Here, click on "**Clothes**".

Lightroom automatically creates masks of the clothes of each person selected, which makes changing the color of clothes so much easier!

CHAPTER ELEVEN

WORKING WITH PRESETS AND PROFILES

What Is A Lightroom Preset?

A Lightroom Preset is an XMP file with picture information that allows you to click once to instantly change a photo's exposure, contrast, color, and sharpness. Because presets include prepared modifications into the file, they assist accomplish certain editing styles, which may expedite the editing process.

Lightroom presets are files containing specific adjustments that make your photo appear a certain way. When applied to your photo, they instantly adjust the settings according to the preset and give your photo a specific appearance. You can make your own presets, download ones others have made, or use the ones that come with Lightroom. Presets exist in the form of XMP files, which is the standard file type for presets across all Adobe software.

Maybe the simplest way to conceptualize presets is as filters. When you want to alter your shot to fit a certain tone or style, they come in handy. For example, you may experiment with various black-and-white exposures or apply a vintage effect to your image. Presets for certain genres of photography, including landscape or portraiture, are also available. With presets, batch editing is significantly faster and simpler since you can edit numerous photographs at once in a few easy steps.

What Is A Lightroom Profile?

A Lightroom Profile functions similarly to a LUT (3D Look Up Table), which is a tool used to make precise adjustments to various elements of an image, including the RGB curves, Color Grading, Contrast, and other enhancements. While profiles may seem similar to presets in that they can apply a set of changes to your photo, they differ in a significant way: profiles do not move the adjustment sliders within Lightroom.

Instead, they are applied directly to the image data, influencing how the photo looks without visibly altering the settings you see in the editing panel.

Interestingly, your camera itself has a built-in profile. This built-in profile is essentially how your camera interprets and displays the image data on its screen. Each camera model has a slightly different way of processing this data, leading to subtle differences in how images appear. You might not notice these differences unless you compared the outputs side by side, as the variations are often quite minor.

Your camera's profile is a reflection of how it chooses to interpret the data captured in an image, determining the final look of the photo as displayed on your camera's screen. While you can change your default profile in Adobe software, doing so would affect every image you import into Lightroom, which might not be ideal. Instead, many photographers prefer experimenting with different profiles within Lightroom. These profiles can be selected from the options available in the software, downloaded from other creators, or even custom-made, giving you creative control over the final appearance of your photos.

To grasp how a Lightroom profile works, it's helpful to understand LUTs a bit more. A 3D Look Up Table, or LUT, is essentially a complex set of instructions that dictates how the colors and tones in an image should be adjusted. These adjustments include things like color balance and RGB curve modifications that go beyond what you can achieve with Lightroom's regular tools. In other words, LUTs and profiles enable you to apply sophisticated color grading and tonal adjustments that would otherwise be out of reach with Lightroom's standard editing capabilities.

This makes profiles an incredibly powerful feature for photographers who want to fine-tune their images with a higher level of precision, often achieving a distinct and polished look that can set their work apart.

Lightroom Profiles are made by editing the LUTs in Photoshop and saving them to apply to photos. They can be added to a photo on their own, or placed on top of a preset. Profiles do not affect the sliders in the Develop Module and are instead controlled by a slider that increases or decreases the intensity of all the adjustments built into the LUT.

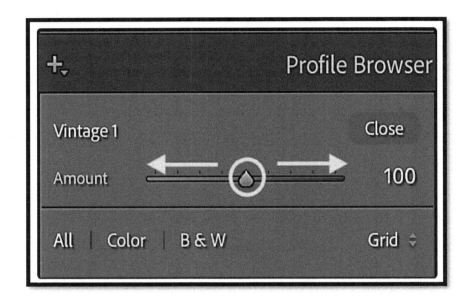

This implies that you may modify your picture using a profile as a basis, and then make changes in the Develop Module without affecting the profile's look. To put it simply, a Lightroom profile is essentially a more sophisticated Lightroom preset that expands upon the features of a preset. The Lightroom profile LUT is really edited when you apply a preset and then go back and tweak it in the Develop Module.

What's The Difference Between Lightroom Presets and Profiles?
Lightroom profiles and presets might first seem to be the same thing. It is true that you may quickly apply some adjustments or general styles to your images using both of them. Presets and profiles may alter your image's exposure, tone, or appearance. For example, they might provide a vintage impression or a certain aesthetic appeal.

Presets and profiles, however, vary significantly from one another in terms of their functionality and the impact they have on the editing process as a whole. Let's examine a few of the more notable variations.

- Presets are adjustments made using the existing editing tools within Lightroom. These tools are the ones you're already familiar with, such as exposure, contrast, highlights, shadows, and more. Presets can be easily created directly within Lightroom by saving a combination of these adjustments that you regularly use.

- When you apply a preset, it automatically adjusts the relevant sliders in the Develop Module, which means you can see exactly what changes have been made and further tweak the image from there. However, the changes made by presets are limited to the range of the sliders in Lightroom. For instance, if a preset pulls the blacks all the way down, you cannot adjust the blacks further beyond the slider's limits.

- Profiles, on the other hand, go beyond the capabilities of Lightroom's standard tools. They include adjustments that are not accessible through Lightroom's usual editing interface. These adjustments can include intricate color grading, textural changes, and specific effects that you might typically associate with cinematic or film-like looks.

- Unlike presets, profiles do not alter the adjustment sliders in the Develop Module. This means that after applying a profile, you can continue to make additional edits without affecting the underlying changes made by the profile. Profiles must be created in Photoshop, which allows for a broader range of adjustments and effects that Lightroom alone cannot achieve.

- Because presets adjust the sliders directly, they are a bit more transparent— you can see what changes are being made and can continue to tweak the sliders after applying a preset. This makes presets straightforward and quick to use, but also somewhat limiting, as you are constrained by the range of the sliders.

- Profiles, by not affecting the sliders, give you more freedom to adjust your photo in ways that might not be possible with a preset alone. They provide a unique look that can be layered on top of your existing adjustments, offering more creative control.

How to install a Lightroom profile and preset

You can download Lightroom presets and profiles (sometimes for free depending on where you source them from). The file type will most likely be a .xmp (Extensible Metadata Platform) file. Click the + icon next to the Preset menu tab to import a preset. Choose Import Presets and open the.xmp file or files that you downloaded.

It will be added toward the bottom of the stack to your Preset menu. Instead, open the "Profile Browser," click the plus symbol next to it, then choose "Import Profiles" and choose the.xmp file of your downloaded profile.

How to create your own Lightroom presets

Setting up your own Lightroom settings is a very simple and easy process. First, make any changes you want to a picture. Select them and click the plus sign next to the "Preset" button. Then choose "Create Preset." There will be a pop-out menu. You can name your Lightroom preset here and then save it as is, or you can choose which parts to keep and which ones to get rid of at this point.

For instance, if you only want your preset to change the tones and grain in your photos and not the contrast or exposure, make sure that contrast and exposure are not checked. Instead, make sure that any grain and color choices are checked.

If you right-click on your preset in the main menu and choose "Update with Current Settings," you can also make changes to it later by choosing the parts of the change you want to update again and then deselecting those parts. To get rid of any imported or made settings, just right-click on them and choose "**Delete**." This also works for profiles.

How To Turn A Lightroom Preset Into A Profile

- Begin by importing your XMP preset files into Photoshop's Camera Raw.

- Inside Camera Raw, locate and click on the Preset icon. This icon is used to manage and apply different presets to your images.

- To create a new profile from the preset, hold down the Option key on a Mac or the Alt key on Windows while clicking on the "Create New Preset" icon.

- A dialog box will appear prompting you to name your new profile and select a group where it will be saved. Enter a descriptive name for your profile and choose an appropriate group to keep your profiles organized.

- Check off the settings that you want to incorporate in the profile. These might include adjustments like exposure, contrast, and color settings.

- Once you've configured the settings and named your profile, click OK to save it.

- Your newly created preset is now converted into a profile and installed back into Lightroom. You can find it in the profile section within the Develop module of Lightroom, ready to be applied to your photos.

Let's break these steps down more in-depth.

You can either use profiles you have downloaded and imported into Lightroom, or you can create your own. To create a profile, you must start with a preset. You can either create and save your own preset or load one into Photoshop.

Once you've done that, open a RAW file in Photoshop and Camera Raw should open automatically (or open a JPEG and head to **Filter > Camera Raw Filter**.) With Camera Raw open, click the preset icon in the toolbar on the right.

Select the setting that you want to use. I picked the "flat" setting that comes with Adobe software. Then, click the tweaks button in the menu and make the basic changes to your profile look the way you want them to.

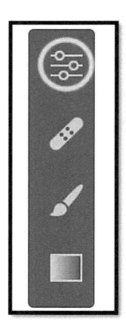

To make a certain color scheme, you can change things like color grade and HSL. As you make changes, keep the style of your page in mind. You should also think about what kind of photo you want to use this profile on, since not all profiles work well with all types of photos.

Let us see how the picture turns out.

To save your changes as a new profile, go back to the second-to-last icon on the presets tab and press Option + Click (Mac) or Alt + Click (Windows) on the New Preset button. This will open the New Profile window.

This is what you should see at the top of the window: Create Profile. Below, you can give your page a name and choose your group from the "**Group**" drop-down box. It will show up as a folder in Lightroom after you choose the group. Check the boxes next to the changes you want to make to the profile, then click **OK**.

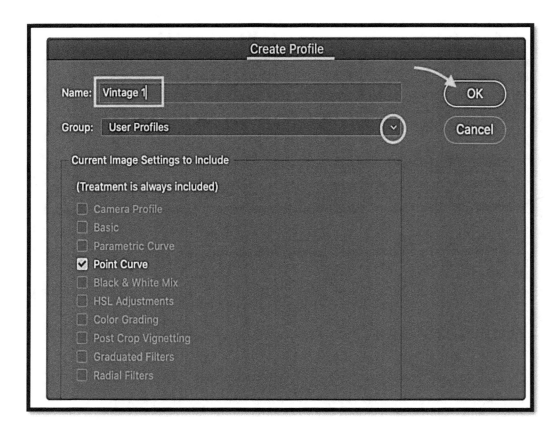

Lightroom will now allow you to locate your profile by directing you to the Develop Module, selecting the drop-down arrow that is located next to the Basic tab, and then clicking the four rectangles that are located on the right side of the screen.

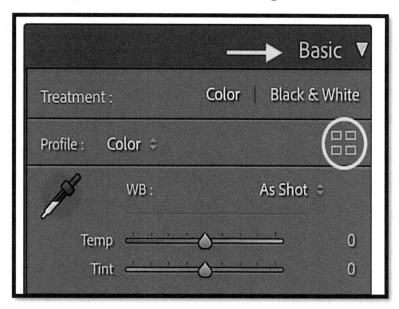

This will open your profile window, where you can find your newly saved profile.

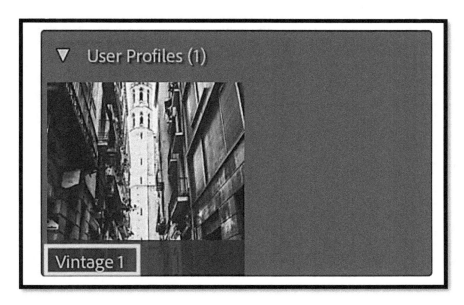

Should You Use Presets Or Profiles?

Whether you use Presets or Profiles depends on how you would like your photo to look, and how much control you'd like to have over the final results.

Presets can be helpful as a starting point because they change the adjustments in the Develop Module. You can then go into individual adjustments and change them. In this case, if you use a template that makes your picture a little too bright but you like the color tone, you can just lower the brightness and leave the other settings alone.

Profiles, on the other hand, give your picture a general look that you can change how strong. In other words, you can add a setup on top of the profile or just change the settings in the Develop Module to finish your picture. You can change a lot about how your picture looks in the end.

Take some time to try out both settings and profiles to find the one that works best for you. Try them out on different photos to see which one gets you the result you want. Both settings and profiles are likely to be used at different times, so it's best to learn how to use them both.

CHAPTER TWELVE

LENS CORRECTIONS AND TRANSFORMATIONS

The Lens Corrections Panel

The Lens Corrections panel in Lightroom Classic looks simple, but there's a lot going on behind the scenes. Most of the time you don't have to pay much attention to it – just make sure you check the appropriate boxes then get on with developing your photos.

But sometimes things don't work the way you expect them to, and that's when it's useful to understand it better.

What is the Lens Corrections panel for?

The Lens Corrections panel gets rid of or lessens chromatic aberration, vignetting, and optical distortion that the camera lens causes in Raw files (but not in JPEGs, which may already have been fixed in the camera).

In the Lens Corrections box, there are two tabs: Guide and Profile.

In Lightroom, lens settings are found and used on the Profile tab.

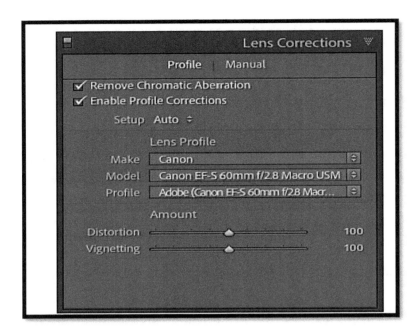

The Manual tab is for adjusting the amount of distortion correction, vignetting reduction, or chromatic aberration reduction yourself.

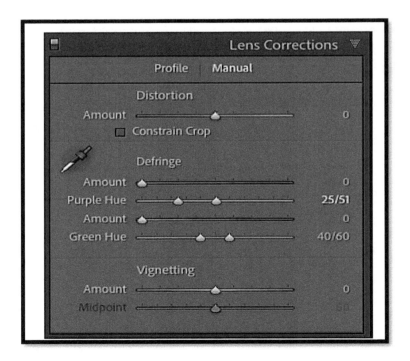

The Profile tab – remove Chromatic Aberrations

A chromatic distortion is a color border that can be seen around the edges of an item in a picture. Older wide-angle or zoom lenses are most likely to give you color swirls around the edges of the frame when the subject is lit from behind. They could be purple/green, red/cyan, or blue/yellow. Most of the time, you need to zoom in 100% to see them.

At 100% zoom, you can see some color banding around the edges of the tree stems in the picture below.

To get rid of them, check the box next to Remove Chromatic Aberration.

The Profile tab – Enable Profile Corrections

Vignetting, barrel distortion, and pincushion distortion are all fixed by Profile Corrections.

Sometimes the sides of the frame are darker than the middle. This is called vignetting. It is normal for vignetting to show up at the widest aperture settings of a lens. As you slow down, it slowly goes away.

The picture below was taken with a 50mm f1.8 lens set to f1.8. The version that hasn't been fixed yet, with full vignetting, is on the left. The fixed form, with no vignetting, is on the right.

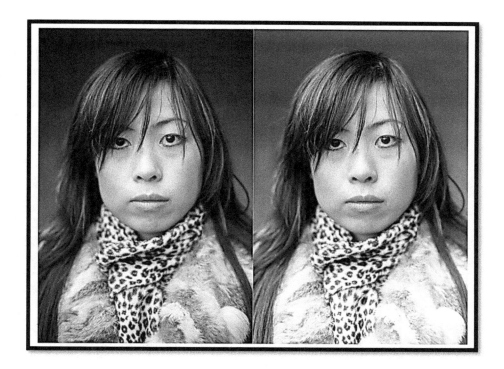

In this case, the version with the background looks better. If that works better for you, you can change how Lightroom Classic fixes vignetting.

The lens bends straight lines outwards, making them look like the sides of a barrel. This is called barrel distortion. Wavy lenses, both fixed and zoom, let you get it. It's more possible that a cheap lens will give you barrel distortion.

This picture was taken at 18mm with an 18-135mm zoom lens.

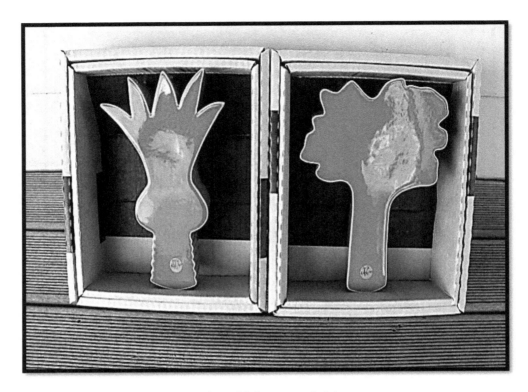

You can see the change between the old form and this one.

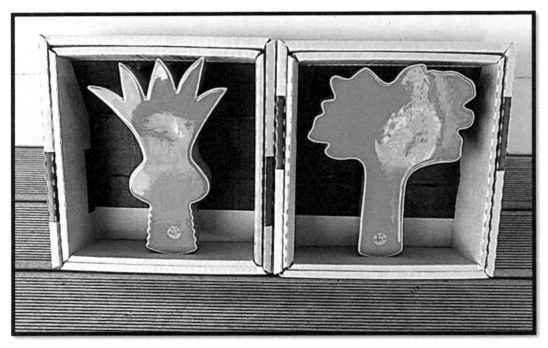

When straight lines curve inward, this is called pincushion distortion. It can happen with some zoom lenses, and unlike barrel distortion, you probably won't notice it unless you look for it. I don't have any cases to show you because it's so rare.

Built-in Profiles

If you have a certain camera and lens, you may see the word Built-in Lens Profile applied at the bottom of the Lens Corrections panel.

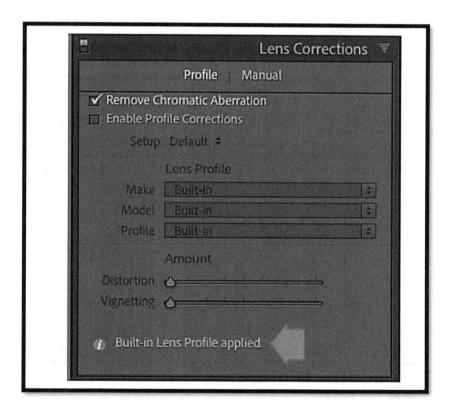

This means that Lightroom is using a lens setting that was saved by your camera in the Raw file. It happens a lot with tiny and small cameras.

If this sounds like you, then great! Your camera did the work for you. You can't find a lens profile in the Lens Corrections panel, so there's no point in looking for it.

Check the Enable Profile Corrections box if it's not already checked. Lightroom checks the EXIF data of the picture and, if it finds the right lens profile, uses it immediately.

Lightroom might not always be able to find the lens type. In that case, you can pick it out by hand from the options.

Some lenses may not be in the database because they are too old or haven't been profiled by Adobe. If that's the case, the Raw file may already have a profile applied, which will show the message "Built-in Lens Profile applied."

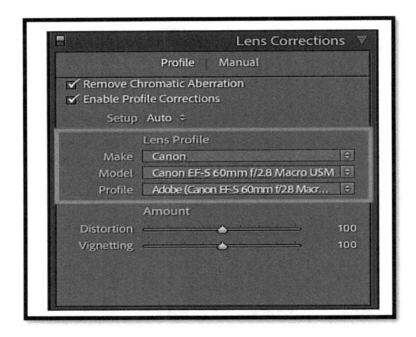

You can change how much distortion or vignetting is fixed by moving the sliders below. Both are already set to 100. You can move a slider to the right to make the adjustment stronger or to the left to weaker.

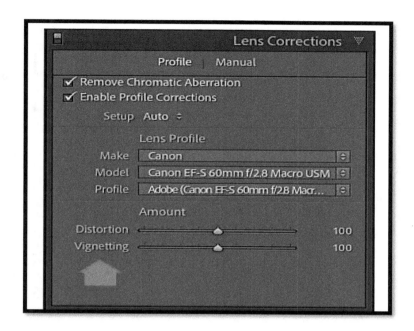

This works well for pictures like the image above, where the frame makes the picture look better.

How to set a default lens profile in the Lens Corrections panel

For sure, Lightroom only uses a profile if it knows for sure what kind of lens was used. It looks at the EXIF data in the picture to figure out what lens was used.

You can pick a setting yourself if Lightroom doesn't use one (as long as it exists).

You can make it the default setting for that lens so you don't have to pick it every time. This is how you do it.

1. Open a picture that was taken with the camera or lens profile you want to use in the Develop section. Then, make sure the box that says "Enable Profile Corrections" is checked. Make sure Lightroom doesn't set the lens on its own.

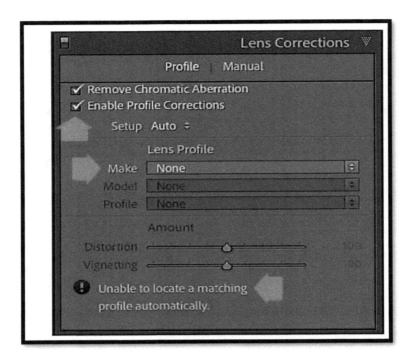

2. Check the box that says "**Enable Profile Corrections**," and then use the options to choose the profile you want to change. You can change the Distortion and Vignetting sliders if you need to.

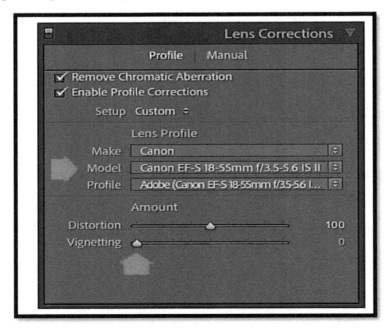

3.   Select **Save New Lens Profile Defaults** from the Setup menu.

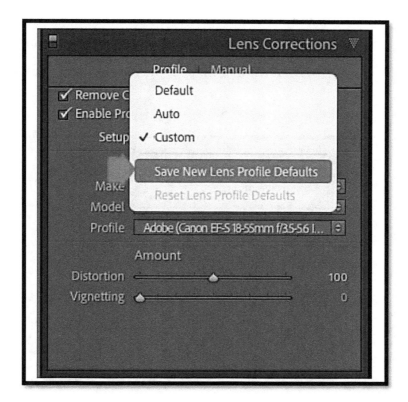

4.   Go to the Setup menu and choose "Preset." The next time you open a picture taken with the same camera and lens, Lightroom will use the setting you just saved. And if you changed them, the Distortion and Vignetting settings as well.

The Setup menu in the Lens Corrections panel

There are three settings in the Setup menu.

- **Default:** Allows you to customize the lens settings.
- **Auto** tells Lightroom to look for a model that matches.
- **Custom** means that you chose a style by hand or changed a setting, such as the Vignetting tool.

The Manual tab

If there isn't already a profile for your lens or if you want to change or ignore the profile settings, go to the Manual tab. Most of the time, this is because checking the box next to Remove Chromatic Aberrations didn't completely remove all signs of chromatic aberration.

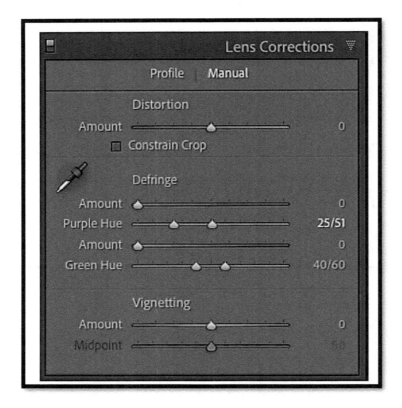

You can make your distortion fixes or changes using the Distortion and Vignetting sliders.

Select the eyedropper icon and then click on the photo's leftover color bands to remove chromatic aberrations by hand. If you need to, you can also move the buttons by hand.

Using the Transform Tool

The Transform tools in Lightroom are often missed by less experienced editors, but they are a very useful way to fix a problem that photographers have had for a long time: perspective distortion. Perspective distortion is one of those small problems that can ruin a great picture, but most photographers don't know how to spot it or, even more importantly, fix it.

The Transform panel is near the bottom of Lightroom's Develop module's list of tools and sliders. Its job is to fix photos that have perspective warping.

But what is confusion of perspective? In real life, it's when lines that should be straight, whether they're horizontal or vertical, start to come together. The sides of the building don't rise straight up into the air; instead, they curve in toward each other, giving the watcher the impression that the building is falling backward.

Look at how the houses appear to be falling away from the view. That's because this picture has perspective distortion!

Perspective error is common and can't always be avoided, no matter how good your gear is. It's because of where you are with the subject. Technically, you can avoid warping by making sure your camera is perfectly level and parallel to the subject, but this isn't always possible.

Perspective distortion is not the same as lens distortion, which is caused by the physics of the lens and is possible to remove in the Lightroom Lens Corrections panel.

Luckily, the Transform panel has two main ways to deal with perspective distortion:

- Upright corrections (via six easy-to-use buttons)
- Transform corrections (via seven handy sliders)

For the most part, the Upright buttons work great. But if they don't do what you want, you can always use the Transform sliders to make more manual changes.

When should you use the Transform panel?

Since the Transform panel is meant to fix perspective distortion, you should use it whenever you take a picture of something with clear vertical or horizontal lines. It's easy to miss perspective distortion until someone points it out, so even if your picture looks fine, you should still try a few Transform buttons just to be safe.

There is some perspective confusion in this picture. Can you find it?

Transform is especially helpful for changing pictures of:

- Building exteriors
- Building interiors
- Trees
- Telephone poles and lampposts

When you use the Transform tools on pictures, you usually want to get a natural result, which means a picture that looks like the scene our eyes and brains would see in three dimensions. Keep in mind, though, that you can use Transform to do the opposite: make some parts look bigger for an effect that isn't realistic or even strange.

You can also choose to leave a photo with all of its warping. I don't usually suggest this, but it can look very dramatic!

There is a lot of perspective confusion in this picture—just look at how the lines of the buildings come together—but it works well here because it makes the picture more dramatic. (It would also be nearly impossible to fix this amount of viewpoint distortion.)

How to use the Transform panel: The Upright options

If you're working on a new picture, start by trying out the Upright buttons in the Transform panel to fix perspective error.

Just a note: To better show how each option works, I'll use this picture, which has some mild perspective distortion:

As it stands, the Off button is already chosen, so click on Auto instead:

Auto tries to look at the whole scene and fix any issues it finds, making sure that perspective distortion is taken into account on both the vertical and horizontal axes. It also does a few other calculations to make sure the results look normal. After you press the "Auto" button, carefully look at your picture to see if any lines are going up or down.

As you make these adjustments, keep in mind that they will always crop your picture, or cause you to crop it. Of course, this shouldn't be a problem most of the time, but if the edges of a scene are important to you, I suggest leaving a little extra space along the edges so you can distort the view later on.

I've found that Auto works well about 70% of the time. If you don't like the result or want to try something different, press the Vertical button. This will only fix vertical lines that are coming together. This is sometimes a good way to fix houses that are slightly warped without cutting out too much of the scene.

The Level button is another choice. It only fixes horizontal lines that are coming together. This tool isn't something I use very often, but it can be useful if you need to shoot stores from an angle.

The Level button didn't do much for this picture because it mostly has vertical lines that are coming together.

Please keep in mind that the Level option might not work right when you are working with straight and vertical lines. The software might be fooled by these lines together, and Lightroom may decide to change the vertical lines and tilt the rest of the picture. If that happens, you'll need to use a different Upright fix or even the Transform sliders we'll talk about below.

You should also check out Full. It fixes both vertical and horizontal lines, so it's also worth a shot. I don't like the Full choice very much because it makes the effects look too good to be true. You might still be able to use it, but be aware that it's very harsh.

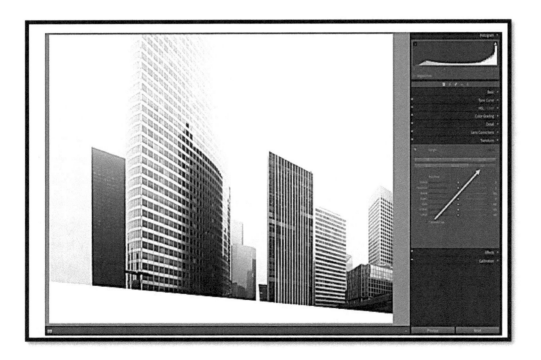

The Full option cropped and changed the picture in big ways.

And finally, you can choose "**Guided**." Guided lets you input data manually and make changes automatically to create a very customized effect. If you're having trouble getting a natural look, this could be a useful tool to try.

The Guided option might take a minute or two longer to get right, but it's likely the best way to make sure you get a good result. When you choose one of the other automatic choices, Lightroom has to choose which vertical and horizontal lines to use to change the viewpoint. These lines may not be the best ones to use. That's where the Guided tool shines; as the shooter, you know which lines need to be straightened and can tell Lightroom how to do it. How it works:

Your cursor will change into markers when you click the Guided button, and you'll be able to draw lines (called guides) on your picture. To begin, draw your guides across two lines that are coming together.

The picture will change right away, but you can also add a third or even a fourth guide across horizontal lines in the picture. You can't add a third vertical guide; if you try, the Transform panel will tell you that the guide setup you entered is wrong.

After making the lines, click on the circle that looks like a guide above the buttons. You're done!

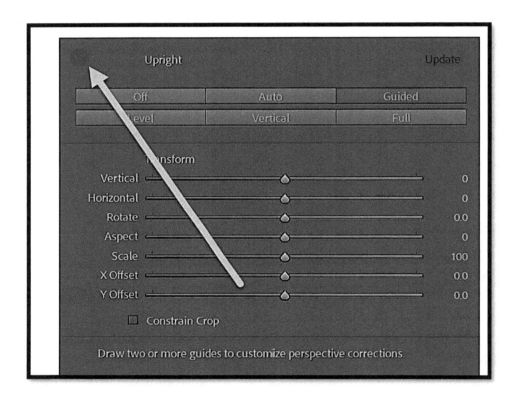

One last piece of advice: make sure there is no white space around the edges of your picture after you've fixed the skew. While the Transform panel will sometimes crop this extra space for you, you may need to remove it yourself. The Constrain Crop button at the bottom of the panel can be checked if you want Lightroom to always cut off any extra space. But I don't like the way it works, so I suggest you crop by hand instead.

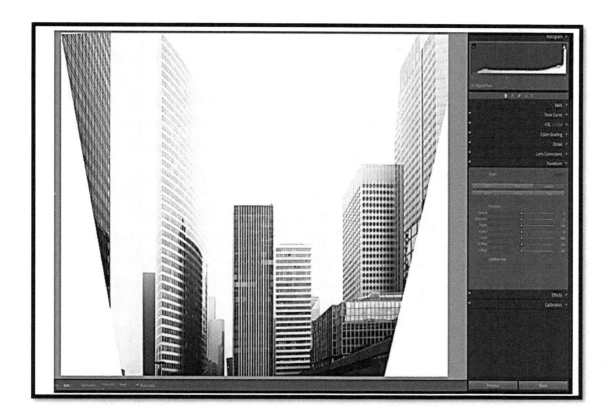

The picture after using the Guided option to fix it.

How to use the Transform panel: The Transform sliders

With the above-mentioned Upright tools, perspective warping should be easy to get rid of quickly. The Transform buttons are a great option, though, if you'd rather make adjustments by hand or if you don't like the results the Upright tools give you and want to change them.

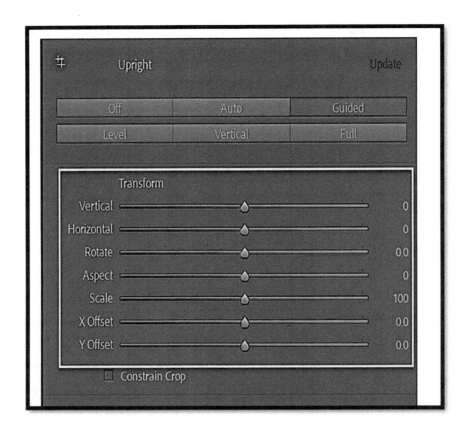

The Vertical and Horizontal sliders are the most useful because they let you fix errors in the width and height of the image. So, if you have vertical lines that are coming together, all you have to do is move the Vertical slider in either direction until the lines look like they are straight. And if your horizontals are coming together, use the Horizontal tool instead.

You can rotate the picture with the Rotate tool, which can also be used to make sure the image is perfectly straight.

Then there's the Aspect tool, which can help you fix photos that are too compressed or too stretched after you've used a different distortion adjustment.

Finally, you'll see the Scale, X Offset, and Y Offset buttons. I don't use these very often because they crop your pictures in certain ways. Feel free to try them out, but don't be shocked if you don't use them much after that.

You might not find that the buttons do much when used by themselves. However, if you use them together and in small amounts, you can successfully change the scales to get the view you have in your mind.

CHAPTER THIRTEEN

ADVANCED COLOR CORRECTION

Part 3: Advanced Techniques and Workflow Optimization

Using the Color Calibration Tool

Adobe Lightroom has a part called "**Calibration**" that has seven sliders. One called Shadows is at the top. You can change the color of your pictures to be more green or fuchsia, based on your taste.

There are six more buttons below that. There are three groups of these: Red Primary, Green Primary, and Blue Primary. There is a scale called Hue and another one called Saturation in each of these.

Lightroom has settings called "Calibration" that you can use to change different parts of your picture. It can be used to bring out the colors in a golden hour picture, and it can also be used for portraits and other types of photos.

When you use the Calibration tool in Adobe Lightroom, you don't have to follow any rules. It can make your edit look sloppy, so we don't recommend using it before making other color tweaks.

Making all of your changes in advance is preferable, and then using Calibration to add the finishing touches when you're satisfied with everything. You'll be able to add more of your creative style to your pictures once you know how to use this tool.

How to Use the Calibration Tool in Lightroom

Let's take a look at how to use the Calibration tool now that you know a bit more about it. Find the feature and add it to your changes by following these steps.

1. Get on your computer and open Adobe Lightroom Classic.
2. Once your program is ready, click on the Develop tab.

3. Just scroll down to the very end of the menu on the right. The Calibration part will be there once you get there.

4. Move the knobs around until you get the look you want. When you add or remove colors, you should try to keep things simple. Adding or removing too many colors can mess up the rest of your edit.

5. There's always the original picture to look back at if you're not sure how different your edited image looks.

Color Correction

1. **Import Your Photo:** To begin, bring your photo into Lightroom's Library module.

2. **Switch to Develop Module:** To go to the Develop module, click on the Develop module in the screen's upper right area.

3. **Basic Panel:** To find the Basic panel in the Develop module, look to the right side of the screen. Here are the main tools for fixing colors.

4. **White Balance:** To fix any color casts in your picture, you can change the white balance. You can select a setting (like Auto, Daylight, Cloudy, Shade, Tungsten, Fluorescent, Flash, or Custom) from the White Balance dropdown menu, or you can make individual changes using the Temperature and Tint sliders. Slide the colors around until they look natural and even.

   These sliders—exposure, contrast, highlights, shadows, whites, and blacks—can change how your picture looks generally, including its color. To improve the colors and tones in your picture, make changes as necessary.

5. **HSL/Color Panel:** What does HSL/Color Panel stand for? It stands for Hue, Saturation, and Luminance. This panel lets you pick out certain colors in a picture and change their hue, intensity, and brightness separately.
   - **Hue:** You can change the color of certain colors in your picture. One way to do this is to change the color of greens to yellow or blue.
   - **Saturation:** Change how bright certain colors are. It's possible to make colors brighter or duller by changing the brightness.
   - **Luminance:** Change how bright certain colors are. You can raise or lower the intensity to change the brightness of colors.

White Balance in Lightroom Classic

When photographers bring in new shots, the first thing they usually do in the post-processing process is change the white balance. It's artistic and sometimes important to change the white balance, even with the most advanced camera gear.

It's not hard to figure out how to use Lightroom's white balance tool, but if you do, you'll find that it has a lot of other useful features. It is the goal of this guide to help you understand your photo's white balance so that you can make good choices when you are editing it.

What is White Balance and What is it For?

The color temperature of the picture is what "white balance" in Lightroom means. The number K, which stands for degrees Kelvin, is used to describe this measurement. Kelvin tells you how warm or cool the light in your picture is.

Understanding that all light sources have their temperature is the best way to get a handle on white balance. Think about times when you were in different rooms and felt how hot or cold it was.

Because it is warm, candlelight has a yellow glow that makes it look warm and welcoming. Fluorescent or halogen bulbs give off a cool blue light that makes things look cold. With these different effects, you can quickly change how your shots look and feel.

On your camera's screen, you may have seen that the white balance settings are different. If you change these, your camera will be told to change the photo's color temperature based on the lighting.

There is a number, typically in degrees Kelvin, that goes with each of these pre-set tasks. Each of the presets is on a color temperature range, which normally goes from blue to yellow. Your camera will try to balance the white balance by coming up with the opposite tone of the light in the room.

Check out the chart below to see what each setting looks like in terms of its Kelvin number.

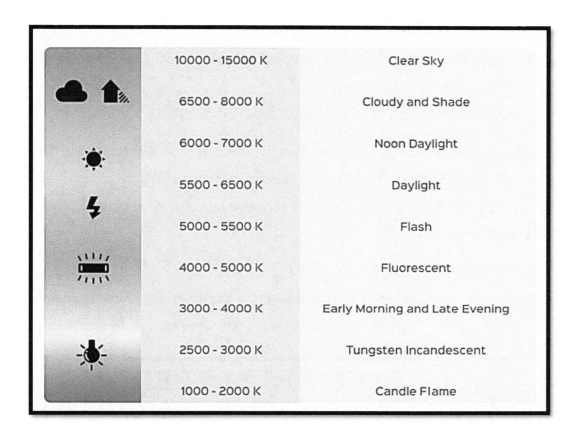

10000 - 15000 K	Clear Sky
6500 - 8000 K	Cloudy and Shade
6000 - 7000 K	Noon Daylight
5500 - 6500 K	Daylight
5000 - 5500 K	Flash
4000 - 5000 K	Fluorescent
3000 - 4000 K	Early Morning and Late Evening
2500 - 3000 K	Tungsten Incandescent
1000 - 2000 K	Candle Flame

When you set the camera to auto mode, the image sensor looks at the picture data to figure out which white balance works best for this shot. A lot of photographers leave it at this setting and then change the white balance in Lightroom.

Don't worry if you think you might have picked the wrong setting or if your camera thought the white balance in your picture was off. It's easy to fix the color temperature after the fact, just like many other camera setting mistakes.

How To Adjust The White Balance in Lightroom

Everyone has a different idea of what the white balance in a picture means. If you view your photos on a computer screen and then on a smartphone, you can see this difference. On the other screen, the picture is likely to look a little cooler than you remember it.

Here are the three most common things that can change your photo's white balance:

- How the computer or screen is color calibrated (or not)
- How it is perceived by the human eye
- The camera white balance settings at the time of capture

Changing the camera settings and then changing the numbers afterward are the only ones on that list that most photographers can directly change. There are several ways to change the white balance in your photos in Adobe Lightroom. Each has its own pros and cons and best uses.

Use the White Balance Slider

In the Develop module, the White Balance tool is at the top of the global changes area. It is in a part called "WB." You should pay attention to the Temp and Tint settings.

Whenever you open a picture, the temperature will be set to 0. As a point of comparison, this shows where your camera's original white balance setting was made.

The temperature scale has tones that change from blue to yellow as you move it. Moving it to the left will give a picture a bluer tint, and moving it to the right will give it a more yellow tint.

You can change the pink and green tints in your picture with the tint tool. Use this to help even out any color casts that are already there in the picture. Besides this, the color settings let you add some creative effects to the mood of your picture as a whole.

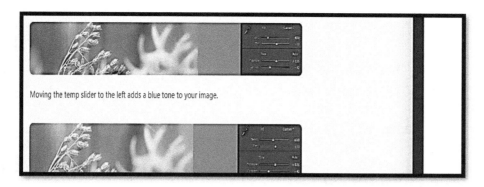

Moving the temp slider to the left adds a blue tone to your image.

Most photographers use this method to make a small adjustment as part of the Lightroom color correction process, and it works every time. As we'll talk about in a bit, you should make sure that your monitor is color-adjusted.

Using the Eyedropper Tool to Set a Neutral Target For White Balance

The eyedropper tool is to the left of "WB." It looks a lot like the tool you'd find in picture editing programs like Photoshop. This picking tool will pick out a small part of the picture and tell you what color a single pixel or a full area is. It works well for focusing on specific tones and fixing the white balance in Lightroom.

If you use the eyedropper, you can find a neutral tone in your picture and set it. You are telling Lightroom that this one pixel is white, regardless of what it thinks. After that, the computer will change the white balance on its own based on what you tell it.

The tool is easy to use; all you have to do is click the eyedropper and move it to a white spot in the picture. The slide will move to the right place for neutral when you do that. Making sure the RGB numbers are as close to the same as possible is an easy trick.

Of course, this method will only work if your picture has a neutral white point. If so, try to get it as close to neutral as you can, and then use the white balance tool to make changes.

Shoot in RAW and Use Lightroom White Balance Presets

As a result, RAW pictures contain all the information that a shot could have. This means that you can change a lot of pixels. If you shoot in RAW, Lightroom has presets that you can use in the same way that you would in the camera settings.

These presets are easy to use because they match the settings on your camera. Lightroom, on the other hand, only applies it to photos that have already been taken. This means that the look can be slightly different than on a camera, where the photo sensor reads the data and makes changes in real-time.

Syncing your White Balance Adjustments Between Photos

If you're a shooter who takes a lot of pictures, you will love being able to sync your white balance settings. It's pretty simple: hold down the shift key and click on the photos you want to sync. Then, right-click and select "Develop settings." Finally, select "sync settings."

By clicking this, a window will appear that lets you choose which settings you want to share between the pictures. Make sure that white balance is chosen. Any changes you make to the first picture will also be made to the others in the batch.

White Balance for Color Correction Vs. Using it Creatively

Some photographers will only use the white balance tool to fix the colors in their pictures. They will then use the other changes to add more colors.

These are the most common ways to add color to a picture:

- The Color Grading Tool (Split Toning)
- HSL Module (Hue, Saturation, Luminance)
- Tone Curves
- Calibration Module

If you keep the change in color temperature of the light in your picture modest, it can look good, but if you make it too big, it can make the picture look washed out.

The targeted adjustment tool is a great way for experienced photographers to change the light in their pic. After adjusting with a radial or linear mask, you can use the white balance tool to bring the color temperature back into balance.

White Balance Tricks You Can Use To Improve Your Photos

Using the Lightroom white balance sliders to get the most out of your photos can involve more than just changing some numbers. To get the most out of Lightroom's white balance tools, try these tips:

Color Calibrate Your Monitor

On different screens, each picture won't look the same. As a photo editor, this is one of the hardest things to deal with because the picture might look great on your computer screen but not quite right on someone else's.

After color calibrating your monitor, it will show the real colors of the picture more accurately. This means that anyone with a screen that is properly set up will see the same thing you do.

It can be done in two ways: physically or electronically. A lot of people use simple, free tools to make sure the colors are correct.

Use it to Adjust the Mood of your Photo

You can sometimes change the white balance of a picture to make it feel different or moodier.

For instance, if your picture is bright and sunny and you want it to look old and worn, you could move the temperature scale to the blue side to give it a soft sepia tone.

Using tools in Lightroom like a reversed radial mask can help make your photo brighter and change how the light hits it. By shifting the exposure to sunny spots, you can give the mask a yellow tint. To get rid of this, move the temperature tool to the left. If you don't do this, your picture might not look right.

Once you know how to change the white balance values without using the white balance selection, you can add it to the basic panel to give your photos a little more color depth.

Frequently Asked Questions

If you've never used these tools before, it can be hard to find the right mix of temp and tint sliders to fix colors. These are the questions we get asked most often about the white balance tools in Lightroom.

Where are the white balance temperature and tint sliders located in Lightroom?

The white balance temperature slider is at the top of the basic panel, and the color slider is right below it.

Is the white balance tool in Lightroom only good for color correction?

No, the Lightroom white balance tool can also be used for artistic tasks. The best way to fix any color casts in your picture is to use the white balance choice tool.

Will using the white balance in Lightroom permanently affect my photos?

Lightroom is proud of the fact that it doesn't change your photos in any way. In other words, you can make changes to your picture that the program will only show when you send it.

CHAPTER FOURTEEN

HDR AND PANORAMA MERGING

Creating HDR Images

A method called **"bracketing"** is used to make HDR pictures. It is possible to get a more accurate and thorough view of highlights, midtones, and shadows by combining several shots taken at different exposures into one picture. Landscape photographers like this method because it can be hard to get details in both shades and highlights when you only use natural light.

Because the scenes need to be as still as possible, landscape photography is also great for HDR processing. Because the pictures are stacked on top of each other during bracketing, the process needs at least three images that are almost exact copies of each other, except for their exposures. When you work with moving things like people or animals, this can be hard. A tripod is also important to make sure you always get the same picture.

You can combine the pictures in Lightroom once you have them. With a few different merge settings, you can get the picture you want.

Step 1: Select the bracketed images

Choose which pictures will be used for the HDR merge first. All of the pictures in brackets are up to you. You might want to use them all. I'll say more about that later. Once you've chosen which pictures to use, make sure each one is chosen. You can do this in either the Library Module or the Develop Module.

Step 2: Photo Merge > HDR

Select the pictures you want to join, then go to Photo > Photo join > HDR. You can also right-click on one of the pictures you've chosen and choose Photo Merge > HDR. To do this quickly, press Ctrl+H on your computer. This opens the HDR Merge Preview window. This window shows a preview of the joined files and gives you three major options to make before the final merge.

Keep in mind, that the sample picture might not look very different from some of the original bracketed pictures. It will probably look flat. That was meant to be that way because the final united picture is still RAW data and needs to be processed.

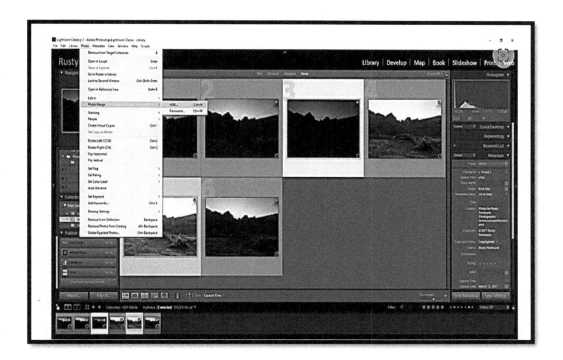

Step 3: Choosing HDR Options

There are three main choices to think about on the right side of the HDR join Preview window before the final join.

- **Auto Align:** If you choose this option, Lightroom will try to match pictures that were moved between shots, and it does a pretty good job of it. This choice might not be needed if the camera was on a stand.

- **Auto Tone:** If you choose this option, the merged preview picture will be displayed with some basic tonal changes. Most likely, the changes will involve lowering the image's highlights, raising its shadows, and changing its white and black points. This makes the picture look more balanced and lets you know how much room you have to play with the tones. In the HDR sample window, the Auto Tone button is the same as the Auto button in Lightroom's Develop Module's Basic Panel. Since the final adjustment will be made later, I usually leave this choice unchecked. Also, I don't like how the picture looks when this is on because it gives it that "HDR look."

- **Deghost Amount:** This feature gets rid of or lessens "ghosting," which is caused by items moving around in the scene between shots. Decaying takes out pixels that have moved between frames and fills them in with pixels from the base image. This can work well for people, cars, clouds, or plants that are moving. The more movement there is, the more deghosting you should choose. If you check the box next to "Show Deghost Overlay," you can see what parts of the picture are hidden. Of course, you will choose "None" if there are no moving items in the pictures. In that case, use the lowest setting to get the best picture quality.

It's important to know that the HDR settings will stay the same the next time you use Photo Merge. The next time, the choices you need to turn on might be different based on the picture.

The HDR Merge Preview window. Note the HDR Options on the right side.

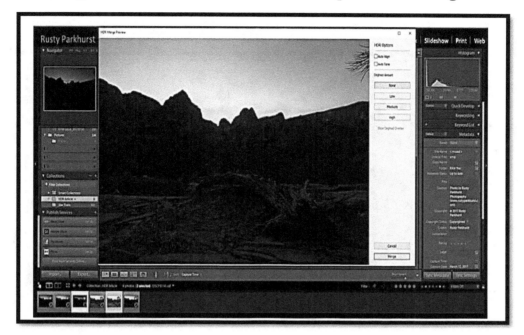

The picture has an "HDR look" because Auto Tone is chosen in the HDR Merge Preview window.

For masking out movement between frames, the Deghosting choice is helpful. If you click on "Show Deghost Overlay," you can see where the masking has been applied.

Step 4: Merging the Images

Once you're happy with how the sample picture looks, hit the Merge button to make the picture official. The choices that were chosen will be used to merge the picture files, and the final merged image will be added to the Lightroom filmstrip. A 16-bit DNG file, which is Adobe's raw file format, is what you get. The merged image keeps all of the raw data from the original pictures, so you can use a lot of that data to edit the end picture.

The pictures with the darkest and lightest brackets are at the top. Before making any changes, the bottom picture is the merged one.

The picture that was joined in Lightroom's Develop Module. In the Basic Panel, the Auto Tone button has been chosen.

Step 5: Edit the Image

The fun starts now. Up until now, the machine has done the majority of the work. Now you can add your artistic touches and edit the final united picture to your liking. As you move the sliders in Lightroom, you'll see that you can get a lot more detail out of the picture. In this case, the brightness scale can now go from -5 to +5 stops instead of just -5 to +5 stops. The highlights slider will bring back detail in the brighter areas, and the shadows slider will do a great job of making the darker areas brighter. It's up to you whether you want to make changes or use presets. These changes won't hurt the original picture, like all of Lightroom's other editing tools. You can undo anything at any time or start over.

Tips for best results

Lightroom's HDR merge tool is pretty easy to use. There are only four basic steps to go from importing a picture to making the final image. There are, however, some tips that will help you get the best results and speed up the process even more.

Tip 1: Shoot in RAW

It may seem like a broken record, but this tip works for almost all kinds of shooting. When you shoot in RAW, all of the picture data is kept, which is very helpful for getting back details in the highlights and shadows. It is very important to use the RAW file format. That's what I think you should use by default. It's okay to shoot in JPEG if you have to. Just remember to change the camera settings back to RAW when you're done.

Tip 2: Use only what you need

This could be true whether you take three, five, seven, or even nine bracketed photos. You might not need all of them to make the HDR. You will have to try a few different things before you find the one that works best for you. Use only two of the pictures: one with two stops less exposure and one with two stops more exposure. This will make the merger go faster, and it might be all you need to get what you want.

Tip 3: Edit after the merge

Don't edit the pictures in the brackets before you merge them. During the merging procedure, the picture changes will not be kept. Before joining, you can make lens changes, and those settings will be kept. Save all other changes for the final picture that has been merged.

Tip 4: Stack bracketed images

This tip might not help you make better HDRs, but it will help you order your pictures better. Workflow is faster when things are better organized. That is, faster means more efficient. Going faster is better. When you have a card full of photos, it can be hard to keep track of all the bracketed pictures and figure out which ones go with what. Putting each group of bracketed pictures on top of each other can help organize things and make them easier to work with.

First, get all of the pictures into Lightroom. **Photo > Stacking > Auto-Stack by Capture Time** is what you need to do. In the pop-up window that opens, you can change how long there is between stacks. The idea behind this is that each set of bracketed pictures is taken in very little time. I find that a setting of 10 seconds works well for night shots. This time setting would need to be a lot longer for longer shutter speeds, like those used for night photos. Once the time is right, click on Stack.

Lightroom will use the pictures' time stamps to figure out which ones should be put together. Go back to the Photo Menu or right-click on any photo to get to Stacking > Collapse all Stacks. A stack will be made of all the sets of pictures that are within the given time. There is a small white box in the top left area of an image that looks like a stack of white boxes. This box tells you that the image is a stack. The number in the box tells you how many pictures are in the stack. At any time, each stack can be made bigger or smaller.

The Stacking feature in the Photo Menu. Do this within Lightroom's Library Module.

In Auto-Stacking, you can set how long to wait between stacks.

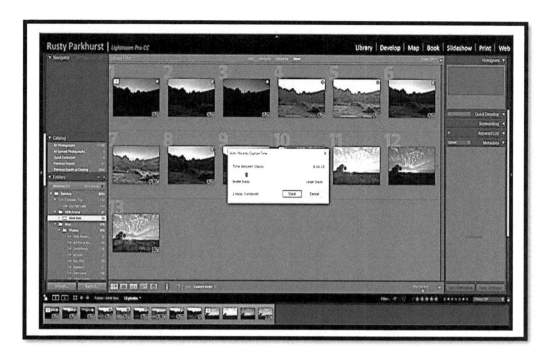

Tip 5: Reset HDR options

When I talked about Step 3, I said that the HDR settings from the last session would be kept the next time Photo Merge is opened. When you're done with the HDR merge, pick any two shots and open the preview window again. To stop making another HDR picture, deselect all of the choices and click "Cancel." This process is quick and easy, and it can help you use tools.

Tip 6: Skip the preview

It seems like I'm always short on time. Not at all. But if there's a way to make the process go faster, I'm all for it. I like the artistic process of editing my photos. You can get around the HDR viewing window in at least a couple of ways. If you hold down the Shift key and click on Photo Merge > HDR, the merger will happen in the background while you do something else.

The same thing can be done by pressing Ctrl+Shift+H on your computer after choosing the pictures you want to join. You won't be able to see a sample if you use these methods. That being said, you don't need to see a preview if the pictures were taken on a stand, the scene didn't move much, and you change the HDR settings as suggested in the last tip. Also, you can always use the sample to do the merge again if something doesn't look right.

Create a Panorama

Panorama Photo Merge

Pick out the pictures you want to use to make a panorama. The finished picture will be a RAW DNG file that you can edit after the stitching is done, so you don't have to edit it. "Photo Merge" is Lightroom's built-in tool for combining multiple photos. It can do two things: make HDR images and stitch landscapes together. We will, of course, be focused on the panorama function in particular. To open the tool, choose the photos you want to join together, then right-click on them and pick **"Photo Merge"** > **"Panorama..." or "Photo" > "Photo Merge" > "Panorama..."** in the Lightroom menu. You can also press "CTRL + M" (or "CMD + M" on a Mac) to open the tool quickly:

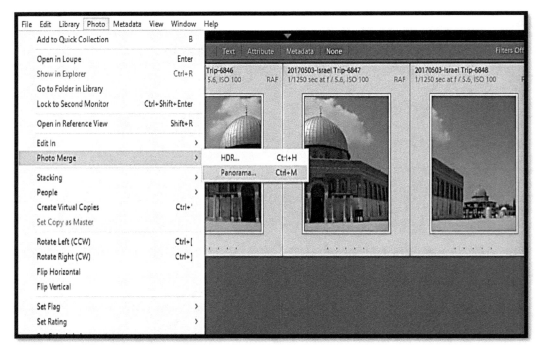

This will open the Panorama Merge Preview, which will look like this:

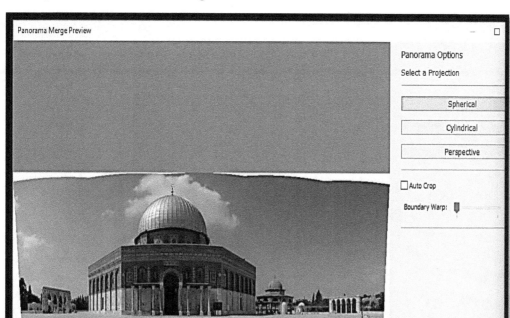

If you compare it to some third-party software, the Panorama Merge tool is very basic, with just a few choices. This makes it great for people who are just starting to stitch images together. Panorama projection comes in three main styles: spherical, cylindrical, and perspective. There are also two other styles: **"Auto Crop" and "Boundary Warp**." Let's examine each tool in more detail.

Panorama Projections

It's set to circular by default, which makes sense since most of the images you'll make with Lightroom will be circular. However, what is the difference between views that are spherical, cylindrical, and perspective? Take a look:

- **Spherical Projection**: Spherical Projection is the usual projection choice. It changes images so that they look like they were mapped to the inside of a sphere. This tool is great for making wide and multi-row images. When shooting close objects, the spherical warp usually gives the most realistic result because it doesn't stretch anything. Look at this round picture of the Dome of the Rock that I took in Jerusalem with my hand:

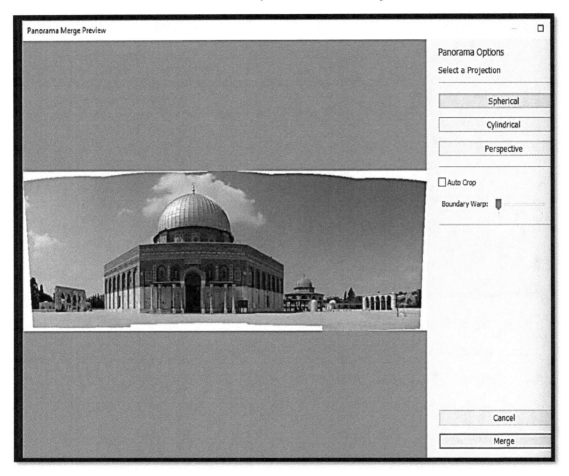

- o The picture that comes out is a little skewed, but it looks pretty real, like something you'd see from the same distance.
- **Cylindrical Projection:** This one changes pictures so that they look like they were mapped to the inside of a cylinder. It's good for wide views, but be careful when you use it because it will try to keep vertical lines straight, which can mess up your subjects a lot. Look at how it changes the shape of the building from the same set of panorama pictures:

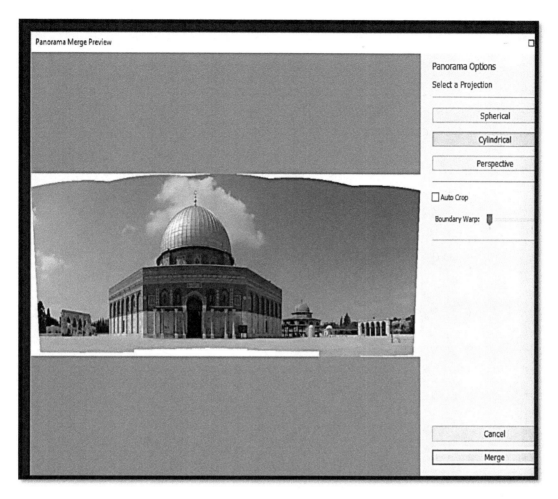

- o The roof doesn't show the truth; it looks like it's stretched too far. I don't think you should use Cylindrical Projection on landscape photos because it could stretch the scenery and make it look very fake. Be careful when you use it.

- **Perspective Projection:** This one is best for taking pictures of buildings and especially for putting together vertical views. When shooting at lower focal lengths, it can be hard to use for wide horizontal building panoramas because the lines at the edges of the picture might get bent. Look at the background of the same scene in Perspective Projection:

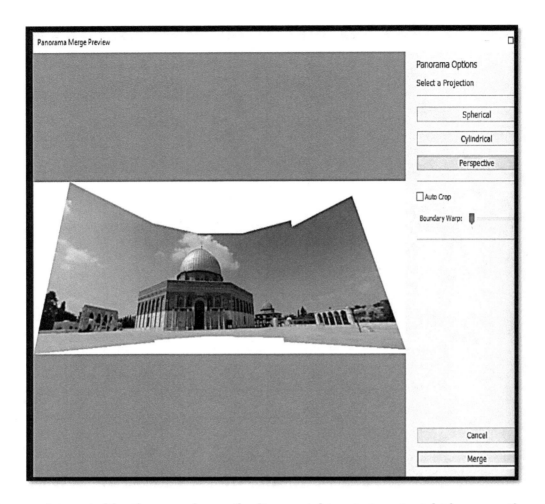

If your picture is like the one above, the lines might not stay straight because they are stretched too much, especially near the edges of the frame. The building is pretty well put together, but everything around it looks like it's going to fall apart. But sometimes the Perspective Projection is the only choice, like when you want to see buildings that go up and down over and over again. Check out the picture below, which was made from 4 vertical photos and is in Spherical Projection:

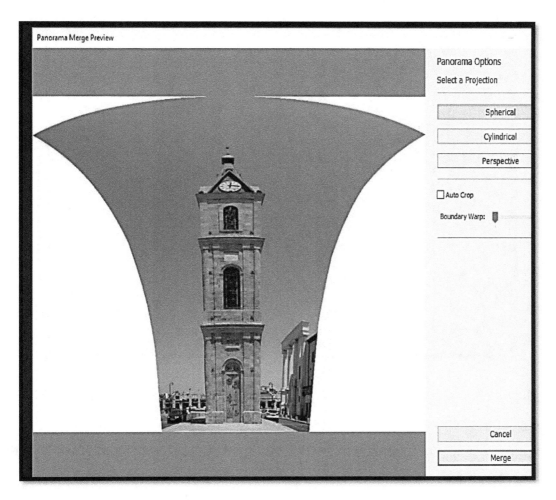

You can see that the clock tower has a strange shape, with the top of the building looking bent and bigger than the bottom. If you switch to Perspective Projection, the problem goes away and the building looks natural, with the right perspective:

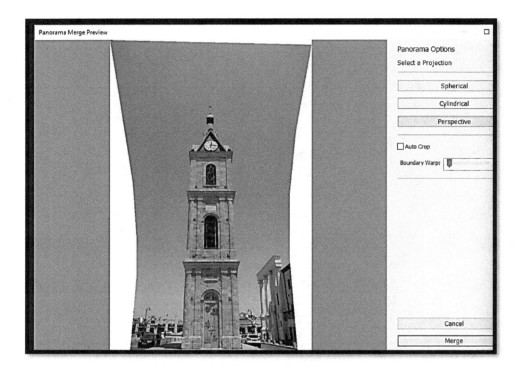

I think you should try out the different ways of projecting to see which one works best for each panorama picture. Some panoramas will only work with one projector method and panoramas that will work with all three. I prefer spherical projection most of the time because the pictures it makes look the most real. But, as you can see above, there are times when Cylindrical and Perspective views work better.

Auto Crop

As you can see in the screenshots above, the edges of the frame are often empty because most panoramas need to stretch pictures to fit the different types of projection. In this case, the "**Auto Crop**" option can be very helpful; it will find the empty spaces and crop the picture to fit them. Check out the picture below, which was made in Spherical Projection with the "Auto Crop" setting turned on:

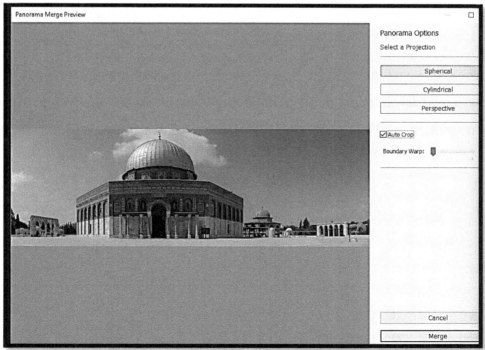

You can see that Lightroom resized the picture immediately to get rid of the white edges. This means I don't have to crop the picture in Lightroom before I can start working on it.

I really like this function and use it a lot, but there are times when you shouldn't use AutoCrop because it might cut out too much of the picture. You will lose a lot of the picture if your panorama is wide and some parts of the stitched panorama look much lower than the rest. To avoid too much clipping, you may be better off cropping pictures by hand in some situations.

I don't like how close the top of the dome is to the edge of the frame in the picture above. On the far right side of the view, there was too much empty room compared to the middle. In this case, I might choose to cut out the picture on the right and only lose a little room at the top of the frame.

"Boundary Warp," which we will talk about next, is another choice you can use in this case.

Boundary Warp

The Boundary Warp feature is fairly new to Lightroom (it's only in Lightroom CC right now), but it's a tool that was badly needed. It bends the whole view so that it fills the space and stretches out to reach it. In situations where lines or a horizon are not clearly defined, the border warp feature can work very well to keep most of the picture and lessen the effect of the Auto Crop feature. Let's look at the same Dome of the Rock picture, but this time we'll move the Boundary Warp to 100%:

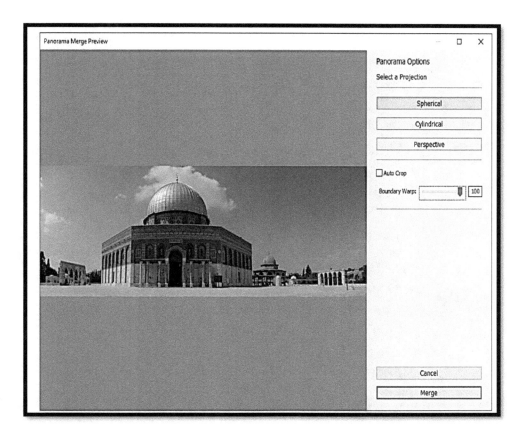

When the picture is set to 100%, there is no need for "Auto Crop" because it is stretched to the edges of the frame. To use this function at such a high level may work in some panoramas, but I think 100% is way too high for most panoramas because it makes lines stretch way too much.

You can see that the skyline isn't straight in the picture above; it looks a little crooked on the left and right sides of the frame. In this case, it's best to look at each picture on its own. I found that the best number for border warp on the picture above was 70, with Auto Crop turned on:

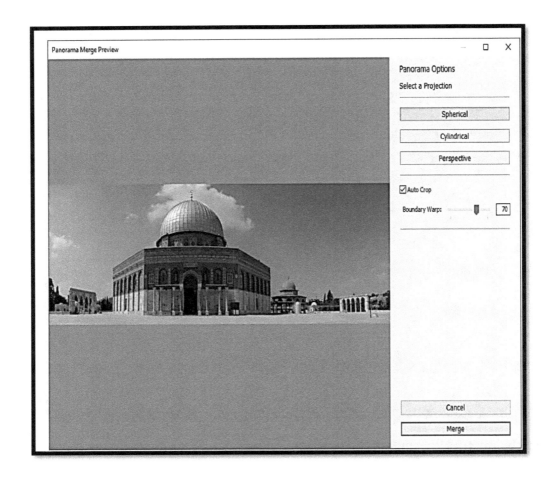

This is the version I'd like to work with because it gives me more "breathing space" at the top of the picture. Still, I'm not happy with the outcome because the cloud is cut off, and I'd like there to be a bit more sky in the picture. I could not zoom out or walk back in the field, so the only thing I could do was make a two-row picture, which is what we will talk about next.

Stitching Multiple-Row Panoramas

A multi-row panorama is made up of two or more rows. This is useful if you want to make a very high-resolution picture or if you want to catch more of the scene than your focal length will allow. And that's exactly what I did for the picture of the Dome of the Rock above: I made a two-row image:

The 8 pictures were stitched together pretty well by Lightroom. There are 4 in the top row and 4 in the bottom row. Before I knew it, I had a high-resolution picture that was bigger than a single-row panorama. But it took a while to stitch. Even though I cut out the backdrop and part of the sky in the final picture, you can see why shooting in more than one row might be helpful in some cases.

I have made a lot of multi-row landscapes in Lightroom so far. Two-row landscapes are what I do most of the time because I want to get more detail out of them. But remember that it will be harder to stitch landscapes if you have more rows. Lightroom might not be able to stitch more than two rows because it needs a lot of memory and resources. Most of the time, I don't go over two rows, but I have tried making three-row landscapes in the past, with mixed results.

Finishing Up in Photoshop

For the most part, Lightroom does a great job of joining photos together, but sometimes you'll need to take a panorama into Photoshop to fix problems with joining and other distortions. While this doesn't happen very often, there are times when you might have small parallax mistakes, too much bending that needs to be fixed, or subjects that need to be copied. When Lightroom was done putting the above picture of the Dome of the Rock together, it was clear that the image was warped. The lines look like they are bent in ways that don't make sense in many places. To fix the problem, I had to bring the image into Photoshop and use the Warp tool to straighten out the lines:

And here is the end picture after I fixed it up in Photoshop:

I made the sky more even, increased the contrast, and cropped the picture even more to make the design a little tighter (click to expand). The picture that comes out is about 20,000 pixels wide and 8200 pixels high, which is enough to print at 150 dpi on a 133-by-54-inch sheet of paper.

CHAPTER FIFTEEN

CREATING A SAVED SLIDESHOW

Saved Slideshow

In the Slideshow module, you were working on a slideshow that hadn't been saved yet, as shown in the bar at the top of the Slideshow Editor view.

The Slideshow module can be used as a makeshift work area until you are ready to save your slideshow. Your settings will still be in Lightroom Classic when you come back from another module or close it. The "**scratch pad**" will be wiped and all of your work will be lost if you change the slideshow template in the Template Browser.

You can save your project as a slideshow and keep the layout and playing settings. Also, your drawing will stay linked to the set of pictures it was made for. Your slideshow is a different type of collection that you can find in the **Collections** panel. You can quickly get to the pictures and things will be back to normal if you choose this offering, even if you cleared the slideshow scratchpad more than once.

1. The toolbar at the top of the Slideshow Editor View has an option to save a slideshow. You can also click on the **plus sign (+)** in the Collections panel's title and then choose Create Slideshow.

2. Give your saved presentation the name Desert Slideshow in the Create Slideshow box. Pick "Inside" from the Location drop-down menu, then pick the "Red Sands" collection from the list, and finally click "**Create**." The "**Make New Virtual Copies**" option lets you easily change the way all the photos in your slideshow look, like using a developing preset, while leaving the original photos in the source collection alone.

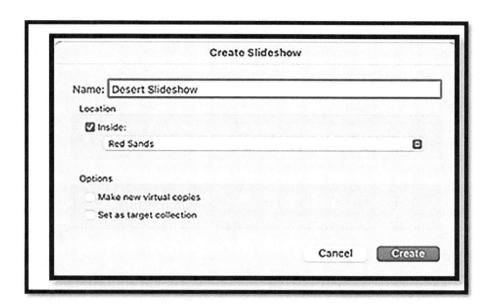

There is no longer a "**Create Saved Slideshow**" button in the title bar above the Slide Editor. It now shows the name of the saved slideshow instead. The saved slideshow can be found in the Collections panel, which has a button that says "**Saved Slideshow**." It's in the Red Sands source collection. With nine pictures, the number of pictures in the new collection shows that it is the same as the source.

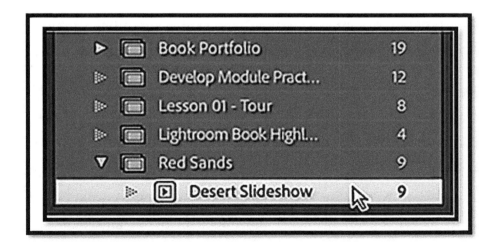

You can save your slideshow at any time during the process. When you go into the Slideshow module, you can save a slideshow with a mix of pictures right away, or you can wait until your talk is over. You can save your slideshow and then make changes to the layout or playing settings. These changes are saved immediately as you work through the slides. You can change the order of the slides in your show without changing the original set if you save the project now.

This picture will no longer be in the Desert Slideshow output collection if you take it out of the slideshow. It will still be in your Red Sands collection, though. If you want to use the pictures in the Red Sands collection to make, say, a print layout and a web gallery, this could come in handy. Even though your main collection stays the same, each project's result collection might have a different set of pictures in a different order.

Refining the content of a slideshow

Pick out all of the photos you want to use in your slideshow before you set the choices for how it will play. If your slideshow is synced with a sound file, you might need to change how the slides and transitions play after you remove a picture. Moving more pictures to a saved slideshow is simple: just click and drag them to the slideshow's listing in the Collections panel.

Place the mouse over the slideshow you want to see in the Collections panel and click the white arrow next to the number of pictures. This will take you from the Library to the Slideshow module where you are making your presentation. These are the steps:

1. To get rid of the background picture you used, right-click on the picture you want to remove from the Filmstrip and choose "Remove from Collection." The picture is no longer visible in the Filmstrip or on any slide in the show. However, it is still part of the background of the slide in the Slide Editor view.

The background picture is now part of the layout of the slides, not just one of the photos that will be shown.

Even if you change every picture in your slideshow, the background picture will still be the same. A straight link to the picture is in the saved slideshow. This link is not affected by the collection from which the photo came or the collection that holds it. The parent collection still has nine photos, but the inner Desert Slideshow output collection only shows eight in the Collections panel.

2. Change where the picture is in the Filmstrip. When the black entry bar shows up, let go of the mouse button.

Adding sound and motion to your slideshow

You could improve your presentation by putting video clips on different slides that follow your layout like you do with pictures. You could then add stroke borders, shadows, and overlays to make them look better. Adding music and film-like pan and zoom effects that bring the pictures to life is an easy way to make a slideshow with still pictures moodier and sadder. In your folder, there is a sound file named desert-rc.mp3. This music will go well with the slideshow's lively and classic theme. You can pick any other song from your library if you'd rather. I think a short piece would work best since there aren't many pictures in the slideshow.

1. Make sure that the Music and Playback panels on the right are expanded. To turn on the music for your slideshow, toggle the switch on the left side of the title of the Music panel. Click on "Add Music," browse to the folder, pick out the

"desert-rc.mp3" file, and then click "Choose." In the Music panel, you can see the name of the sound file and how long it lasts.

2. Select the Intro Screen and Ending Screen choices by expanding the Titles panel. Do not select the option to add an ID plate on either screen. Now it's time to change the slideshow's timing by making the slides and transitions last the same amount of time as the music file.

3. When you click the Fit to Music button, the Slide Length and Crossfades numbers in the Playback panel will change. If you get a message saying the message is too long, shorten the time between Crossfades. The timing is perfectly set so that the eight pictures and two opening screens play at the same time as the music file.

4. Change the Crossfades scale to make the fade changes a little longer, and then press the Fit to Music button again while keeping an eye on the Slide Length value. Lightroom changes the length of the slide to match the length of the music file, even if the fades are long.

5. Uncheck the boxes next to Repeat Slideshow and Random Order in the Playback panel. Choose the first picture in the Filmstrip in the Slideshow Editor view. Then, press the Preview button at the bottom of the right panel group to see how the slideshow will look. When you're done, press the Esc key to play something else. Adding music to the show makes it more like a story. Moving parts will be added next to turn it into a journey from a story.

6. From the Playback panel, pick the **Pan and Zoom** menu item. Move the slider about a third of the way to the middle of the range between Low and High to set the effect level. A higher setting on the Pan and Zoom tool makes the

movement faster and wider. A lower setting makes the movement slow and more like a full-frame view.

7.   Make sure the first picture is chosen in the Filmstrip. This will make the slideshow show up in full-screen mode. Click the Play button at the bottom of the right panel group. If you press the space bar, you can start and stop playing. When you're done with the slideshow, just press the Esc key.

You can make your slideshow's music play with up to 10 different songs. Just move the files around in the list in the Music panel to change the order in which they play. You can improve a slideshow by adding sound files that aren't part of the lesson project. To do this, press the "**Add Music**" button.

There may be more than one sound file in your slideshow. If you press the "Fit to Music" button, the slides and transitions will be adjusted to fit all of the music tracks. The Fit to Music button, the Slide Length and Crossfades settings, and Sync Slides to Music will all be turned off if you do this.

Lightroom changed the time of the slideshow to match the beat and key sounds in the music after it looked at the sound file. This tool in the Playback panel lets you mix the sounds of the video clips in your slideshow with the music.

The Playback Screen area will show up at the bottom of the Playback panel when you add a second display. You can then choose which screen will play your slideshow in full screen and choose whether the other screen should stay blank while the slideshow plays.

Saving a customized slideshow template

Your slideshow template will now be a new option in the Template Browser after you have saved it after making changes to it. Before, you saved your slideshow, but this is not the same thing. They were saved with certain settings, and now they are in a saved slideshow. When you save a custom template, it only remembers the layout of your slides and the playback settings; it doesn't connect to any pictures.

Adjusting and arranging user templates with expertise

Explore the various options available in the Template Browser for organizing your templates and template folders as outlined below:

Changing the name of a template or folder

You can't change the name of the Lightroom Designs folder, any of the built-in designs, or the User Templates folder that comes with Lightroom. Simply right-click on a template or folder in the Template Browser and choose the Rename option from the menu to change the name of any of your made templates or folders.

Moving a template

Just drag a template to the folder you want to move it to. Simply right-click on a template and select **"New Folder"** from the menu that appears to move it to a different folder. The chosen template will be moved to the new folder as soon as it is made. There will be a copy of the template in the new folder while you move it. The first copy will stay in the Lightroom Templates folder.

Adjusting settings in a personalized template

In the Template Browser, find one of your custom designs and click on it. Then, use the controls in the right panel group to make changes. To keep the changes you made, just right-click on the template in the Template Browser and choose Update with Current Settings.

Making a copy of a template

You could make changes to a template without changing the original by making a copy of it. Press the Create New Preset button (+) in the Template Browser panel title to make a copy of the template you are currently viewing in an existing template folder. Give the copy a name in the New Template dialog box and pick a folder from the Folder menu to put it in.

Then click on **Build**. Simply hit the **Create New Preset** button (+) in the top right corner of the Template Browser panel to make a copy of the template you've selected in a new folder. After that, name the copy in the New Template box and pick New Folder from the Folder menu.

Next, in the New Folder box, type a name for your folder. After that, click Make. You can now see the new folder in the Template Browser. Click the Close button in the New Template box when you're done. A new folder will be made and the copied template will go in it.

Exporting a custom template

Right-click on the name of the custom slideshow template in the Template Browser and choose Export from the menu. This will let you use the template in Lightroom on a different computer.

Adding a custom template

To bring in a custom Lightroom template made on a different computer, just right-click on the User Templates menu or any template in it, and then choose Import from the menu that comes up. To use the Import Template box, find the template file and click Import.

Getting rid of a template

As you move your mouse over the template name in the Template Browser, a menu will appear. Select "Delete" from that menu. To get rid of a template, just click the "Delete Selected Preset" button in the Template Browser's bottom right corner. The designs in the Lightroom designs folder can't be deleted.

Making a new templates folder

In the Template Browser, right-click on the title of any folder or template and choose "New Folder" from the menu that comes up. This will make a new empty folder. It's easy to add layouts to the new folder.

Getting rid of a templates folder

First, remove or move all of the models in a folder to another folder. Then delete or move the folder itself. Right-click on a folder and pick "Delete Folder" from the menu that appears. It will save you a lot of time to save your customized slideshow template. You can then use it to make a similar presentation or as a starting point for a new design. Your personalized template will be shown with the other user designs in the Template Browser panel.

1. The **Create New Preset** button is at the top of the Template Browser panel. You can click on it or go to **Slideshow > New Template** while your slideshow is still open.

2. You should name the new template "Centered Title" in the "New Template" box. From the Folder menu, make sure that the User Templates folder is selected as the file to be sent. After that, click Make. It's a good idea to give a modified template a specific name before you save it. As you add more templates to the Template Browser, this will help people find them more quickly.

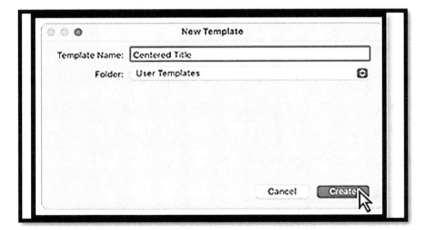

The custom template you made has been successfully put into the User Templates part of the Template Browser panel.

Exporting a Slideshow

You have the option to download your slideshow as either a PDF file or a high-quality video file if you want to send it to a friend or client, play it on a different computer, or post it online.

1. In the Slideshow module, click on the Export PDF button at the bottom of the group of panels on the left.

2. The Export Slideshow To PDF box has a lot of choices. Pay close attention to the size and quality settings. Press the Cancel button. It works when you look at a PDF slideshow in Adobe Reader® or Adobe Acrobat. Still, PDF copies of slideshows won't have music, the ability to set the length of each slide, or the ability to play them in any order.

3. Follow the steps again for the "Export Video" button. Look at the Export Slideshow To Video text box and pay attention to the Video Preset menu's different options. As you select an export option, a short explanation will show up below the Video Preset menu. You can save slideshows as MP4 movies in Lightroom Classic. This makes it easy to share them on video sites or cell phones. 480 x 270 pixels can be used for a mobile media player or email, but 1080p is the best setting for HD video.

4.   When you move your slideshow to a video, you need to give it a name and pick a folder to save it in. From the Video Preset menu, choose an option. Then, click Export to move on.

In the top left area of the workspace, a progress bar shows how far along the export process is.

Playing an impromptu slideshow

Even if you're not using the Slideshow module, you can still show a slideshow on the spot. In the Library module, it's easy to see a full-screen sample of the pictures you just added. Choose **"Use For Impromptu Slideshow"** from the menu that comes up when you right-click on a template in the Slideshow module Template Browser. For the last-minute slideshow, this will let you change the slideshow template.

It is easy to start the slideshow right away with any of the Lightroom Classic features. For the last-minute presentation, the template picked in the Slideshow module will decide how the slides are put out, when they play, and how they move from one slide to the next. If you haven't picked one yet, the Slideshow module will use the ones that are already there if you haven't changed them.

1.   You should go to the Library module. Pick the **"Previous Import"** option in the Catalog panel. You can change the order of your pictures by using the Sort menu and the Sort Direction button (which looks like an "A" above a "Z") in the Grid view toolbar.

2.   Press **Command+A or Ctrl+A**, or go to Edit > Select All, and then click on the first picture in the Grid view. This will select all the pictures from the last import. The Toolbar has a button called "Impromptu Slideshow" that you can

use in the Library and Develop sections. Pick Slideshow from the menu at the right end of the Toolbar if you can't see the Impromptu Slideshow button.

3. To begin the unplanned slideshow, select Window > unplanned Slideshow or press Command+Return/Ctrl+Enter on your computer.

4. To stop and restart playback, press the space bar. The chosen pictures will keep showing in the slideshow until you press the Esc key or click anywhere on the screen to stop it.

You have learned more about the Slideshow module and how to use the control panels to make a slideshow template on your own.

Suggested Settings for a Slideshow

It is important to remember that you do not have to use all of the features, even though they are all there. Most of the time, when we make videos, we keep things simple and make small changes to fit my brand.

Pick the Simple template from the Template Browser since most of the time we want to talk about pictures. Setting the borders to 72 pixels is easy. Just click on the Layout panel. In the Options panel, change the stroke's edges to a dark gray color (R=20%, G=20%, B=20%) and make them 1 px wide. Make sure that the Background panel only has a black background option. In the Overlays panel, none of the choices have been picked.

We added starting and end screens in the Titles panel for a while. There's a lot that can go wrong when you show a slideshow to a client or a group of people. We'd rather pick when the first picture in my slideshow appears. We might think about introducing ourselves or setting the scene before the project starts. On the Intro Screen, you can add a plate with your company's information on it. Picking "Use A Styled Text Identity Plate" is the simplest option.

We put in the name of my company and picked the font Helvetica Neue Condensed Bold. Use the Scale tool in the Titles panel to change the size of the text once your ID plate is ready. This will make sure it looks great in the presentation. The writing is helpful, but I need to change it to fit my needs. You might be able to use Photoshop too if you can use Lightroom.

I signed a name graphic in Photoshop with a tablet and pen. The graphic had one text layer as well. This picture was saved as a see-through PNG file. The colored fill at the bottom is only there to show how the white type looks. The Graphical Identity Plate option can be found in Lightroom's Identity Plate Editor. After that, click "Find File" and pick the PNG image.

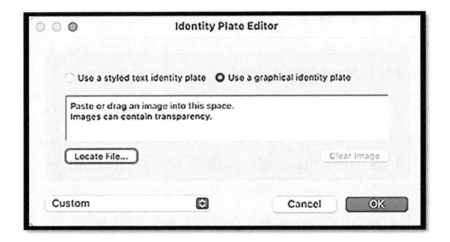

The slideshow is now unique to me because I added my logo to it. Pick the "**Ending Screen**" option and leave it blank. Make sure that the "**Add Identity Plate**" button is not checked. You have the option to start the show and then pause it right away during the presentation. If you leave your name or image on the screen, you can professionally introduce yourself or your work before the show starts.

CHAPTER SIXTEEN

USING PEOPLE VIEW

People View

Lightroom Classic features a standard interface. Lightroom's user interface features a new slider in the updated **'People View'** section.

Activating 'People View' in Lightroom

The Lightroom icon is in the upper left corner of the screen. Open Lightroom and click on it. Just click on Tools and then on Preferences. To use Lightroom, open the Preferences window and pick it from the list on the left. Select the "**Advanced**" option from the right column. In the "**People View**" area, make sure that "**Feature Photo**" is set as the usual **People View**.

How to Adjust the People View Effect in Lightroom

The People's view allows for minor adjustments to the way that features of people show. It is normal to make three adjustments:

- When you press Ctrl+M, a new editing window will appear. Use the selection tool in this window. To go from "People View" to "Background," click on a picture in the dropdown menu and drag the pick to the new spot. Close the window and go back to Lightroom Classic to finish your choice when you're done with the job.

- Press **Ctrl+Shift+L** in Lightroom Classic to get to the Look menu. The things you picked will be on the menu when you look at it. Select tools can be found by clicking on "**Refine Selection**." The tool that makes things bigger is in the bottom left area. In the People view, you can use it to get a better look at your pick. The pick can be turned with the zoom tool. Change the things you're doing until you get what you want. After you close Lightroom Classic, go back to Lightroom CC.

- There is a new Edit window in Lightroom Classic that you can open by pressing a set of keys. This window lets you get rid of the item you chose and set the people view back to how it was before. Don't forget to press the "**Save & Quit**" button in the top right area to get out of edit mode.

Quick Develop and Auto Tone

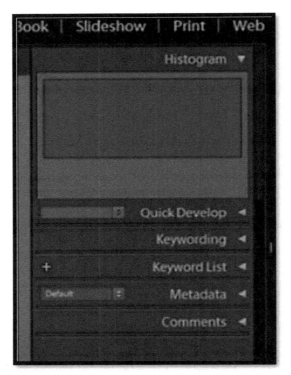

Even though Lightroom is designed for a particular kind of shooter, some people have asked about adding a "**Quick Develop**" mode and an "Auto Tone" feature. If you're having trouble, this can help you find the Quick Develop or Auto Tone sliders in Lightroom CC. People often want to know if they can turn on the Auto Tone button in Lightroom Classic CC. Yes, that's correct. Right-click on the Auto Tone and choose "**On/Off**." It is now possible to change the auto tone in Lightroom CC.

How to activate the Quick Develop button in Lightroom Classic 2025

You can find the Quick Develop button in the Develop Module, located in the sidebar.

- To turn on the Lightroom Classic "Quick Develop" button, just right-click on the Develop Module and pick "Edit."
- Go to the Edit panel and find the things that say "Enable/Disable Developer Panel." To turn on the module in the Connections group, click the radio button in the upper right corner next to it.
- On the Group page for the Develop Module, turn on the "Quick Develop" item.

How to Enable the Auto Tone Key in Lightroom

You can get to this key in the Develop Module by going to the Project page and then to the Group page.

- In Lightroom, find the "**Auto Tone**" button and press it to turn it on.
- Once you find the Auto Tone button, all you have to do is click on it.
- On the Group page of the Develop Module, press the Auto Tone button.

Simple steps on how to use "**Quick Develop**" and "**Auto Tone**" in Lightroom Classic

Color changes can be made quickly, which is one of Lightroom's best benefits. For effective color changes, you should use this tool with care and planning. It's better known as "Quick Develop" and "Auto Tone." Either way, these two terms describe how you can improve your photos in Lightroom so they stand out.

1. **Quick Develop**

   Select "Quick Develop" from the "Photo" menu to begin. Next, pick the color space you want to use.

2. **Auto Tone**

   After that, go to the "Photo" menu and choose "Auto Tone." Then, click on the "Auto Tone" tab.

3. **Speed Dial**

    Choose your first picture, then use the "Speed Dial" feature.

4. **Bevel/Grind Tool**

    You can find the "Bevel/Grind Tool" tab on the right side of the screen.

5. **Focus Mask**

    Press the "Focus Mask" button on the right side after picking out your subject.

6. **Darken**

    Find the "Darken" button on the left and press it.

7. Mask for Light

    In the upper right corner, click the "Luminosity Mask" button.

8. **Luminosity Mask**

    On the right side, click the "Hue/Saturation Mask" button.

9. **Vibrance**

    In the upper right corner, click on the "Vibrance" button.

10. **Power**

    On the right side, press the "Strength" button.

Merging Photos with HDR Panorama

It can be hard to make an HDR shot with Lightroom and Photoshop if you have ever tried. People often use post-processing to make HDR pictures look more real. Lightroom is set to Automatic by default. This gives you one photo where you can change only the shadows, one photo where you can only change the highlights, and one photo that you can just look at as is.

Right now, things are not going well. These two apps let you take an HDR shot, and then you can mix them to make the process go faster. If you want to make a beautiful full-color picture with better clarity, try the great HDR picture Photo Merge tool.

When you follow these steps, you can effectively merge your HDR Panorama Photos in Lightroom:

- Go to the Lightroom online interface to begin. Go to File > Site Preferences in Lightroom after opening it. Click on Advanced in the bottom right area. Click the "**Merge Photos**" box on the left when the window comes up. To save your work, click the "**Save**" button.

- Next, get out your phone and open the Lightroom app. In the top left area, click on the camera icon. Pick out a picture in **Capture One** and then go to Keyframe to make a picture of it. Pick the picture in the list that is right next to the default picture and has an HDR image.

- Wait a minute. Just click in the bottom right part of the screen to finish. A purple cloud is needed. The new picture will show up when you click on the cloud button.

- Select "**Merge and Retouch**" as your option. You should see two buttons on the right side. These are called Merge and Retouch.

Merge and Retouch

When you click the "**Merge and Retouch**" button, the combined picture will be chosen immediately. There is a Retouch button right below the join button. Pick up the Retouch button. To make a seamless HDR panorama picture, the shot should be combined and the shadows and highlights should be changed individually.

To change the direction of the shadows and highlights, use the small arrow going to the right. You should try things out on both sides to get the best results. With just one click of the Unite button, you have the option to combine all of your HDR Panorama Photos.

Installing Presets

It takes a long time to set up Lightroom Classic (64-bit) or Lightroom CC (32-bit), which is a problem with the preset system. If you want to quickly add your profiles to the "custom presets" pane, click on the plus sign (+) in the top right corner of your Lightroom window after that. After adding the Lightroom presets, you can change how each one looks to make your pictures look better.

When you save original files in the Camera Roll and change the file type to JPG, the camera may use different settings when rendering the JPG file instead of the RAW file. Your original RAW files should be changed to JPG files before you use a preset. This way, you can still use your original pictures in that preset.

Configuring Presets in Lightroom Classic (64-bit) and Lightroom CC (32-bit) Personalized Settings:

- Use the sliders to crop, blend, clone, change the roundness, tilt, and work with stacked negatives to change the picture.
- Making a copy of a part of your picture and moving it to another area makes it easy to edit and change. For this method to work, you need to duplicate your experience.
- Use the buttons to fine-tune the brightness of different parts of the shot and make sure the brightness is the same everywhere. Then, make the necessary changes to the contrast levels.

Presets in Lightroom

The following are some of them:

- They are Proxies, Levels, Contrast, Tonal Contrast, DaVinci Resolve, and The Element. These presets will be used on your raw files.

- Moving the main and secondary buttons will change how bright the picture is. This helps when the subject is dark or can't be seen because of a bright window.

- In video editing, a background that looks like a cartoon character is often used to put the person in the shot. A lot of the time, this is changed to keep their attention on the most interesting part of the frame. When taking shots of animals, this is a great way to make your Bokeh look softer all the time. Most of the time, this will also affect the person's eyebrows.

Post-Processing Tips: Using Presets and Rounded Edges

You can change Lightroom presets, which makes them hard to use with JPEG files. In Lightroom, presets work well with raw files. This guide will teach you how to use Lightroom presets to improve the sharpness of your photos and how to trim the edges of your photos to make them look better. Hold down the word icon next to the adjustment icon on the right side of the layer you're at the moment. After that, move the circle clip to where you want it to appear.

Leave it where it is and let Lightroom do its thing. There will be no effects on any other layers in the stack because of the changes. Don't forget to apply the Lightroom custom effects to those levels. Hold down the angle sign and drag the arrow next to it to the right. Then do what you need to do. In this case, the Level scale was used. If you want a flat look, try the N (Neutral) slider instead of the Linear Bias slider.

When you use the **Right-Hand Tool**, always remember the right way to do it. It is important to always pick the sliders that match your adjustment goals. The angle slider helps you finetune how sharp your picture is generally. You can change the numbers by moving the button next to the click icon and then moving the click icon itself to the right.

To make the rounding feature stand out, hold down the sign icon and move the middle icon, the cloud, to the right. As the usual setting, enable the "shake" option. Most people would rather not wear it because the smooth edges can be annoying.

Enhancing Highlight Correction on JPEG Images

If your pictures are JPEGs, Lightroom has an adjustment layer called Highlight Corrector that you can use to make them brighter or clearer. If the rest of your picture isn't clear, this might help. Select Highlights in the menu and then add the Highlight Corrector Adjustment Layer on top of the picture layer. The Highlights button lets you change the amount of the Highlight Corrector Adjustment Layer as you move the Highlight Color slider.

Place your images on the map.

This module makes it easy to place items on the map and combine multiple pictures on top of each other. You can move the map around and choose which layers are visible or hidden. To pick an item, just click on it. To make sure everything goes together perfectly, click the "Resize" button at the bottom. If you haven't already, make sure to add the Map module before going any further.

Installing Lightroom Map Module

1. Select your Camera Profile in Lightroom CC, then click the "**Import New Folder**" option at the top. This is what will add to the module.

2. Click "**OK**," and Lightroom will put the.zip file in your library for you. This will let your camera's map module work. If you can afford it, you might want to get a professional DSLR because it is much harder to add map features to a consumer DSLR. Remember to save the file as MAP.plist to make the process go faster.

3. Save the file and then go to Lightroom's settings and pick "Map Pro." Make the square 2048x 2048 in size. Press "OK" to save the changes.

Lightroom Tip: Enhancing the Map Pro with Distance Markers

Once you have the Map Pro Module, you need to take certain steps to set it up so that it can be used in Lightroom. In the "File > New Map" module, find the Map Pro Map file. Change the map's spacing to 4096 by 4096.

- "**File > Open**" will let you get to the file. Get rid of the map's usual center mark and only show the GPS name.
- Click "**File > Open**" to go back to the Map module.
- Press the button to add an object to the map, and then pick where you want the object to place it. So that the GPS can properly figure out where your object starts and ends, you should give it a specific place instead of picking a random spot on the map. To do this, click on the "Convert to a coordinate map" button. To save the changes, press the "OK" button.

CHAPTER SEVENTEEN

ADVANCED PHOTO EDITING TECHNIQUES

Spot Removal

Step 1. Find the Spot Removal Tool

The tool for getting rid of spots is in Lightroom's Develop module. It's the second tool from the left, next to the Histogram.

You can choose to Clone or Heal in the upper right corner once that set of sliders opens.

Every gray dot shows a spot that needs to be fixed, and you can drag any of them to move the pick.

Step 2. Create a Spot to Correct

A white shape shows up when you click on the area that needs work. This is the spot that will be fixed.

At the same time, a white area with lines around it appears, and an arrow points to it from the first spot. The sampled spot is this second place.

You can click on a spot to pick it out and fix it, or you can click and drag to pick out a bigger area. The chosen area and the sample area will show up either way.

Step 3. Adjust Your Spot Selection

Once you've chosen the spot you want to fix, you can move the buttons! You can change the brush size, feathering, and density with the tools.

You can also move the sample area or the spot that was chosen to be fixed. Lightroom will pick a sample area that it thinks is a good match for the area to fix on its own. This isn't always the best place to take samples.

Click and drag either place until it's where you want it to be!

If you need to clone or fix more of an area, all you have to do is click on it again, and Lightroom will make a new spot removal brush there.

The spots that need to be fixed can be moved, removed, or changed at any time.

Tips and Shortcuts for the Spot Removal Tool

In order to be extra sure that all of the spots on a picture have been fixed, you can turn on the Visualize Spots option.

The Visualize Spots setting is in the bottom left area of the Develop module once the spot removal tool is open.

The picture will turn black and white if you check that. You can change how sensitive it is by moving the scale next to the option. This is the best way to see if any more small or hidden spots need to be fixed.

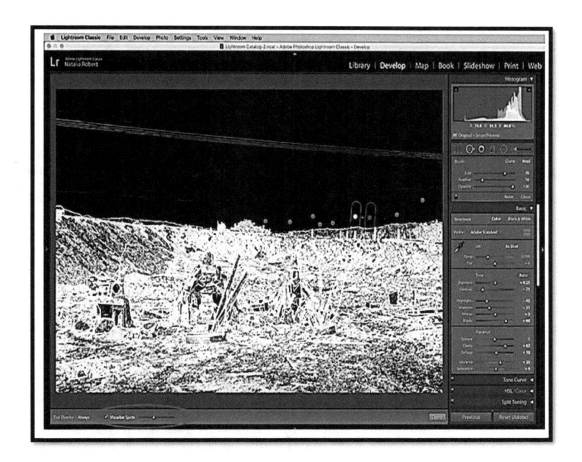

With the Visualize Spots tool, you can check to see if you missed any spots that need to be fixed.

How to Remove Blemishes And Soften Skin

Removing Blemishes

Step 1: In The Develop Tab, Click The Spot Remover Icon

When you open the picture that you want to change in Lightroom Classic's Develop tab, you'll see a bar with a few items above the Basic edits. To get rid of spots, click the button that looks like a Band-Aid.

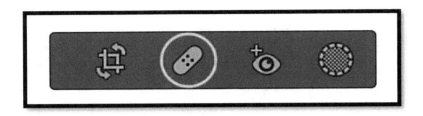

Note: If your picture goes black and white, it's because the bottom toolbar's "visualize spots" option is turned on. When getting rid of flaws, make sure Visualize Spots is not checked. That way, you can still see your subject.

Step 2: Pick Either The Heal Or Clone Spot Removal Brush And Adjust The Brush Settings

Up at the top of the right panel are the different settings for getting rid of spots.

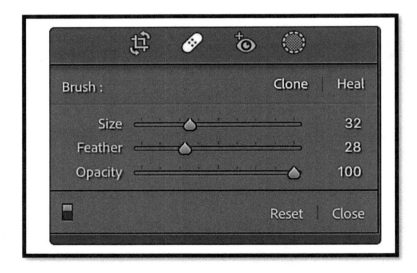

You can choose Clone or Heal next to Brush. The Clone setting copies pixels from an area around the area you brush over to fill in the blanks. The Heal setting, on the other hand, blends the colors and patterns of the area around the area you're fixing.

For now, let's choose Heal, which is the most common brush setting for getting rid of spots. You should change the brush settings to the best ones for your needs before you start to brush over spots. I think you should keep the Feathering level fairly high so that the healed area fits in well with the rest of the area.

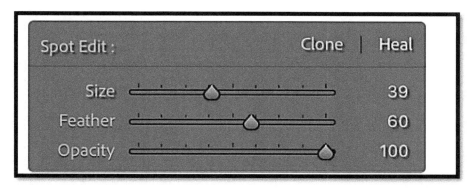

Step 3: Click The Blemish You'd Like To Remove

After setting up the settings, all you have to do is click on the spot you want to fix. The circle will show up on the spot, and there will be another circle close that will pull in sample color and texture to help the spot heal. To get a better healing spot, you can click and drag the example circle.

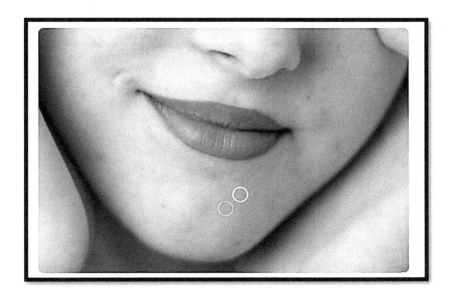

If there aren't any round spots, you can just click and drag the brush over them to fix them. You can quickly get rid of a spot adjustment by clicking it while holding down Alt (Windows) or Option (Mac). There will be a pair of scissors in your pointer at that point. Hold down Alt (Windows) or Option (Mac) and drag over the spots to get rid of them all at once.

Before

After

How To Soften Skin

Step 1: Click The Mask Icon And Select The Brush Option

Softening skin is another simple thing you can do in Lightroom to fix up your skin. We will do this with the adjustment brush, which you can find in the Pane of Masks. In the bar above the Basic tab, click the Mask button.

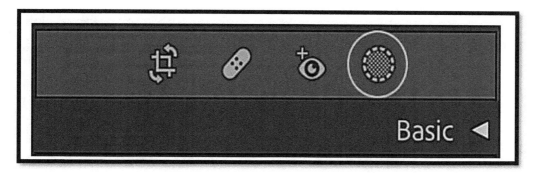

This will take you to the Masking panel, where you can choose from different masks to add a new one. Choose the "Brush" button.

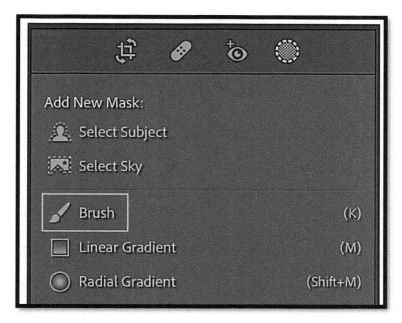

Step 2: Click The Drop-Down Menu Next To Effect To Select The Soften Skin Preset

We are now going to use the brush effect presets that come with Lightroom. These are a fairly recent edit that let you add brush lines to your picture that change how it looks. Click the drop-down button next to Effect to get to these presets. This is a list of the different brush presets that Lightroom has to offer. Soften Skin and Soften Skin (Lite) are the ones we'll talk about.

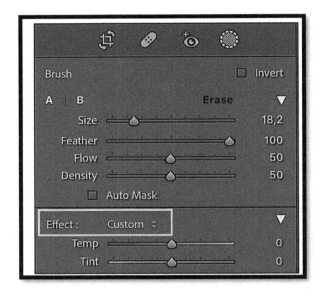

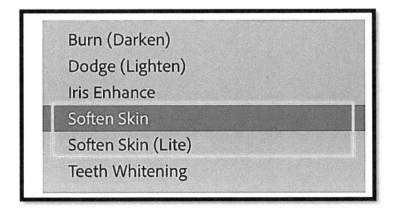

When these two effects are used together, the brush will lighten the area you block. They do this by setting the default changes to less grain or sharpness.

Step 3: Create Your Mask To Use The Soften Skin Preset

To easily paint over your subject's skin without covering any detail, such as their eyes or teeth, you should set the brush settings to a size big enough to do so. If you want the most realistic look, set Flow to 50 to 75 and Density to 100. You can also set Feather to 100 since we won't need any feathering with this brush. You could also check Auto-Mask, which helps keep your mask in an area with the same color or brightness so that you get a better result.

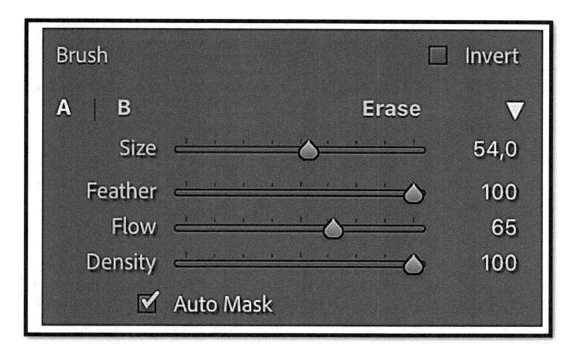

When you put the effect on the subject's face after masking the skin, you will see how smooth it looks.

Step 4: Reduce The Intensity Of The Preset (Optional)

It's possible to change the Texture and Clarity sliders to change how much or how little the skin-softening effect is felt. You can click and drag the toggles on the two effects in the brush changes area. If you drag the button to the left, it will make the skin look smoother, and if you drag it to the right, it will make it look rougher.

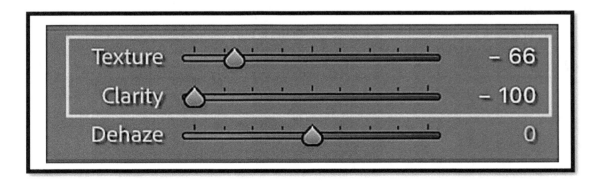

CHAPTER EIGHTEEN

INTEGRATION WITH PHOTOSHOP
Round-tripping between Lightroom and Photoshop

Going back and forth between Lightroom and Photoshop is a great way to work that lets you improve your photos using the best features of both. This is a step-by-step guide on how to quickly switch between these two Adobe programs:

1. **Start in Lightroom**

   o **Import and Organize**: Bring your pictures into Lightroom and use its powerful library management tools to put them in order.

   o **Basic Adjustments**: In Lightroom, make the first changes like exposure, white balance, cropping, and basic color fixes. These changes can be made later and are not permanent.

2. **Edit in Photoshop**

   o **Open in Photoshop**: Right-click a picture in Lightroom and select Edit In > Adobe Photo Shop to edit it in the program. With the Lightroom changes preserved, this will open the picture in PhotoShop as a smart object.

   o **Advanced Edits**: Use layers and masks, fix, and do other advanced editing tasks in Photoshop. For thorough and intricate changes, Photo Shop's tools are superior.

   o **Save and Return to Lightroom**: When you're done changing, go to File > Save in Photoshop and save the picture. You can continue to make changes in Lightroom after the edited picture has been saved back there.

3. **Back in Lightroom**

   o **Refine Adjustments**: You can continue fine-tuning the picture in Lightroom after saving the picture Shop changes. You can make more changes without changing the PhotoShop edits because Lightroom tweaks are non-destructive.

    ○   **Export and Share**: Once you're happy with the picture, you can send it out of Lightroom to share or print.

Tips for a Smooth Workflow

- **Use Smart Objects**: If you open a picture in Photoshop as a smart object, you can make changes in Lightroom and then save the file again in Photoshop.

- **Preserve Layers**: When you save a picture from Photoshop to Lightroom, make sure you save it in a file that keeps layers, like PSD or TIFF, so you can still edit it easily.

- **Stay Organized**: To keep track of which photos have been changed in Photoshop, use Lightroom collections and keywords.

Use Photoshop with Lightroom Effectively

How do I access Photoshop from Lightroom?

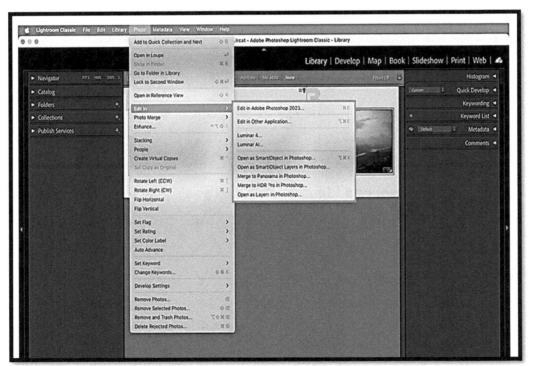

You likely use Lightroom Classic to edit photos as well as arrange files. But there are some things you can't do in LRc.

Lightroom processing is over, but you may want to do some cleaning or more advanced editing afterward.

You will need an editing program with image-changing tools, like Adobe Photoshop, to do this. This is why Lightroom lets you send pictures straight to Photoshop. You won't have to export your files again, so you can keep working.

You can go ahead and edit the pictures as you please, or you can do it for certain changes, like making an HDR or Panorama.

Edit In

You can keep working on your photos in Photoshop even if you only use Lightroom to handle your files or do simple edits.

To do this, go to Photo > Edit In > Edit in Adobe Photoshop. This will bring up the modified picture in Photoshop.

You can also do this by right-clicking on the picture. Then, from the choice that comes up, choose Edit In > Edit in Adobe Photoshop. This works in both the Library and the Develop module.

Keep in mind that when you work with raw files, Adobe Camera Raw won't be used.

This is important because when you open raw photos in Photoshop, the Adobe Camera Raw panel comes up. Plus, you can start changing the picture this way before you go to Photoshop.

If you send raw files from LR to PS, this won't happen. The raw file was already opened and "developed" by Lightroom before it was sent.

Open as a Smart Object

A Smart Object is a special kind of element in PS that lets you edit without destroying the original. In Photoshop, you can turn any picture into a Smart Object.

You can, however, open your Lightroom picture in Photoshop as a Smart Object right away. This improves the flow of work and speeds it up.

To do this, open Photoshop and go to Photo > Edit In > Open as a Smart Object.

Open as Smart Object Layers

You likely already know that Photoshop lets you use layers. You can then stack different parts of the same picture on top of each other. If you want to make one picture out of several, you can open them in LR as Smart Object layers.

Look through the Library and choose the pictures you want to use. Then, open Photoshop and go to **Photo > Edit In > Open as a Smart Object Layers**.

It will open a new Photoshop file for each shot. You can change one picture at a time without changing the others because each one will be in its own Smart Object layer..

Merge to Panorama

Lightroom has a tool that lets you combine several shots into one image. There aren't many ways to customize this function, though. Instead, Photoshop lets you handle the process better.

So, there is a tool you can use to send the photos from Lightroom to Photoshop. Pick out the pictures you want to use first. After that, open Photoshop and go to Photos > Edit In > Merge to Panorama.

This will start up Photoshop's tool for changing panoramas. In the Source Files area, you'll see that the pictures you chose in Lightroom are already there.

You can now start the process and change the settings. The panorama will open in Photoshop when it's done.

Merge to HDR Pro

High Dynamic Range (HDR) is a way to mix pictures that were taken at different settings after the fact. This way, even in scenes with a lot of contrast, you'll get the most detail in the highlights and blacks.

Lightroom does have an HDR tool, and you can also add plug-ins to make it even better. HDR Pro in Photoshop, has more skilled tools.

In Lightroom, you can pick which shots you want to mix. If you want to open them in HDR Pro, go to Photos > Edit In > Merge to HDR Pro in Photoshop.

Open as Layers

I already told you that Smart Object layers let you open more than one picture in a single Photoshop project. But you can also open them as layers with raster images.

To do this, just go to Photoshop and click on Photo > Edit In > Open as Layers. When you edit, remember to use layers so that you don't lose anything. You will change the source file if you work on the picture layer.

CHAPTER NINETEEN

BATCH PROCESSING AND AUTOMATION

Using the Quick Develop Panel

You can quickly make picture color and tone adjustments to one or more photos using the Quick Develop panel in the Library module without leaving the library. When you use the Quick Develop panel to make changes to multiple shots, those changes are relative, not absolute. Any Quick Develop settings you make are saved in the History panel of the Develop module. In the Basic panel, the sliding controls that go with those settings are also saved.

1. Choose at least one picture from the Grid view in the Library module.

2. Do any of these things in the Quick Develop panel:

   o From the Saved setting menu, pick a Develop setting. When you make changes to other settings in the Quick Develop panel, the option moves to Custom immediately. By selecting the Default Settings preset, photos are returned to the original settings used when they were imported into Lightroom Classic.

Tip: To quickly get to a different part of the Saved Preset list, type a letter. For instance, type S to get to the Sharpening setting.

- o To crop pictures, use the pop-up menu to select a new crop ratio. To make the list bigger, press Enter Custom, type in new crop sizes for the width and height in the Aspect Ratio boxes, and press OK.
- o To turn pictures into grayscale, go to the **Treatment** tab and choose **Grayscale**.
- o Pick a white balance setting from the White Balance menu that pops up and use it.
- o Change the **Temperature and Tint** settings to fine-tune the white balance. You can slowly raise or lower the Kelvin temperature, green tint, or magenta tint by clicking the direction buttons.
- o Change the tone settings for each person by clicking their arrow buttons. For instance, you can change the general brightness of the picture by pressing the Exposure buttons. With each click, the brightness is changed by one full stop or a third of an f-stop.
- o To use Lightroom Classic's default settings for Exposure, Blacks, Brightness, and Contrast, click the "**Auto Tone**" button.

Tip: To change the tone of photos instantly, go to Presets and choose the "**Apply Auto Tone Adjustments**" option.

- o Change the Clarity setting to make the image's mid-tones stand out more.
- o Change the Vibrance setting to change the intensity of all colors that aren't very saturated. This will have less of an effect on very saturated colors.
- o Press Alt (Windows) or Option (macOS) to see the settings for Sharpening and Saturation. You can change how sharp and deep the colors are in your picture with these settings.

The settings can be changed more slowly with the single-arrow buttons than with the double-arrow buttons.

Reset Quick Develop adjustments

- Press Ctrl+Z (Windows) or Command+Z (Mac OS) to undo changes you make in the Quick Develop panel as you try them out.
- To get a picture back to the way it was when it was imported into Lightroom Classic, click the "Reset All" button at the bottom of the "Quick Develop" panel or go to "Photo > Develop Settings > Reset."
- To get rid of all settings, choose General - Zeroed from the Saved Preset pop-up choice in the Quick Develop box.

CHAPTER TWENTY

PRINTING AND PRESENTING PHOTOS

Preparing Photos for Print

1. **Calibrate Your Monitor**

   Color Calibration: To set up your monitor, use a hardware calibration tool, such as the X-Rite i1Display Pro or Datacolor SpyderX for color calibration. This makes sure that the colors you see on your screen are the same as the colors that are printed.

2. **Edit Your Photos**

   Basic Adjustments: Changes to the Basics Use simple changes like exposure, contrast, white balance, black balance, highlights, and shadows.

   Color Corrections: Make changes to the white balance, brightness, and vibrance to make sure the colors are right.

   Detail Enhancements: As needed, sharpen and reduce noise, but don't sharpen too much because it can cause print flaws you don't want.

3. **Set the Correct Resolution**

   Resolution for Print: Make sure your picture has a resolution of 300 DPI (dots per inch) in the Develop module. This is the standard for good prints.

4. **Soft Proofing**

   Enable Soft Proofing: To turn on soft proofing, go to the Develop module and check the box next to the picture that says "Soft Proofing." This makes your picture look like it will when it's printed.

   Choose a Profile: Pick the ICC profile that works with the paper and printer you want to use. You can get the information from the website of the printer or paper maker if you don't already have it.

Adjust for Print: Make any necessary adjustments to ensure that the colors and tones look good in the soft print sample view. If you see any colors that aren't in the right range, they might not print right.

5. **Output Sharpening**

    Export with Sharpening: Use output sharpening when you export your picture to print it. Under "Output Sharpening" in the Export window, choose "Sharpen For: Matte Paper" or "Glossy Paper" based on the type of paper you want to use, and then choose how much sharpening you want (Standard is usually a good choice).

6. **Export Settings**

    File Format: Pick either TIFF or JPEG. The best-quality copies should be made with TIFF, but JPEG at its best quality can also work.

    Color Space: If you want a bigger range of colors, set the color space to Adobe RGB (1998). If your printer needs sRGB, you can also do this.

    Image Sizing: Make sure the size is set to 300 pixels per inch (PPI).

    Dimensions: Choose the exact sizes of the print you want to make. To avoid cropping problems, make sure the aspect ratio fits the size of the picture.

How to Make A Print In Adobe Lightroom

After setting up your equipment correctly and getting your pictures ready, you're ready for the magic step: printing them with Adobe Lightroom. Take a quick look at the Print module in Adobe Lightroom. First, pick out a picture, then just click on Print.

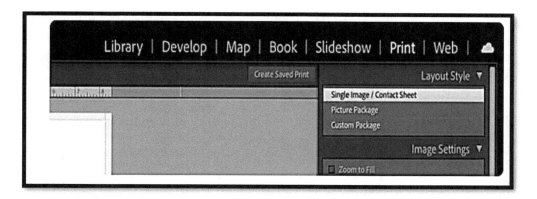

Even though we're only going to talk about printing one picture here, it's important to know that Lightroom can print more than one picture on the same sheet of paper, like a contact sheet.

1. **Set Your Paper and Printer**

   As soon as you get to the Print module, you need to set a few simple choices for the print to work. In Adobe Lightroom, start by picking on Page Setup in the bottom left area.

   When you click on the Paper Size dropdown, pick a setting that fits the size of paper you want to use. To enter a custom page size, select **Manage Custom Sizes** instead.

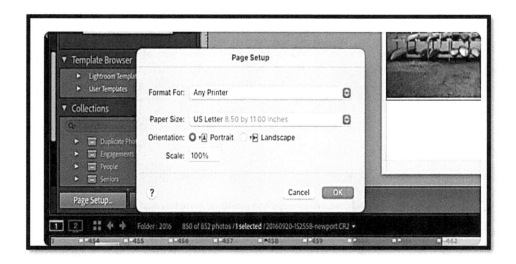

Click on Print Settings now. If you're already linked, start by picking out your printer.

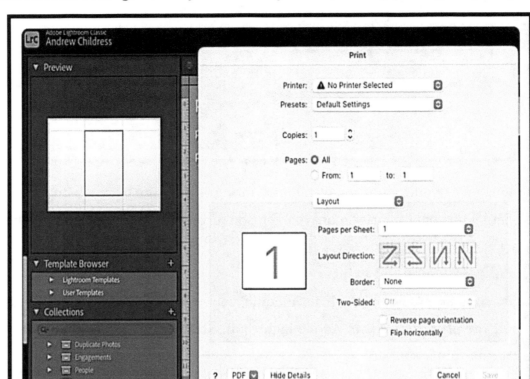

These settings are pretty simple to use if you only need to print one picture. Do not change the Layout Direction. Just leave one page per sheet if you want to keep things easy. Change the number of Copies if you want to print more than one.

2. **Set Your Margins**

   Now we can work on changing how our picture prints and how much paper it takes up. Allow us to begin by setting our Margins. You can find the choices on the right side of the Develop module.

   Margins give you room around the page's edge for safety. I'm going to put in a 0.50-inch space on all sides for my case. Check the printer's settings to see what it can do, then set the page to match.

Do not change the size of your image's edges yet; we will do that next. Think of them as a "margin of safety" that will keep you from cutting off your picture by mistake. A very wide space could also help you move your picture away from something like a scratch or wrinkle on one side of the page.

3. **Set The Cell Size**

    It looks like your page has a lot of empty room now. The Cell Size needs to be changed so that the end print is bigger.

    Make the print the size you want it to be by changing the Height and Width settings. If you know just how you want your print to look, you can type in a size. The size you typed in is shown by the black box in your image.

Remember that the aspect ratio is a very important part of how your picture looks. In the end, the cell size must have the same aspect ratio as the source picture, or you will have to cut off some of the images.

You could also just mess around with these options and make them as big as they can be on the page. Keep in mind that the Guide we set in the last step will stop you from making the picture bigger than the guided area.

4. **Set the Print Job**

    We are almost done. Set the Print Resolution as high as your printer will let you for the best quality. Check the printer's specs to make sure the pictures work. Epson printers, for instance, can print at 360 dpi (dots per inch), but they can also do fine at lower multiples: It's fine to make copies at 240 dpi; it uses less ink.

Then, change the settings for sharpening. A little sharpening makes the picture shine.

5. **Create Your Print**

The only thing left to do is start the print job. To print the job, press Print. On the pop-up window, you can also save it as a PDF. If you're not near the printer right now, this is the best choice.

You can also make a test print if you're not sure about the look or the settings. Before you print the whole page, change the cell size to print a narrow band of your picture, like a 1- or 2-inch strip on an 8x10 print. Test strips are very important if you want to make big, high-quality prints to show off or sell.

CHAPTER TWENTY-ONE

TROUBLESHOOTING AND TIPS

Common Issues and Solutions

Adobe Lightroom Updates Issues

Two important things should be done before updating Adobe Lightroom: make sure your machine can run the latest version and make a copy of your data. This keeps your work safe and makes sure that updates go smoothly.

Checking OS Compatibility

Compatibility is very important for an update to work. The newest version of Lightroom might need certain operating system (OS) requirements. It's easy to check:

- **For Windows users:** If you use Windows, make sure you have at least Windows 10 (64-bit).

- **For Mac users:** If you have a Mac, your OS should be at least Mojave (number 18.14).

If your OS doesn't meet these needs, you might want to update it first. To avoid problems with installing Lightroom, this step is very important.

Backing Up Your Lightroom Catalog and Images

It's like having insurance for your work when you back up your info. Here are some steps to take before updating:

1. Make a backup of your Lightroom album, which has all of your changes and settings. On a PC, go to **Edit > Catalog Settings**. On a Mac, go to **Lightroom Classic > Catalog Settings**. Choose how often you want to back up by clicking on Back Up Catalog.

2. Make a copy of your photos: For extra safety, keep them on a different drive or in the cloud.

The Update Process

It's not as hard as it might seem to update Adobe Lightroom. This part will walk you through the steps one by one, making sure the update goes smoothly and quickly.

Navigating the Adobe Creative Cloud for Updates

To begin, Adobe Creative Cloud is where you should go to keep Lightroom up to date. Here's how to get around it:

1. **Open Adobe Creative Cloud:** You can usually find it in the system tray or the program folder.
2. **Locate Lightroom:** Under **"Installed Apps"** in the "Apps" tab is Adobe Lightroom.
3. **Check for Updates:** It will say next to Lightroom if there is an update available. Then click "**Update.**"
   Click the "**Check for Updates**" button if you can't find them. It takes a while for new changes to show up sometimes.

Troubleshooting Common Update Issues

The update process may run into problems from time to time. What are some usual problems and how do you fix them?

- **Update not showing:** Make sure that the Creative Cloud app is up to date. If not, make changes first.
- **Installation errors:** Make sure you can connect to the internet and that your gadget has enough room. It might also help to restart the machine.
- **Incompatible system:** Think back to the check for suitability in the last part. You might need to first update your OS.

Post-Update Steps

After updating Adobe Lightroom, there are a few important things you should do to make sure everything is working right. These steps will help you make sure the update works and get used to the new version quickly.

Verifying and Testing the Update

It's important to make sure that the new version is put properly and working as it should after updating. How to do it:

1. **Check the Version:** Do this: Open Lightroom and click on **Help > About Lightroom**. This will show the version number that is currently in use.

2. **Explore New Features:** Read the update notes to find out about any new features or changes. You should try them out to see how they improve your workflow.

After an update, testing the software makes sure that all of the new features work and that your current processes don't change.

Adjusting Settings and Preferences in the New Version

Some basic settings might change when you get a new update, and you might also get new preferences. To make them custom:

1. **Review Preferences:** On a Windows computer, go to Edit > Preferences. On a Mac, go to Lightroom > Preferences. You can change settings for things like speed, layout, and how files are handled by going through the tabs.

2. **Update Catalog Settings:** Updates can occasionally modify catalog settings. You can change the settings for backups, information, and more by going to **Edit > Catalog Settings** and checking them out.

Lightroom keeps Crashing

Optimize the Catalog

When you choose to optimize the catalog, Lightroom will look at the catalog's data format to make sure it is right and clear.

It's not likely that your catalog is crashing, but if it is, installing this should fix it. In addition, it will make sure that your catalog keeps working well after you restart Lightroom.

Open the catalog and click on "**Optimize Catalog**" in the File menu. Wait a moment for it to do its thing.

After it's done, restart Lightroom and check to see if the problem still exists.

Turn off the GPU

If you've already done steps 1 and 2 and are still having issues, it's possible that Lightroom isn't getting along with your graphics card driver.

Graphics card drivers that are broken or don't work with Lightroom have been one of the biggest problems for a long time, causing everything from speed problems to frequent crashes.

To turn off the GPU on a Mac, go to either

- (Mac) *Lightroom Classic > Preferences > Performance*
- (Windows) *Edit > Preferences > Performance*

and uncheck the box next to Enable Graphics Processor. This will turn off the GPU. This might also help Lightroom work faster.

That might fix the issue, then you might want to get a GPU that works with Lightroom.

Glossary

Adjustment Brush

A Lightroom tool that lets users apply adjustments like exposure, contrast, and clarity to particular sections of a picture by painting them with a brush. This tool is quite handy for performing targeted adjustments without changing the overall image.

Aspect ratio

The ratio of an image's width to its height. Common aspect ratios include 4:3, 3:2, and 16:9. Changing the aspect ratio might help you better frame your topic and prepare photographs for multiple display formats.

Backup

To prevent data loss, transfer your Lightroom library and photographs to another place. Regular backups guarantee that you have a secure duplicate of your work in the event of hardware failure or other problems.

Batch Processing

A function that lets you make the same edits or actions to numerous photographs at once. This can save a lot of time when working with a large number of photographs that need to be edited similarly.

Catalog

Lightroom uses a database file to hold information about all photographs you import, such as their location, metadata, and any modifications or alterations you make. The catalog does not include the photographs themselves, but rather a record of where they are kept and what alterations have been made.

Clarity

A slider in the Develop module boosts mid-tone contrast, giving photos a more defined appearance. Increasing clarity can improve texture and detail while reducing clarity might result in a softer, more ethereal impression.

Clone Tool

A tool for replicating pixels from one area of a picture to another. It is commonly used to remove imperfections, dust spots, or undesired items from photographs by duplicating and mixing adjacent pixels over the region to be eliminated.

Collections

Lightroom's Collections tool organizes photographs without relocating them from their original place on your hard disk. Collections may be used to categorize photographs for better access, as well as to establish specialized projects or albums.

Color Grading

A function that lets you modify the color balance and tones in the shadows, midtones, and highlights separately. This powerful color-correcting tool aids in creating a certain style or atmosphere in your photographs.

Contrast

A setting for adjusting the contrast between an image's darkest and brightest areas. Increasing contrast darkens shadows and brightens highlights, adding depth to the picture, whilst diminishing contrast makes tones more comparable, creating a flatter look.

Crop Overlay.

A tool for trimming and adjusting the frame of your image. The Crop Overlay tool allows you to modify the aspect ratio, correct the horizons, and remove undesired borders.

Dehaze

A slider that decreases or increases haze in your pictures. It may be used to recover information from foggy or hazy photographs, as well as to produce an artistic haze effect.

Develop Module

The portion of Lightroom where you make the majority of your image tweaks and modifications. This module has tools for exposure, contrast, color correction, sharpening, and more.

DNG (Digital Negative)

Adobe developed the open-source RAW file format known as DNG (Digital Negative). Converting your images to DNG can assist in ensuring future compatibility and minimize file size while maintaining image quality.

Export

The process of saving modified pictures to a certain format and place. You may prepare your photographs for sharing or printing by selecting the file type, size, quality, and other settings during the export process.

Graduated Filter

A tool that makes progressive alterations to an image, commonly used for sky or other regions that require a slow change in exposure or color. It may be used to darken a brilliant sky or warm up a sunset.

Histogram

A graphical depiction of your image's tonal values. It displays the distribution of shadows, midtones, and highlights, allowing you to better understand your photo's exposure and contrast.

HSL / Color Panel

A panel in the Develop module lets you change the hue, saturation, and luminance of certain colors in your image. This allows you to precisely regulate how each hue is portrayed.

Import

The process of importing photographs into your Lightroom collection. During the import process, you may add metadata, apply presets, and group your photographs into folders or collections.

Keywords

Keywords are descriptive keywords used to organize and search photographs later. Keywords can be inserted during import or at any time within the Library module.

Library Module

Lightroom's area for organizing, sorting, and managing pictures. The Library module provides tools for rating, flagging, keywording, and building collections.

Luminance

The intensity of a color in a picture. Adjusting brightness can help you brighten or darken individual colors without changing their hue or saturation.

Metadata

Camera settings, date and time, location, and other data about your images are all included. Metadata may be added and changed in Lightroom to help you organize and manage your photo collection.

Noise Reduction

A method that decreases the appearance of grain or digital noise in pictures, particularly those taken at high ISO settings. Lightroom has controls for minimizing brightness and color noise.

Overlay

A visual assistance that allows you to apply adjustments more accurately. For example, the crop overlay displays grid lines to aid composition, but the adjustment brush overlay displays where modifications have been made.

Panorama Merge

A function for combining many pictures into a single panoramic image. Lightroom automatically aligns and combines the photographs into a seamless panoramic.

Perspective Correction

Adjustments to rectify distortions produced by the camera's angle. This is especially important for architectural photography, which requires lines to be straight and parallel.

Photo Merge

A collection of features, including HDR Merge and Panorama Merge. Photo Merge combines numerous photographs into a single image with a higher dynamic range or a larger field of view.

PPI (Pixels Per Inch)

PPI (Pixels Per Inch) is a measure of picture resolution, indicating the number of pixels per inch. more PPI values indicate more resolution and detail.

Presets

Predefined settings can be applied to pictures to rapidly achieve a certain style or impact. Lightroom has several built-in presets, and you may build and store your own.

Publish Services

Lightroom's Publish Services feature enables direct upload and sharing of photographs to internet sites including Flickr, Facebook, and Adobe Portfolio.

Radial Filter

A tool for applying modifications to an oval or circular section of your image. It may be used to emphasize or enhance particular aspects of a photograph, such as generating a vignette effect.

RAW Files

RAW files are unprocessed images taken by your camera sensor. RAW files include all of the sensor's data, allowing for greater post-processing flexibility than JPEG files.

Resolution

The level of detail in an image is usually measured in pixels or PPI. Higher-resolution photographs have greater detail and may be reproduced in bigger sizes without losing quality.

Sharpening

A technique that improves the definition of edges in your photograph, making things look sharper. Lightroom has several sliders for controlling the quantity, radius, and detail of sharpening applied.

Smart Collections

Smart Collections automatically update based on specified criteria, such as keywords, ratings, or information. Smart Collections are dynamic and can help you keep organized as you add more photographs to your database.

Soft Proofing.

A function that shows you how your images will seem when printed on various devices or paper kinds. Soft proofing allows you to make revisions to guarantee that your printed photographs meet your expectations.

Spot Removal

A tool to remove minor flaws, dust stains, and other defects from your images. The Spot Removal tool may clone or repair portions, blending them perfectly with the surrounding pixels.

Sync

The technique of using the same edits or settings on many images. This may be done manually or automatically using Lightroom's synchronizing tools, which saves time when dealing with large groups of similar pictures.

Targeted Adjustment Tool (TAT).

A tool that lets you click and drag right on your photo to change certain tones or colors. TAT is available in a variety of panels, including Tone Curve and HSL/Color.

Tone Curve

A tool that allows you to precisely manage the tone range of your images. You may use the curve to brighten or darken certain regions, such as shadows, midtones, or highlights.

Virtual Copies

Virtual copies are duplicates of photos that may be edited without producing a new file. Virtual copies relate to the same original photo but can have completely different changes done.

Vignette

An effect that darkens or lightens an image's edges to focus emphasis on the center. Lightroom's Post-Crop Vignetting tool allows you to create and edit vignettes after cropping your image.

White Balance

A setting for adjusting the color temperature of your image to guarantee correct colors. To obtain your preferred white balance, utilize presets, sliders, or the eyedropper tool.

XMP (Extensible Metadata Platform)

This is a standard for storing metadata in files. Lightroom may preserve edits and settings as XMP sidecar files that accompany RAW files and can be read by other programs.

Zoom

You may zoom your shot to view more detail. Lightroom has a variety of zoom capabilities and tools to let you analyze and edit particular areas of your image.

CONCLUSION

Thanks for reading this. I hope this guide helped you learn how to edit and organize your photos in Lightroom Classic. You now know how to organize your photo library, use different editing tools, and make beautiful pictures.

Don't forget that practice makes perfect. You will get better at editing photos as you use Lightroom more. Try out a bunch of different tools and methods until you find the ones that work best for you.

You can improve your photos with Lightroom Classic, which is a strong tool. Keep looking around, keep learning, and most of all, enjoy your journey as a photographer!

INDEX

Y

Z

www.ingramcontent.com/pod-product-compliance
Lightning Source LLC
LaVergne TN
LVHW080110070326
832902LV00015B/2513